Sociology of the Arts

This series brings together academic work which considers the production and consumption of the arts, the social value of the arts, and analyses and critiques the impact and role of cultural policy and arts management. By exploring the ways in which the arts are produced and consumed, the series offers further understandings of social inequalities, power relationships and opportunities for social resistance and agency. It highlights the important relationship between individual, social and political attitudes, and offers significant insights into the ways in which the arts are developing and changing. Moreover, in a globalised society, the nature of arts production, consumption and policy making is increasingly cosmopolitan, and arts are an important means for building social networks, challenging political regimes, and reaffirming and subverting social values across the globe.

More information about this series at
http://www.palgrave.com/series/15469

Jane Frank

Regenerating Regional Culture

A Study of the International Book Town Movement

palgrave
macmillan

Jane Frank
Griffith University
Nathan, QLD, Australia

Sociology of the Arts
ISBN 978-3-319-65035-7 ISBN 978-3-319-65036-4 (eBook)
https://doi.org/10.1007/978-3-319-65036-4

Library of Congress Control Number: 2017954889

Cover illustration: Cultura RM/Alamy Stock Photo

Printed on acid-free paper

This Palgrave Macmillan imprint is published by Springer Nature
The registered company is Springer International Publishing AG
The registered company address is: Gewerbestrasse 11, 6330 Cham, Switzerland

For my sons, Euan and Alastair Cummiskey.

Acknowledgements

My sincere thanks go to Sharla Plant, Jack Redden and the series editors at Palgrave Macmillan for their professionalism, advice and enthusiastic response to this project. Along the way, there have been other critical readers and significant contributors who have helped shape my research and ideas. In particular, I would like to thank my colleagues Kay Ferres and Stephanie Green from Griffith University—my doctoral supervision team—but also Ian Woodward, who offered concrete support and encouragement, David Inglis, Tony May, Susanna Chamberlain, Rosslyn McCarthy and Hugh McMillan. I am also most grateful to Susan Jarvis for editing my manuscript prior to submission.

Exploring the world's book towns was a labour of love. However, the research was made possible by the many experts in Australia, New Zealand, Scotland, Wales, England and the Republic of Ireland who shared their experiences, knowledge and time in interviews. Many of them welcomed me warmly into their book towns; introduced me to fascinating writers, booksellers and locals; and offered me hospitality. Their willingness to have their ideas, recollections and opinions expressed in this book greatly strengthen it, so I extend thanks to Pamela Bakes, Leo Berkelouw, Richard Booth MBE, Patrick Buckridge, Joanna Chambers, Ian Cochrane, Ros Derrett OAM, John Edmondson, Lincoln Gould, Daniel Gschwind, Bill Hauritz, Kate Mead, Paul McShane, Laurie Muller, Carole Nelson, Anne Nioa, Jane O'Hara, Peter Playden,

Brian Roberts, Peter Schiotz, Steve Rosa, Ted Sharkey, Robyn Sheahan-Bright, Gill Swales, Adrian Turpin OBE, Joyce Watson, David Williams and Carolyn Yates.

Many other people contributed material, or offered advice and support, over the course of the project; they include David Adair, Anne Barclay, Kenny Barr, Joan Benson, Helen Bird, Catherine Black, Amanda Boyce, Mary Bromilow, Cate Campbell, Susan FitzGerald, Roger Frank, Margaret Gibson, David and Pamela Gulland, Chris Lee, Donna Little, Shane McCarthy, Georgina McKeown, Sheila Minet, Pete Monk, Wendy Mort, Martin O'Brien, Barbara Pini, Maria Porter, Carol Saffer, Chris Schmidt, Tui Snider, Patricia Wise and Beverley Wood. My thanks goes to each of them, as well as to my husband, Peter Cummiskey, and young sons, Euan and Alastair. I acknowledge a lifetime of encouragement and support from my parents, Alexander and Kathleen Frank.

I am also thankful, of course, for the myriad conversations in bookshops—both at home and away, and spanning decades—where I've worked, immersed myself in books or simply passed through and memorialized the bookshop, place and discussion with the book/s I collected that day.

Pro captu lectoris habent sua fata libelli

Terentianus Maurus, *De Litteris, De Syllabis, De Metris* (c. 300 CE)

Contents

About the Author

Jane Frank is a lecturer in the School of Humanities, Languages and Social Science at Griffith University, Australia, with research interests in the fields of cultural studies, cultural sociology, and book and print culture.

List of Figures

Introduction

During the 1990s, I worked in Scotland as a book publicist, and in book export and distribution. As part of my work, I attended book fairs and expos, and became aware of Hay-on-Wye, the world's first book town, and other book towns that were then emerging in Europe. The successful transformation of this Welsh town had inspired others to follow its lead. In 1996, I read a Scottish newspaper report about a competition to establish a national book town in Scotland. Wigtown was declared the winner in 1997 (Fig. 1).

This initiative grew out of a feasibility study conducted through the Scottish Tourism Research Unit (STRU) by A.V. (Tony) Seaton. Between 1992 and 1998, Seaton was Reader in Tourism at the University of Strathclyde and in 1993 founded Scottish Tourism Research, a programme that provided advice to governments on cultural tourism, thanatourism (dark or grief tourism) and book town development. Seaton's research supported a book town venture in a peripheral location, the main driver being that a book town would provide a major opportunity for economic development and be a flagship tourism and cultural development for a rural town in Scotland (Seaton 1997, p. 2). This rural regeneration strategy would be funded by the National Lottery. Seaton and others developed a selection process designed to allow entrant towns to compete on an equal footing. Selection criteria included organizational strength, transformational scope, the economic

Fig. 1 Wigtown—Scotland's National Book Town official road signage (2011) (Source: Photo by author)

importance of the book town to the region, speed of implementation, the potential to attract book dealers, strategic value and regional benefit, existing book trader expertise, the scenic appeal of the town, the availability of book supply, historical/cultural features, accommodation/tourism infrastructure, events programme and available retail property (Seaton 1999, pp. 394–5).

Seaton's research was reported in the Glasgow *Herald* in 1996. In Wigtown, it sparked the interest of Meta Maltman from the organization Machars Action (Watson and Cochrane personal interview 2011). Maltman gathered support for Wigtown's bid to be Scotland's National Book Town. Seven communities placed bids in February 1997 (Press 2001, p. 34). Of these, three came from small towns closely situated in the south-west of Scotland: Dalmellington, Gatehouse-of-Fleet and Wigtown. When Wigtown was declared the winner, I drove to the town, located on a remote peninsula known as the Machars. Everywhere I looked, buildings were crumbling and paint was flaking off the walls. The town was very down at heel. Visiting writers and journalists would also see drabness and dilapidation, 'as if all that was lacking was tumbleweed rolling down the street' (Pow 1999, p. 39). It was difficult to imagine this depressed, marginalized and lonely community by the sea as a bustling book town in the spirit of Hay-on-Wye.

While there are differing opinions about how complete and effective the transformation to book town has since been for Wigtown, I sensed a dramatic change in the physical appearance of the town when I revisited it on 5 September 2011 after an absence of almost 14 years. The official road signage on the A75 signalling the turn-off to 'Wigtown – Scotland's National Book Town' was the first indication of that change. As I reached the town itself, I found that the distinctive County Buildings had been restored to their former glory and now housed the Wigtown Book Festival headquarters, the museum and the local library, providing a central point of reference. Built in 1862 in the flamboyant French Gothic style, these buildings—which mark the siting of the County Seat of Wigtown—were both unexpected and wonderfully out of place in the small Scottish market town (Brewster 1996, p. 64). Bookshops lined the two main streets alongside the town green, sporting names like The Box of Frogs, The Creaking Shelves, Reading Lasses, The Old Bank and The Bookshop: Scotland's Largest Bookshop. The forlorn sense of neglect had been replaced by a feeling of bookish comfort. Despite it being a bleak, cold, damp Monday afternoon, well past the peak summer tourist season, there were people browsing in the shops and it was clear, as I talked informally to booksellers and visitors, that the Wigtown Book Festival—due to occur in a few weeks' time—was keenly anticipated. It would feature Maggie O'Farrell, Fergal Keane, Celia Imrie and a host of other national and international figures, most (although not all) of them literary. The festival offered a feast of content designed to appeal to local audiences, including regional history as well as celebration of local achievements and traditions. The scale and depth of the programme were impressive. I was eager to analyse this apparent transformation and to discover why such a project, and others like it around the globe, had become a growing trend—especially as the imminent death of the book was mooted daily in the media.

Since my time in Scotland, I have worked in arts and cultural policy development, and regional arts delivery, with a special interest in the capacity of the arts to drive rural and regional cultural development and renewal, which enrich community life. Although I no longer work in publishing, I continue to cultivate an obsessive book-collecting habit and a passion for secondhand bookshops that date back to my youth. The idea of the book town intrigued me. For a decade, this interest lay dormant; however, one day, as I read Charles Landry's *The Creative City: A Toolkit for Urban Innovators* (2008), I came upon a case study titled 'Creating Something Out of Nothing: Hay-on-Wye Book Town, UK'. Landry's comments about the impacts of culture on economic and community development—and, in Hay-on-Wye's case, the impetus of books in this process—stimulated my own research on the book town phenomenon which has escalated to incorporate more than 58 villages in 29 countries.

My aim in this book is to highlight the significant role that increasingly is being played by book towns as sites of contemporary public culture, through exploring their diversity, their hybrid cultural values and their relevance in both international and local contexts. My discussions interlock with other academic work in the realm of sociology and the arts that is focused on the potential of creative pursuits to drive transformation—not only in the way that they can build resilience to change but also in their potential to explore social constructions and the significance of place, space and identity (Evans and Shaw 2004; McCarthy et al. 2005; Stephenson and Tate 2015). The advantages of creative community enterprises like book towns extend beyond initial processes of engagement to the achievement of longer term benefits, which include the establishment of identity and a sense of place; the engendering of resilience, confidence and new understandings; and the provision of fresh opportunities for social agency and for the challenging of previous approaches. While more intensive research has been dedicated to creative cities and their cultural economies (Cooke and Lazeretti 2008; Florida 2008, 2002; Kong and O'Connor 2010; Landry 2008; Landry et al. 1996; Markusen 2014; Pratt 2008; Scott 2006), a growing body of research is also addressing these ideas in the context of rural and regional communities, which are equally prone to the impacts of globalization. Chris Gibson's (2012;

Gibson and Connell 2011, 2012) empirical and theoretical explorations relating to the power of culture in Australian rural transformation, and the way cultural production and consumption are embedded geographically, together with related studies of cultural economic development in rural areas (Griswold 2008; Hall et al. 2003; Lade and Jackson 2004; McGranahan and Wojan 2007; McHenry 2011; Trotter 2001; Wojan 2007; Wood and Thomas 2008) are important contextual markers.

In a similar vein, this book examines the contributions of community events and festivals that occur in the global sub-set of book towns—small, rural or regional, vibrant book-loving locales—with relation to their social and economic life. It explores the proliferation of book town activity and festival culture as a part of what has been well documented as a global swell in the number of annual festivals since the last decade of the twentieth century (Bennett et al. 2014, p. 1) and the potential this creates for enhancing cultural diversification. Book town festivals, and book-related dynamics more broadly, are proliferating as sustainable means for the increasingly mobile audiences and local communities that consume and experience culture, deliver cultural products for countryside consumption and generate tourism (Burns and Novelli 2008; Rojek 1993, 2000; Sheller and Urry 2004; Urry 2007). Book towns thus become 'a significant aspect of the socio-economic and cultural landscape of contemporary everyday life' (Bennett et al. 2014, p. 1) that enables opportunities for shared consumption of book culture, local history, lifestyle activities and hospitality. In a macro sense, this cultural buoyancy provides transformative consumption experiences for social engagement 'across cultural, geographic and social borders, and within and across scales of social interaction from the local to the global' (Bennett and Woodward, in Bennett et al. 2014, p. 16).

The intersection of the global rise of cosmopolitanism—usually associated with growing urbanism and increased levels of education—and the global rise of the Book Town Movement as it has primarily developed in rural and peripheral locales is an important one. This book recognizes book towns as junctures: points of confluence for both individuals and communities, local and global issues, realism and idealism. The Book Town Movement and its expansion therefore occupy a significant space to explore a range of intersecting contemporary sociological trends. I explore developments in international cultural tourism and, more recently, post-tourism to contribute to current understandings about global and local cultural engagements. In doing so, I will demonstrate how bringing together a range of approaches, strategies and processes based in cultural and social theory can enhance how we think about local or regional experience and potentials in relation to what are too easily generalized as global trends. The growing importance of marginal book town locations as centres for cultural activity is highlighted. Festivals and events occurring in book towns such as Hay-on-Wye in Wales, Wigtown in Scotland and Australia's Clunes are highly acclaimed, and the peripheral location in itself is an attraction and a drawcard to increasingly global audiences and participants.

This book breaks new ground in its cultural and material analyses of the role of the book as catalyst in these transformative events. While discussions about whether the book will survive the digital revolution are impossible to avoid in contemporary discourse, and there is lingering scepticism about the book's future, the expansion of book towns around the world at this time is a surprising development in the history of print culture. While it would be wrong to ignore wider changes in book culture, book towns provide ample evidence that hard-copy books have played, and will continue to play, a vital role in shaping our lives. They are artefacts with a deep, abiding history that not only have relevance as objects but also impact on other forms of popular culture (Carrière and Eco 2011; Darnton 2009; Murray 2012). While incorporating new book technologies and formats into our relationship with books and print, many of us experience a feeling that two different ways of life are 'colliding with each other like tectonic plates jostling for position' (Striphas 2009, p. 176).

I will present book culture in book towns as a paradigm of the means by which communities evolve a dialogue concerning the history of the book and the reasons why books are collected. Collections of books speak to where we wish to go as well as to where we have been. Antiquarian and secondhand books are significant in the construction of localness because they carry memory traces that propel visitors back in time. In contemporary culture, time is a source of constraint and people bridle against its limitations. Activities such as browsing in bookshops and reading demand space and time, drawing us back from the primacy of the moment to a more leisurely pace. Books, which are tangible objects—sometimes of great beauty—constitute infinite imagined presences in these communities. Book towns allow the protection of books from time and from technology, but are also part of the cultural filtering process: books that don't sell eventually perish and society moves on. Books are at once objects and artefacts, and reading is a three-dimensional, tactile experience in which the way the text looks or feels or smells influences engagement with it. It is the fact that they are repositories of these unique and distinct items with multiple dimensions that infuses the world's book towns with richness and diversity.

What especially interests me is the analysis of how book towns have been established and how this intersects with critical issues about how book culture is consumed. I therefore examine book towns in the context of the increased cultural mobility of individuals and address books as cosmopolitan symbols. I argue that meaningful belonging is derived from relationships with places, objects and ideas, and explore this notion in relation to the significance of books as well as geography in the case of book towns, to show that books, allied with cultural heritage, coffee and countryside, can both stimulate a book-based economy and promote an alternative cosmopolitan model in a localized context. This includes seeking to understand how people exploit travel as an opportunity to infuse their lives with greater meaning—and how they value books, collecting books and sharing public discourse about books—and highlighting the difficulties and opportunities that can arise in any discussion of culture as a measure of community cohesion.

There is evidence of the appeal of book towns relying on a growing democratization of culture. By analysing Hay-on-Wye book town founder Richard Booth's philosophy of book towns as economies of poverty, I categorize book towns as promoting egalitarianism, exploring their emphasis on both low and high cultural forms, and demonstrating their accessibility to all through provision of multiple entry points for engagement. They are hubs that cater to a myriad of different special interests, idiosyncrasies and even eccentricities, constituting meaningful experiences for all kinds of people seeking engagement at different levels. Significantly, book towns are magnets for people with eclectic tastes, hives of special interest, and therefore targets for special-interest tourism. They thrive due to the passion of their eccentric founders and the eccentric tastes of collectors, and they answer the post-tourist need for extreme novelty. Yet many are established through utopian ideals—opportunities for booksellers, in particular, to live more perfect lives, where they can escape the mainstream and where residents and visitors alike can embrace a rural idyll through avoiding the relentlessness of city living.

Starting Points

The global expansion of the Book Town Movement and its contemporary dynamics constitute an under-researched field. To my knowledge, there are no other dedicated academic studies from the past 15 years that holistically address the movement's cultural significance and its relationship with other international trends such as globalization, changing book industry technologies and trends, consumption of print culture, peripheral community development and increased specialization in tourism. Few contemporary comparisons of book towns in different countries and continents have been compiled, other than in journalistic commentaries and weblogs. One exception is Paul McShane's (2002) Churchill Fellowship Report, which was the outcome of a tour of book towns in Europe and North America. This report's aim was to apply international models as examples for developing a book town in Australia's very different geographic and cultural conditions. However, as it was completed prior to the last decade of expansion, it takes no account of book towns in Japan, Malaysia, Korea, South Africa, Eastern Europe and Australia. Another is Audra Merfeld-Langston's (2007) doctoral thesis, 'The Villages du Livre', which investigates French and Belgian book towns, but also provides illuminating insights into the expansion of the movement across Europe. Merfeld-Langston's work is important for its scholarly historical research of French society and print culture and for identifying why book towns have developed so prolifically in France. While her doctoral studies provide new detail about the cultural phenomenon of the *villages du livre* 'exploding through the Hexagon' (p. 8) of France and Belgium, they draw specifically on political and historical factors unique to France to explain why the movement developed there in a particular way.

Richard Booth's (1999) autobiographical account of the rise of Hay-on-Wye and his involvement in the spread of book towns across the globe provides a level of detail lacking in other sources. As well as recounting his worldwide search for books and his insights into the book trade, this autobiography reflects on society as it was changing during the period that book towns were being established and the effects of this change on the Book Town Movement itself. Booth depicts this society as increasingly centralized and dominated by distant authorities, both bureaucratic and capitalistic. However, because the account relies so heavily on Booth's unorthodox political and social views, which inevitably colour his recollections of how events unfolded, I have counterbalanced these ideas with the critiques of others where available, particularly the memoirs of Paul Collins (2003) and Paul Minet (1989), and Kate Clarke's (2000) history of Hay-on-Wye. Merfeld-Langston (2007) also offers helpful insights into the thinking of Nöel Anselot, the founder of Redu, Belgium's book town, expressed in his autobiography, *Un Village à Livre Ouverts* (2004). The founder of Archer City book town Larry McMurtry's three volumes of autobiography, *Walter Benjamin at the Dairy Queen: Reflections at Sixty and Beyond* (1999), *Books: A Memoir* (2008) and *Literary Life: A Second Memoir* (2009), are more than accounts of McMurtry's passion for antiquarian books and the establishment of a book town in the vast emptiness of the Texan landscape. Using the writings of Walter Benjamin as a starting point, his work encapsulates valuable material about the book trade, not only in Texas and the United States but globally. Of course, Seaton's research of the 1990s—thorough and ground-breaking at that time—was pivotal, yet it was largely quantitative, primarily focused on the role of book towns as stimulators of tourism, and is now dated.

These were all important references and starting points for my exploration of why book towns are a growing phenomenon in the early twenty-first century. In this book, I return to the source of the movement in the United Kingdom and explore holistically, for the first time, the social and cultural factors that triggered, but also combined to sustain, this enduring global phenomenon. I particularly focus on book towns in Wales, Scotland, England, the Republic of Ireland, New Zealand and Australia to closely explore their particular reasons for development and their diverse specializations. Wales is the site of the world's first book town, and

I particularly wanted to interview founder Richard Booth as a significant component of the research for this book. It was also important for me to revisit Wigtown in Scotland to witness the changes that had taken place there since that book town's inception. I was also particularly interested in the comparison of Australia's and New Zealand's fledgling book towns with longer established examples in the United Kingdom in terms of local cultural policy considerations. The specific first-hand accounts of book towns are therefore limited in number but investigated in depth and enriched by my personal exposure to book town environments, events and happenings.

In my observations of book towns, I paid particular attention to the town settings themselves, and the bookshops within those towns and villages: their physical, spatial, temporal and social organization. I observed community dynamics at events and festivals, but also in the day-to-day lives of the towns. My own impressions are therefore built into the discussions in this book: my observation of spatial and behavioural aspects of book towns thus providing a social and cultural inquiry into the dynamics of book towns to reveal new understandings.

An important aspect of my site analysis was exploration of book towns as 'cultural landscapes', where book town activity has imbued rural and regional locales with cultural values. Through combined elements of time and space, and representing political as well as social and cultural constructs, book towns have acquired significant layers of meaning that I analyse through historical, sociological and cultural perspectives. The character of book town landscapes and townscapes reflects the values of the entrepreneurs and shapers of projects, as well as those who live in these places. Book towns are landscapes of cultural exchange where practices and processes become forms of cultural heritage. The creation of themed book town communities creates the community's image of itself, yet I also address the different ways in which non-book-related groups and individuals regard book town initiatives. I examine travel and tourism to book towns, built around a quest for particular experiences, and explore the experience of place and landscape as key elements of that quest. This book therefore analyses my observations of tourism-driven representations of book towns as cultural landscapes through an exploration of issues connected with globalization and localization.

Book town case studies make it possible to analyse book town examples in geographically disparate regions, providing a level of depth, richness and complexity not provided in earlier numerical studies commissioned by government and tourism bodies. They were an ideal means for me to examine the underlying reasons *why* events are taking place in book towns and *how* processes are occurring. I conducted 28 in-depth interviews in book town locations. These interactions enabled me to gain insights into the social reality of book towns: social processes, social change, social organization and social meaning. I selected some interviewees for their specific book town expertise as project founders, managers, festival directors or booksellers in the towns I identified for particular focus. Others were purposely selected from sectors that intersected with book town projects, such as publishing, libraries, government, tourism, event management, the cultural industries and academia. However, I was able to widen my pool of interviewees by using snowball sampling—simply asking these original experts who else to interview, so the 'snowball' grew as I encountered many other people in the book towns themselves who were knowledgeable about the history and establishment of book town projects.

During these in-depth conversations, I was interested in exploring a range of different approaches and themes from the perspectives of both cultural production and consumption to understand why cultural diversity thrives in these places. Working more specifically at the intersections of cultural studies, cultural policy, social science and print culture, my research considered where, how and why book towns exist within cultural and community contexts. Visits to book towns, in-depth conversations with book town experts and a focus on the practices of book town events, festivals and the day-to-day existence of those who work in book businesses and visit book town enterprises enabled me to develop an approach that built a more revealing understanding of book town culture, encompassing both the contemporary and historical cultural practices that have occurred and the social reality of individuals, groups and communities that engage in book town life. I explored and analysed the interviewees' perspectives, but also looked at their values—their deeply held beliefs about what is important to book town experience. I considered how people made decisions and participated in social action in these communities. My own background in book and print culture was also highly relevant to these discussions, helping to shape my understanding of book town dynamics. In many respects, therefore, this book provides a relationship model of social and cultural inquiry.

A rewarding outcome of writing this book has been the opportunity for mutual learning and the transfer of knowledge. As well as benefiting from the first-hand knowledge and project expertise of experts and stakeholders, I was able to share theory and practical information from other book towns. The material I could share offered opportunities to create stronger networks between book towns. Established book town leaders were interested to learn of other projects and often were willing to provide advice about how to overcome obstacles. It thus follows that, in many cases, I didn't simply conduct isolated interviews with respondents but have maintained a continuing dialogue. For this reason, an important outcome of writing this book will be maintaining connections and sharing intelligence of contemporary international trends that are working around the world. This is a way of providing in-kind support to energetic and innovative people working in an often under-resourced environment.

Cultural policy is an important focus in this book's analysis of how book towns achieve cultural diversity. The research aims to inform cultural policy frameworks through investigation of how book towns orient their cultural policies in contexts of diversity, with particular attention paid to the social dimension of these policies. The book town is presented as an example of a cultural resource and a public good that has the potential to contribute significantly to future public policy and to regional culture around the globe, promoting innovation. As peripheral townships with increasingly eclectic populations and approaches, book towns promote new dynamics for community and cultural practices in rural and regional areas. This book analyses the ways in which book towns use cultural strategies to reinvigorate failing economies and strengthen cultural capital. The notion of a themed community based on books and book culture is examined as a development strategy capable of consolidating a rural town's reputation as a cultural attraction. The work examines how the social dynamics of rural life are harnessed in book towns to enhance the authenticity of the visitor experience.

In particular, I examine book towns as effective examples of culture-led regeneration in regional areas throughout the world: as policy instruments that deliver cultural unification as a means to protect national and regional cultures, and in their capacity as bastions of social capital, economic multipliers and tourism hubs. I also survey book towns in the context of their importance to citizenship and civic discourse by highlighting the role of bookstores in everyday existence as vital 'sinews of civil society … the common thread of civil life' (Gopnik 2015, para. 7). To do this, it was necessary to closely scrutinize a range of government documents and reports sourced from a number of countries. These included Hansard, ABS statistical data and international equivalents, central and local government development reports and meeting minutes, and government reports on sustainable rural tourism, business clustering, sea change and tree change, community development, cultural heritage and regeneration, and volunteerism in country towns. I consulted many documents specific to book town development, including feasibility studies, economic impact studies, event audits and outcome reports, business plans, project evaluations and forecasts. While secondary resources and ethnographic research were important to my book town research, I also drew on a wide range of unpublished texts, including reports, newspaper and magazine articles, brochures, festival programmes, newsletters, web materials, and radio and television media. Many of these materials were only made available through site visits and shed important light on the social environment of book town communities.

Using these materials, this book explores book towns as significant to growing regional agendas informed by social, economic, cultural and demographic change. These communities have often found themselves in economic situations dictated by the vagaries of world financial markets and industrial change that have placed them under siege. They are examined as models of resilience and sustainability through implementing place-based strategies where they are themed as 'places for books', ultimately leading to broader social benefits including community cohesion, community-mindedness, increased tolerance and cultural diversity, a pride and attachment to the town, and a strong sense of the future. Book towns are also investigated as projects that explore and define communities of book-based interests. Part of this discussion considers the motivations of those who have moved from metropolitan existences to live and work in book towns and their reasons for doing so: cheaper property, a themed community of like-minded booksellers, more space to work, a more relaxed lifestyle and a rural environment. My findings demonstrate that these benefits counteract difficulties such as distance from city venues, markets and networks, and that in fact there are still fruitful linkages with urban cultural life. The rise of book towns is linked to the dispersal of cultural capital related to globalization and localization, the breakdown of high cultural authority and the growing sophistication of media cultures.

Book towns are positioned as centres of social change through the power bases they establish in their building of partnerships with governments, businesses, the publishing industry and the media. They play an important role in bringing communities together by sustaining local traditions and experimenting with innovative festival programming that places them at the centre of cultural debate. This includes attention to how book towns embrace young people in their programmes—which is essential to maintaining their future relevance.

While this book aims to afford an insight into the core values upon which it seems most book towns have drawn, and presents a range of key ideas and processes for thinking and theorizing that are likely to prove the basis for successful book town projects, it does not present a model for book town development. The book and the results it conveys are reliant on specific investigations in a selection of the world's book towns. Book town development and emphases vary considerably in each of the world's book towns, so it is not possible to regard any book town as wholly typical of those elsewhere. While book towns often adopt national, regional or local characteristics relating to geography, cuisine or culture, each is unique. However, where possible, patterns of development or success observed across various examples are identified.

Besides focusing on the history of the Book Town Movement and the lives and experiences of book town entrepreneurs, my research also incorporated a close study of issues and topics related to books, book culture (the ideas) and print culture (books as objects). As well as subjects including the history of books and book collecting, I investigated the central role played by books in human social communication structures including the publishing industry, book and writer's festivals, the future of secondhand bookshops, reading trends around the world and the nexus between books and citizenship. This research, gleaned not only from reports, books and journal articles but also from extensive media sources, was essential to understanding why, despite having been overlooked previously in schemes of economic and social regeneration, books as cultural and cosmopolitan items are fundamental to the phenomenon of the book town. This is not only because of the part they play in bridging industrial and digital worlds, but due to the social and economic impacts they create when book-based economies are established.

This research was important for recognizing the relationship between issues facing the publishing industry and the growth of book towns. Changes in publishing as a result of the digital age mean a significant residue of printed items is left in their wake. These items are sought after, desirable and have an exchange value. Book towns are burgeoning in light of these changes, with books at their nucleus stimulating creative possibilities that enable innovation, meet a global demand for special interests and self-fashioning and allow the gathering of book enthusiasts in the countryside. I use this research material to demonstrate that books in book towns act as conduits for global connectivity but simultaneously work as trigger points for nostalgia that draws people to these places. An unprecedented growth of literary festivals and a strong interest in literary prizes are part of a sustained interest in book culture expressed in book towns. These wholesome, convivial communities are thus increasingly important components in the commercial and media structures significant to contemporary book culture and provide evidence of shifting patterns of cultural consumption.

It is my hope that the work I have done to analyse book town examples from opposite parts of the world will provide a foundation for those involved in the existing or future development of book towns. This research should assist the broader book community and inspire open-minded local communities to consider a book town development as a means of injecting new life into peripheral communities suffering social or economic hardship or deterioration. Research into book towns as examples of regional or peripheral development would also assist future book town establishers by highlighting that book town successes rely on unique regional and local characteristics and an avoidance of homogenous culture. Communities will succeed by remaining true to their intrinsic character. Through the development of book-based economies, book towns are emerging as unique and idiosyncratic centres of sustained social, cultural and economic growth. Strong links established between book town development and tourism are significant generators of economic activity and catalysts for alliances between government and creative communities, so this account of the Book Town Movement may also provide guidance for governments, entrepreneurs or tourist bodies seeking a tailored opportunity to advance a peripheral community with potential.

Outline of Chapters

Chapter 1 defines the term 'book town' and identifies the factors that have combined to create circumstances whereby book towns have proliferated. It locates book towns at the intersection of a number of local and global trends that impact on the consumption of book culture. It deploys the concept of book culture to foreground the intertwined relationship between books, collecting, themed communities and specialized tourism practices that positions the book town as significant in contemporary life as a mechanism for regional and cultural vitality. In establishing the beginnings of book towns, and recognition of them, the chapter addresses the first book town research by Tony Seaton, which focused on the economic model of specialized retail clusters in Hay-on-Wye and the early European book towns as a driver of regional tourism development, leading to sustainability. It also documents experiments in Europe, where book towns developed online organizational networks to enhance their profile in step with increasing globalization and opportunities newly available due to emerging technologies. A number of agendas for book town formation are established, including European unification, UNESCO's global creative policy-making strategies recognizing places of cultural and literary activity, political motivations in France associated with preservation of national book and literary culture, and the appeal of book towns as utopian locales, or cohesive peripheral territories, that celebrate community values and a unique identity based on book culture infused with the ambience of rural landscapes. At the same time, the chapter establishes that book towns create a point of difference from city-based book culture and offer an appealing lifestyle. Charles Landry's (2008) work on cultural clusters is applied to the clustering of books in book towns to appeal to the imagination of book-enthused entrepreneurs and generate travel demand from both cultural tourist and post-tourist cohorts.

In Chap. 2, the entrepreneurial and organic theories of book town development are discussed with reference to the Welsh town of Hay-on-Wye as a foundational example of how book towns can operate successfully as sites of cultural as well as economic renewal. This chapter details the inception and progression of Hay-on-Wye, investigating why it has sustained itself successfully for over half a century and uncovering the nexus between that success and the eccentricity of its founder, Richard Booth. The chapter details Booth's notion of a peripherally based book empire that inspired the flourishing of the global Book Town Movement, leading to a variety of idiosyncratic and strategic approaches in nations around the world. Key philosophies applied by Booth in his creation of a book empire were the book town as an 'economy of poverty', and respect for and protection of a traditional rural way of life, which are explained. However, the remarkable success of the initiative is also attributed to a number of other factors particular to the 1960s, including specialization and decentralization of the UK book trade and Booth's early appreciation of the international trade opportunities that later became widespread due to sweeping globalization. Importantly, the chapter clarifies the trades in new titles and secondhand books as distinct from each other: the secondhand economy is centred on merchandise that is not confined by time restrictions that govern a new book's 'lifespan'. This issue accounts for the disconnect between the Hay Festival, established in 1988, and the community of secondhand book dealers in Hay-on-Wye led by Booth. In most subsequent book towns, the establishment of festivals that celebrate the book and the ideas contained in it have been embraced eagerly. For this and other reasons, the chapter documents why Hay-on-Wye is a surprising and unique development in the history of print culture, rural tourism and community dynamics, but at the same time an organic model that is a complex and dangerous exemplar for replication.

In Chap. 3, I examine the juncture between book towns as attractive destinations and the emergence of the Slow Movement in the late 1980s to explain further how book towns developed as sites of cultural renewal. The qualities of book town culture that demand experiential immersion—such as slow reading, browsing and fossicking in bookshops, as well as the conviviality of events and activities associated with writing, reading and book crafts that they promote—unlock the pleasure and enchantment that are integral to the notion of slow culture. This chapter explores bookshops and book towns as third places that encourage relaxation, creative interaction, inclusivity and community unification. Book festivals and fairs in book towns are unique in these rural locales that operate as secular forums for considering issues that are not only book related, but refer to broader societal and ethical concerns. They create distinct identities, focusing on cultural heritage and nostalgic rural pasts as well as providing a utopian counterpoint to impersonal 'mass' offerings and the increasing commercialization and standardization of large cities. The hand-crafted, organic country goodness of the experiences—recycled books, fresh air, locally grown produce and the 'heart' behind the festivals hosted in these locales—appeals to travellers in search of more meaningful experiences as well as to local inhabitants. This chapter aims to unpack the link between book towns and the intimacy of experience that is achieved when there is an opportunity to create connections with people, place and culture in a leisurely way. The value of historic heritage and the 'character' of book towns as cultural tourism drawcards, destinations for nomadic travellers and prospective sea-change and tree-change locations has heightened their social and economic potential. They have therefore been identified as places deserving of policy focus.

This leads into Chap. 4, which investigates book towns as sustainable culture-led rural regeneration projects. The chapter explores key motivations for the support of book towns by governments and development agencies as 'edge-of-the-map' attractions that 'create something out of nothing', as Landry (2008) recommends. The peripheral nature of book towns and their distance from urban centres of culture is identified as intrinsic to their success. Book-based economies are flourishing in rural communities where, unlike in cities, entrepreneurs and booksellers can afford spacious, unoccupied properties—often with considerable charm—that, when grouped together, create specialized book clusters, the like of which is unlikely to occur in the metropolis. This distinctiveness establishes book towns as unique destinations that not only sell books but are thriving centres of regional culture. Book towns encourage regional cultural expression of language, literature, geography, history and specialties such as local produce and cuisine. These place-centred specifics colour visitor experiences so that the desirable landscapes in which book towns are located become an important component of the image these communities project. The chapter thus addresses book towns as place commodities where image-building is vital to tourist consumption in a global world: the unfamiliar, exotic and picturesque are highly marketable. While the problems posed by themed town identities are explained in this chapter, I also reinforce the point that the increased social cohesion, and the cultural and economic capital made possible by the resultant multiplier effect, provide a means of effectively galvanizing communities behind book town initiatives. The chapter poses the challenges for themed villages when it comes to addressing the needs of the non-bookish elements in their communities. Book towns attract and retain change-makers and other talented individuals who operate businesses and curate events with programmes that dually appeal to local populations as well as culturally savvy people willing to travel long distances to be part of exciting literary and intellectual dialogues.

Chapter 5 explores the dimensions of book culture exploited and enhanced by book towns. In this chapter, the success of the book town phenomenon is attributed largely to the book as a unique commodity, a beautiful artefact, a container of ideas and a marker of history, nostalgia and the substantiality of print culture. The chapter unpacks the unique relationship between book collectors and their books, distinguishing books from other items of consumption. I argue that collecting books is an egalitarian occupation, with the collector understanding, cherishing and preserving the concept and ideal of the book—its historical, material and sentimental value. The tangibility of books as objects of desire is investigated: antiquarian books embody history and provenance revealed in their aesthetics—jackets, bindings, inscriptions, book plates, imperfections and previous ownership. The wanting of these objects is connected, in this chapter, to a middle-class nostalgia for a romanticized past, while at the same time the book is regarded widely as a cosmopolitan symbol representing intellectual debate and meaningful human interaction. The connection between books, memory and the literate person's literary DNA is highlighted in this chapter to explain why pilgrimages to book towns are sought both as a means to desired identities and as pleasurable experiences, in which the sight, touch and smell of books are central. The 'treasure hunt' that is secondhand book shopping is thus a metaphor readily used by book villages. However, a link is established in this chapter between new book publishing and the secondhand book economy as the continuation of the first will continue to impact on the future potential of the second. Contemporary engagement with print and literary culture is explored, as is the valuable role performed by independent bookstores as vibrant hubs of physical and cerebral experience.

Amid the success of the global Book Town Movement, Chap. 6 draws attention to book towns that have not achieved sustainable outcomes. The chapter applies Tony Seaton's list of critical success factors to the failed projects of Blaenafon in Wales and Atherstone in England, as well as Graiguenamanagh in the Republic of Ireland—an emergent book town experiencing financial hardship despite possessing other desirable attributes. Book towns constantly tackle a range of economic, political, social and book industry-related issues that threaten to render their futures uncertain. The chapter examines a range of challenges faced by book towns, not only in their infancy but also with the inevitable ageing of the entrepreneurs who created and sustained them. The often eccentric individuals who envisage idealistic or utopian book town communities, as well as booksellers who relocate to book towns to be part of such projects, are categorized in this chapter as non-conformist and reluctant to be part of initiatives that are overly prescriptive or constraining. Their lack of conformity is the very spark that ignites the project, but it can also make book towns problematic models in a strategic management sense when requirements from governments and business stakeholders need to be met. The chapter discusses the hybrid approaches book towns will need to incorporate and consider as they evolve and further engage tourists in pursuits associated with book culture and innovation, with specialized secondhand bookshops likely to remain one aspect of a multi-faceted identity. It is argued that engagement with a younger demographic will be integral to their success, as will the need to make a difference to the town's fortunes as a means of recovery and reinvigoration, and the importance of growing a network of towns around the world that are increasingly recognized as significant sites of cultural diversity.

References

Bennett, A., Taylor, J., & Woodward, I. (Eds.). (2014). *The festivalization of culture*. Farnham: Ashgate.

Booth, R. (1999). *My kingdom of books*. Ceredigion: Y Lolfa Cyf.

Brewster, D. (1996). *Wigtown: The story of a royal and ancient burgh*. Wigtown: The Galloway Gazette.

Burns, P., & Novelli, M. (2008). *Tourism and mobilities: Local/global connections*. Cambridge, MA: CAN International.

Carrière, J.-C., & Eco, U. (2011). *This is not the end of the book: Two great men discuss our digital future*. London: Harvill Secker.

Clarke, K. (2000). *The book of Hay*. Little Logaston, Woonton Almeley: Logaston Press.

Collins, P. (2003). *Sixpence House: Lost in a town of books*. New York: Bloomsbury.

Cooke, P., & Lazzeretti, L. (Eds.). (2008). *Creative cities, cultural clusters and local economic development*. Cheltenham: Edward Elgar Publishing Ltd.

Darnton. (2009). *The case for books: Past present and future*. New York: Public Affairs.

Evans, G., & Shaw, P. (2004). *The contribution of culture to regeneration in the UK: A review of evidence*. A Report to the Department for Culture, Media and Sport. London: DCMS.

Florida. (2002). *The rise of the creative class: And how it's transforming work, leisure, community and everyday life*. New York: Basic Books.

Florida, R. (2008). *Who's your city?* New York: Basic Books.

Gibson, C. (Ed.). (2012). *Creativity in peripheral places: Defining the creative industries*. London/New York: Routledge.

Gibson, C., & Connell, J. (Eds.). (2011). *Festival places: Revitalising rural Australia*. Bristol: Channel View.

Gibson, C., & Connell, J. (Eds.). (2012). *Music festivals and regional development in Australia*. Farnham: Ashgate.

Gopnik, A. (2015, June 12). When a bookstore closes, an argument ends. *The NewYorker*.http://www.newyorker.com/news/daily-comment/when-a-bookstore-closes-an-argument-ends. Accessed 18 June 2015.

Griswold, W. (2008). *Regionalism and the reading class*. Chicago: University of Chicago Press.

Hall, D., Roberts, L., & Mitchell, M. (2003). *New directions in rural tourism: Local impacts, global trends*. Farnham: Ashgate.

Kong, L., & O'Connor, J. (Eds.). (2010). *Creative economies, creative cities: Asian European perspectives*. New York: Springer.

Lade, C., & Jackson, J. (2004). Key success factors in regional festivals: Some Australian experiences. *Event Management, 9*, 1–11.

Landry, C. (2008 [2000]). *The creative city: A toolkit for urban innovators*. London: Earthscan.

Landry, C., et al. (1996). *The art of regeneration: Urban renewal through cultural activity*. London: Comedia.

Markusen, A. (2014). Creative cities: A 10-year research agenda. *Journal of Urban Affairs, 36*(S2), 567–589.

McCarthy, K. F., Ondaatje, E. H., Zakaras, L., & Brooks, A. (2005). *Gifts of the muse: Reframing the debate about the benefits of the arts*. Santa Monica: RAND Corporation.

McGranahan, D., & Wojan, T. (2007). Recasting the creative class to examine growth processes in rural and urban counties. *Regional Studies, 41*(2), 197–216.

McHenry, J. A. (2011). Art will save the city, but what about country towns? The role of the arts in rural towns of Western Australia's Mid West region. In J. Martin & T. Budge (Eds.), *The sustainability of Australia's country towns: Renewal, renaissance, resilience* (pp. 327–349). Ballarat: Victorian Universities Regional Research Network Press.

McShane, P. (2002). *To further Australia's understanding and involvement in the international booktown movement through a program of visits and interviews*. Winston Churchill Memorial Trust of Australia. http://www.booktown.com.au/ChurchillReport_Booktowns_2002.htm. Accessed 27 Feb 2010.

Merfeld-Langston, A. L. (2007). The *villages du livre*: Local identity, cultural politics and print culture in contemporary France. PhD thesis, Pennsylvania State University.

Minet, P. (1989). *Late booking: My first twenty-Five years in the secondhand book trade*. Old Knowle: Frantic Press.

Murray, S. (2012). *The adaptation industry: The cultural economy of contemporary literary adaptation*. New York: Routledge.

Pow, T. (1999, October 11). Whisky and writers in Wigtown. *New Statesman*, p. 39.

Pratt, A. C. (2008). Creative cities: The cultural industries and and the creative class. *Geografiska annaler: Series B—Human Geography, 90*(2), 107–117.
Press, S. (2001). Reading Wigtown: Place identities in a Scottish book town. MA thesis, University of Oregon.
Rojek, C. (1993). *Ways of escape: Modern transformations in leisure and travel.* Basingstoke: Macmillan.
Rojek, C. (2000). *Leisure and culture.* Basingstoke: Macmillan.
Seaton. (1997, July). The book town concept: Retail specialization and rural tourism. *Insights* [British Tourist Authority/English Tourist Board].
Seaton. (1999). Book towns as tourism developments in peripheral areas. *The International Journal of Tourism Research, 1*(5), 389–399.
Scott, A. J. (2006). Creative cities: Conceptual issues and policy questions. *Journal of Urban Affairs, 28*(1), 1–17.
Sheller, M., & Urry, J. (Eds.). (2004). *Tourism mobilities: Places to play, places in play.* London: Routledge.
Stephenson, M., & Tate, A. S. (2015). *Arts and community change: Exploring cultural development policies, practices and dilemmas.* New York/London: Routledge.
Striphas, T. (2009). *The late age of print: Everyday book culture from consumerism to control.* New York: Columbia University Press.
Trotter, R. (2001). Regions, regionalism and cultural development. In D. Carter & T. Bennett (Eds.), *Culture in Australia: Policies, publics and programs* (pp. 334–335). Melbourne: Cambridge University Press.
Urry. (2007). *Mobilities.* Cambridge: Polity Press.
Wojan, T. (2007). The emergence of rural artistic havens: A first look. *Agricultural and Resource Economics Review, 36*(1), 53–70.
Wood, E., & Thomas, R. Festivals and tourism in rural economies. In J. Ali Knight, et al. (Eds.) *International perspectives of festivals and events* (pp. 149–158). Oxford: Elsevier.

1

Book Towns: Expanding Literary Connections

What Is a Book Town?

A book town or a location that has forged a new life through the book business—secondhand and antiquarian bookselling, writing, reading, festivals, publishing and celebration of the written word—uses its book-based economy to provide a unique, themed identity to the town or village, bolstering local, national and international tourism. In particular, book towns both rely on and contribute to the global increase in cultural tourism. Their existence means not only that the survival of hard-copy books is assured, but also that the specialized crafts and skills associated with their historical production are kept alive. This is because they appeal to an emergent nostalgia for preserving traditional print culture in an age of new technology and globalization that threatens the potential loss of traditional books. This nostalgia stems from a general renewal of interest among the middle class in handcrafted goods, in models of how people previously lived, in historic technologies and in 'slow food', found in farmers' markets in cities, hinterland areas, coastal resorts and local produce stalls in rural areas. The book town concept—particularly as it has evolved in Europe—has proven its capacity to revitalize communities via multiplier effects from a book-based economy, cultural tourism and

J. Frank, *Regenerating Regional Culture*, Sociology of the Arts,
https://doi.org/10.1007/978-3-319-65036-4_1

increased social capital for communities. It has therefore emerged as an innovative tourism solution to the economic, social and cultural issues associated with geographic peripherality and unification.

As an international phenomenon, book towns[1] are also known as *Boekenstad* (in the Netherlands), *Paese dei Librai* (in Italy), *Villages*[2] *du livre* (in France and Belgium), *Bücherstadt* (in Germany) and *Noshe Bokbyen* (in Norway) and dozens of other names in the languages of their various host countries around the world. Booth (1999, p. 274) makes the crucial point that it is hard to provide an exact definition of a book town because they are all so different. Book towns developed through unique processes and by dint of their own geographic, topographical and book-generated uniqueness—by the coast (Bécherel, France; Wigtown, Scotland; Sidney-by-the-Sea, Canada), far inland on prairies and in (almost) ghost towns (Archer City, USA; Clunes, Australia), on islands (Gotland, Sweden); in mountainous terrain (Montereggio, Italy); in forests (Redu, Belgium; Waldstadt Wünsdorf, Germany); with cross-border emphasis (Bredevoort, the Netherlands); as districts or quarters in larger regional locations (Montolieu, France); with seasonal limitations (Fjærland, Norway); as eco-experiments (Torup, Denmark); focused on children (Kembuchi and Miyawaga, children's picture book villages, Japan; Mellösa, Sweden); as a small cluster of communities all focused on book-related activities (Southern Highlands, Australia); specializing in theology (Stillwater, USA); related to graphic arts (Montolieu, France); education-oriented (Kampung Buku, Malaysia); and connected to publishing (Paju, South Korea). This book will demonstrate that their differences and their ability to embrace national, regional and local particularities and cultural uniqueness are what make book towns attractive and successful holiday and leisure destinations.

When Seaton (1999) first defined the book town, he provided an account of how these towns initially had developed across Europe—the cradle of the concept—with a retail emphasis focused on economic development and the tourist profile of certain towns:

> The basic concept of a book town consists in converting a substantial amount of commercial properties, or defunct public ones, in declining rural towns and peripheral regions, into units for the retailing of second

> hand and antiquarian books, thus creating a critical mass of single-commodity retailing which ultimately allows the town or region to be packaged and marketed as a novel and unique entity – a town of books. Through the attraction of this kind of specialist retail development visitors are motivated to visit peripheral areas that previously offered no unique *raison d'être* as tourist attractions. (p. 390)

Seaton and Alford (2001a, b) later broadened the scope of the concept beyond retail to embrace complementary cultural facets of these literary townships related to memory, identity and tradition. These included artisan retail enterprises associated with the production of books: paper production, calligraphy, printing, book design and illustration and traditional bookbinding. This expanded definition also includes the staging of events with a literary or artistic theme that allows book towns to be centres of cultural tourism. Seaton and Alford regard book towns as places that particularly appeal to the educated, affluent audiences who constitute the market for antiquarian and secondhand books. Other authors have focused more holistically on what a book town is able to provide and how it establishes a point of difference that transforms the character of a village or town, and propels the rejuvenation and renewal of towns in need of economic rescue. Hanna (2005, p. 1), for example, remarks:

> What is a book town? It depends who you ask. A few definitions follow: a small rural village with lots of bookshops; a themed village with books as a focal point; lots of businesses selling books alongside their other stock; a village or town whose economy is bolstered substantially by the sale of books; a place of culture, of books and music and theatre. If I am asked, I will answer all of the above. I care less about the definition than I do about the overall effect a book town has upon the village or town where it is born … Book towns benefit the local economy by giving an identity to the town or village and increasing local, national and international tourism. The theory is that people won't go out of their way to visit one bookshop but will travel many miles to visit a book town. To light a fire when a town is 'down on its luck' it needs a new image and a fresh start; the book town initiative provides that.

Hanna emphasizes the multiplier effect that book town projects have on regional economies, impacting not only on book-related businesses, but on a host of other—often unrelated—businesses in the community. What is implied, but not directly stated, in this definition is that book town projects are valuable for kick-starting the sense of a town's growing social capital. Macaskill (2007, p. 2) describes what many contemporary book towns try to achieve in this regard, stating that a book town is a location that celebrates the written word and welcomes travellers whether they are avid readers, writers or merely browsers, wanting to visit a town with an extra twist. These towns and villages have a delightfully disproportionate number of secondhand and antiquarian bookshops, and sometimes also have other associated businesses based on writing, reading and publishing. The idea is that a mainly rural town—in attractive surroundings and with historic interest—will find a new life through the book business by attracting well-read visitors.

Any contemporary definition of a book town needs to be inclusive of a range of valid models and viewpoints, and this book will contribute a further dimension to these understandings. For example, Wigtown Festival Director Adrian Turpin (personal interviews 2011, 2017) is interested in the 'grassroots' role of the book town as a resilient literature organization for a region, a national resource and destination for cultural tourism and a point of diversity and connection. He emphasizes the evolving role of the book town as it adapts to a range of broad local and global influences, forecasting that book towns will increasingly become centres of learning and places where ideas are traded. This is so despite the peripheral locations of these towns, or even because of their geographic situations. In contrast, Hay-on-Wye founder Richard Booth (personal interview 2011) identifies the market for secondhand books primarily as an international one, driven by special interests and scarcity of certain secondhand titles in specialized subject categories. His broad view is that book towns need to be the axis points of an international economy and a springboard for greater international understanding through educational exchange. He argues that the advantage of specialized subject areas and linkages with wider international networks is that they will improve the service provided by book towns and widen their global market share.

The emergence of the Book Town Movement is inextricably tied to the key role of individuals—often eccentric ones—beginning with Booth, the founder of the concept. Beginning in 1961, he single-handedly inspired the development of the world's first book town, Hay-on-Wye in Wales. I investigate how others were inspired by his lead and how book towns emerged in Europe and beyond, leading to the formation of international networks and collaborations. Book town founders have identified and developed the potential of their community and region to sustain book-centred activities and attract a book-loving public, as well as understanding and utilizing interactions between not-for-profit and for-profit enterprises in the contexts of tourism, hospitality, cultural production and cultural consumption. While recent book town models have been inspired by certain flamboyant bibliophiles, they also rely for their success and survival on entrepreneurship, government investment, targeted philanthropy and sophisticated communication and networking systems. An interesting juxtaposition is that book towns rely heavily on the internet and a range of modern technologies to conduct their business affairs, including maintaining virtual networks with other bookshops and book towns around the globe. They are both able to preserve past technologies, yet actively take part in contemporary global communications that rely on cutting-edge technologies. In many ways, they are as much a product of contemporary technological and cultural change as they are a reaction to it.

Why Are Book Towns Proliferating Across the Globe?

The popularity, growing importance and expanding functions of book towns, located in peripheral locales, magnify their role in facilitating a wide range of connections between writers, event organizers, book collectors, publishers, the media and the book-loving public, as well as interchanges between communities around the globe. Book towns and the books at their nucleus, as central to overlapping literary, community and commercial interests, spark the central question of this study: why, at a time when the book industry is arguably experiencing a transformation that is more profound than at any time since Gutenberg introduced printing from moveable type in the 1450s, are book towns a growing phenomenon in the early twenty-first century, sustaining and adapting the relationship between book culture and regional locations?

Print and Book Culture

The first factor is the continued buoyancy of book and print culture. Book towns are repositories of secondhand books. Yet my examination of existing scholarship and findings from visits to book towns has revealed a surprising gap in the existing research: the lack of analysis of the current significance of books within book towns. None of the remarkable book-based tourism, economic or peripheral development activity that has occurred would be possible without the continuing draw of books and the sustained need for people to engage in a complex series of relationships with them. The work of this book therefore aims to engage with and contribute to a growing body of research on book history that, together with book/print culture and publishing studies, emphasizes the role of the book as a material object. Books remain key artefacts through which we 'articulate and struggle over specific interests, values, practices and world views' while book culture can be defined as the 'meanings, values, practices, artefacts and ways of life associated with books' (Striphas 2009, pp. 3–9). More broadly, print culture embodies all forms of printed text and other forms of visual communication, and can be contrasted with oral culture (Ong 1982). It is defined as the conglomeration of effects on human society created by printed forms of communication and encompasses many stages as it has evolved in response to technological advance. Over the last 25 years, there has been a new interest in examining print culture, evidenced in the work of Robert Darnton and others who have followed his lead. 'Cultural history approaches' have embraced the study of institutional, industrial and cultural contexts of reading and writing (Carter and Galligan 2007, p. 2). This trend is driven partly by recognition of the key role played by print in our culture for the past 500 years, but also a realization that the book's status is being challenged by other media. Its overwhelming dominance is increasingly being questioned in the literature, and Finkelstein and McCleery (2002, pp. 2–3) believe that this has licensed the study of the book's past as a means to better understand a potential eclipse of the print era.

With Ted Striphas, I strongly question any commonsense understandings of a crisis of book culture. Books still remain at the nucleus of a complex social infrastructure. This infrastructure 'comprises a network of intersecting material, technical, interpersonal, institutional and discursive relations that provides for the production, distribution, exchange and consumption of books' (Striphas 2009, p. 14). Although the production and propagation of books have undoubtedly entered a new phase, printed works are still very much a part of our daily lives. In fact, the 'everyday life of book culture' includes the institutional arrangements, social relations and historical processes that enable books to be perceived as everyday entitlements or 'objects that can be counted on to be wherever and whenever we expect them to be' (pp. 10–11). The book is still the quintessential capital good, having evolved alongside capitalism itself, and both the book and book industry are key foci for innovation: 'late capitalism is still vigorous capitalism, so books and other printed materials in the late age of print are still common and enjoy considerable prestige' (Bolter quoted in Striphas p. 3). Books have a unique role in our culture—an unusual double life. In one sense, they are regarded as important tools of our culture and fundamental to education, subject to intense government and media scrutiny or else disregarded as a form of elite taste; yet at the same time they are considered throwaway items—disposable, familiar, everyday commercial products that are subject to the fluctuations of the market. Similarly, in the case of publishing, there is a dualism between commerce and culture, with publishing considered a commercial industry subject to all the forces and constraints of the marketplace, yet one whose 'products carry messages of social and cultural significance' that many people seek despite the inconsistencies and constraints of the commercial sector (Carter and Galligan 2007, pp. 3–5).

Considering that context, in the writing of this book I have engaged with the following questions: how are people engaging with print culture? What role do books play in our lives? And, importantly, what implications do these connections have on the growth of the Book Town Movement? While investigating these questions, I was confronted by two opposed and initially perplexing collections of evidence, leading to very different conclusions about the future of print culture and engagement with books. Some people describe a current renaissance in book culture, yet others just as vehemently reject this argument. Darnton (1999) rather ironically comments that 'the "conventional" book has been pronounced dead so often that we shouldn't be surprised to find that it seems in excellent health':

> Rarely in Britain has the book trade seemed so vigorous ... Britain's literary microclimate is tropical in its fever and Elizabethan in its profusion. Book festivals from Folkestone to Edinburgh heave with visitors; book clubs and reading groups have become middle England's bingo; book prize news breaks ceaselessly. And that's not to mention the broadcasters, from *The South Bank Show* and Richard and Judy to *Book at Bedtime*. No genre of contemporary writing escapes the programmers. (McCrum 2006, para. 2)

Buzbee (2006, pp. 213–14) observes that 'we're publishing more books than ever, and while there is a good deal being published that we probably won't be reading fifty, or even five, years from now, this has always been the case.' However, just as many commentators and researchers—including Birkerts (1995), Gekowski (2011) and McMurtry (quoted in Lanham 2009)—cite the rising sales of e-books as evidence of a crisis and deride the nostalgia of book-loving baby boomers. New York-based Bob Stein, who visited Australia in 2009 to establish a branch of his Institute for the Future of the Book, states:

> If you think about the book as an object made of printed pages, there is no future for the book, and it's an uninteresting discussion. What's more interesting is to try to understand what role a book plays in our lives ... The book is a vehicle humans use to move ideas around time and space. In all these conversations about the book, what makes it difficult to talk about what's coming is to get over people's attachment to what was. One of the hardest things is separating out the nostalgia. (Quoted in Sorensen 2009, paras 6–7)

Stein's position is extreme—even among those who are enthusiastic about the prospect that technology will change publishing and reading. A more moderate way of looking at this issue is to acknowledge that printed books will continue—and not merely as antiquarian collectibles—insofar as they still have utility, readability, marketability and authority. History proves that new media forms such as television and radio don't completely replace existing forms; rather, they shuffle their place and purpose in the cultural field (Bartmanski and Woodward 2015, p. 4). Thus there are others confident of the book's future: Striphas (2009), Carrière and Eco (2011), Zaid (2004), Darnton (2009), Basbanes (1995) and Florence (quoted in Lindores 2010).

When contemplating the future of books, it is important to note that books and the publishing industry do not exist in isolation. They are, and always have been, intrinsic to a broader symbolic and information-centred environment or culture, where for a millennium they have played a vital role as material forms in which content can be embedded, packaged and communicated to others. Books continue to demand considerable attention in newspapers, in other media and on radio, as well as providing a staple source of inspiration and raw materials for films and other forms of popular entertainment. Therefore, books have a rich public life beyond the printed page. Book content circulates through a range of other related cultural mediums, such as international book fairs, screen festivals and writers' weeks: 'these phenomena incubate the adaption of book content into other media, and such adaptions are then marketed back to book-centric audiences' (Murray 2009). Ongoing literary prestige therefore creates a ripple effect through the deployment of a range of adaptions from original literary works. The links not only with books but also other related media forms, ensure that writers are still endowed with stature in our society—an accolade arguably accorded to few other professions.

The prophesized 'death of reading' would appear to be at the heart of much of this debate, with Griswold (2008) observing that in the twenty-first century, reading seems to be both honoured and abandoned. She asks (p. 65), 'How can the proliferation of reading groups, Trollope websites, book superstores, festivals of the book, and the Oprah effect be part of the same universe as the National Endowment for the Arts (NEA) report's plummeting percentages of readers?' Dana Gioia, then chair of the NEA, in his Foreword to *Reading at Risk: A Survey of Literary Reading in America* (Bradshaw and Nichols 2004, p. vii), links American engagement with literature to people playing a more active role in their communities through volunteerism, philanthropy and even political involvement. He warns of the danger of 'losing the intellectual skill and social habit' of reading, resulting in a nation that becomes less informed, active and independent-minded, and speaks of the 'dumbing down' of cultural engagement and growing preference for forms that require only passive participation, such as television and radio, or electronic media that foster shorter attention spans and accelerated gratification: 'Print culture affords irreplaceable forms of focused attention and contemplation that make complex communications and insights possible' (p. vii).

So, with regard to the question 'How can books be both ignored and sacred?', Griswold (2008) is confident that the answer lies in the emergence—or re-emergence—of a 'reading class' that consists of highly educated, affluent and young people. The members of this group are both heavy readers and early adopters of the internet who, 'exhibiting the concentration effect', read more voraciously than readers of the past. This cohort of avid readers, strong communicators, cultural omnivores—a segment of Florida's (2002) 'creative class'—combines with older, less technologically advanced, long-committed readers to make up this 'reading class'. Books, Griswold argues, are increasingly valued by this cohort. She (2008) uses the term 'reading class' rather than 'reading culture' and claims that it applies in developed countries such as Australia for a whole range of reasons, including increased levels of tertiary education, the need for people to engage in public discourse and perhaps the quest for knowledge via a journey 'elsewhere' that books provide (Kenner 1998, p. 3). While it is book culture and this quest for intellectual engagement that clearly galvanize contemporary book towns around the globe today, this was not how the entity first identified as a book town was initially identified.

Tony Seaton: Book Towns and Tourism

The potential of book towns to boost regional tourism has become a major rationale for their establishment and a significant driver in the growth of the movement. However, the positive impact of book towns on tourism was not really recognized until Seaton's work of the late 1990s. Despite being a magnet for bibliophiles, throughout the 1970s and much of the 1980s, Hay tended to be regarded as an eccentric town of books that successfully injected business activity into a moribund rural area, but not as a centre for 'cultural tourism' as that term is now understood (Seaton 1999, p. 391). When, between 1984 and 1993, four new European book towns were established in Redu (Belgium), Montolieu (France), Bécherel (France) and Bredevoort (Holland), the regional economy was the main focus. Seaton (1997a) stresses that these projects were conceived as a strategy to economically rejuvenate a rural area, using the Hay-on-Wye formula of specialized retailing. However, Seaton also noticed an emergent link between book-based economic strategies and tourism, commenting that the French towns were positioned as 'unique destinations', even if that remained 'virtually unnoticed' elsewhere. It needs to be recalled that Booth's original conception of Hay-on-Wye was as a specialist retail opportunity rather than a tourist development—indeed, his apparent hostility towards tourism in general and the Wales Tourist Board in particular meant that no monitoring of Hay as a tourist attraction occurred for almost 25 years (Seaton 1997a). Nevertheless, with Hay as a model, the steady expansion of book towns in Europe increasingly drew attention to the accompanying growth of tourism. It was Seaton who undertook the first systematic study of book towns as tourist attractions. This study, which began in 1992, was funded by the Scottish Tourism Research Unit (STRU), the Scottish Tourist Board and Scottish Enterprise, with a view to assessing the potential of a book town in Scotland (Seaton 1997a).

Seaton's research, which was completed in two parts, focused on book towns in relation to the generation of tourism. The first report, which examined Hay-on-Wye, delivered detailed findings to support the conclusion that it had 'in 35 years … been transformed from a minor destination into a "honeypot" centre with a strong international niche market clientele' (Seaton 1996a, pp. 26–30). In this work, Seaton enumerated the book town's exemplary advantages as a model of sustainable rural tourism. He discovered that book towns use existing resources to achieve economic growth; are small in scale, requiring no environment-threatening changes that impend the town character; involve relatively small business risks compared with other tourism initiatives; generate revenue that remains in the local community rather than benefiting developers or going elsewhere; stimulate a multiplier effect that benefits a range of other businesses in the town; have the power to raise the national profile of the country as well as the local profile of the town; are less seasonal and weather-dependent than other tourism products; are 'ceaselessly self-renewing attraction[s]' that encourage repeat visits and are a means of creating employment (Seaton 1996a, pp. 29–30). He also argued that they have the capacity to stem an exodus of talented people from a community. This first research report demonstrated that the growth of Hay as a book town had an overwhelming impact on its region, and to some extent on Wales as a whole. Seaton compared Hay-on-Wye's significance to Wales with Stratford-on-Avon's importance to England (Seaton 1996a, p. 18).

In-depth socio-demographic analysis of visitor trends in Hay-on-Wye was completed as part of the first report. Survey data showed that Hay attracted a high percentage of lecturers, teachers, doctors, senior managers and book dealers—often educated people in upper-income groups known in the tourism literature as 'quality tourists' and 'cultural heritage tourists'. The study revealed that females visited more frequently than males, and that although most visitors were day-trippers, visitors to book towns were prepared to drive longer distances than visitors to other attractions, stay longer and make repeat visits, depending on the calibre of books encountered (Seaton 1996a, p. 18). More recent research has determined that this micro-market, which is interested in culture, education, religion and architecture, is often affluent, older, more highly educated, likely to be 'empty nesters' and probably subscribes to the National Trust (Seaton 2010). While most commentators regard book town visitors as eclectic, Seaton (1996a) postulates that the cohort that frequents book towns appreciates forming personal relationships with knowledgeable booksellers. He asserts that they are also more likely to be aware of, and respect, the cultural heritage embodied in the buildings and other landmarks of book towns, and to patronize the cafés, art galleries, craft shops, restaurants and museums that enhance and complete a book town experience.

The second part of Seaton's 1996 research examined the early achievements of the first generation of book towns in France, Belgium and Holland, focusing on their locational features, organizational structures and tourism performance. As discussed in the Introduction, this document recommended the book town as a significant and low-cost regeneration development for a Scottish rural town (Seaton 1996b).

Seaton's pioneering research of the 1990s, conducted both individually and with others, was the springboard for contemporary analysis of what has occurred. Most of Seaton's research focused on the economic, demographic and tourism benefits of the establishment of book towns, as well as the part technology played in developing communication systems and SME[3] cultural tourism networks within and between towns in Europe. This largely quantitative research particularly analysed the economic viability of Hay-on-Wye and other European towns at the bequest of various governments, cultural bodies and tourism organizations. However, this research is now quite dated, and book towns have multiplied far outside the bounds of Europe.

Cultural Tourists/Post-tourists

The initial impetus for developing book towns was to create tourist destinations. Seaton (2002) wrote about various tourist typologies, reinforcing this view of the cultural tourist—aesthete, litterateur or epicurean, associated with good and responsible behaviour and actions—as seeking authenticity and quality of experience, and therefore standing apart from mass tourism. This group more broadly includes people interested in culture and education, and there is an association with a pattern of increasing moral worthiness (Peterson and Kern 1996, p. 906). These tourists like to form personal relationships with specialist booksellers, are more likely to be aware of and have respect for the history and heritage implicit in the buildings and locations of book towns and are likely to frequent the tea rooms and museums that complement a book town visit. The 'purposeful cultural tourist', however, is only one sub-sector of a wider spectrum of tourists who may populate book towns. Bob McKercher's (2002, pp. 32–3) research identifies five different types of cultural tourist, of which 'purposeful' is only one; the others are sightseeing, casual, incidental and serendipitous cultural tourists, with the experiences sought ranging from deep to shallow and a wide-ranging difference applying when considering the importance of cultural tourism as part of the decision to visit a destination.

Recent studies of post-tourist trends apply to the growth of the most recent generation of book towns and ongoing support of more established book towns worldwide. The rise of post-tourism, perpetrated by post-tourists or new leisure tourists, has featured extensively in sociological, travel and tourism studies' literature over the past 20 years. The new leisure tourist thus demonstrates an aesthetic cosmopolitanism that includes an innate 'ability to locate one's own society and its culture in terms of a wide-ranging historical and geographical knowledge, to have some ability to reflect upon and judge aesthetically between natures, places and societies', as well as a 'certain semiotic skill – to be able to interpret tourist signs, to see what they are meant to represent and … to know when they are partly ironic' (Urry 1995, p. 167). The members of this group, through their multiple mobilities, form a culture of cosmopolitan citizenship, where physical, imaginative and virtual travel are interchangeable (Szerszyncki and Urry 2006, pp. 115–16). In part, this is because tourism has become a significant modality through which globalized modern life is organized. Further, tourism is central to understanding social (dis)organization, where it is not constrained to specific locations or cordoned off in particular time periods (Franklin and Crang 2001, pp. 6–7). It is therefore appropriate to view vacationing as:

> a cultural laboratory where people have been able to experiment with new aspects of identities, their social relations or their interactions with nature and also to use the important cultural skills of day-dreaming and mind-travelling. Here is an arena in which fantasy has become an important social practice. (Löfgren 1999, pp. 6–7)

Tourism, then, is partly about the invention and reinvention of cultural traditions.

Equally important, however, are the 'production and consumption of myths and staged inauthenticities' (Selwyn 1996, p. 28). Mention of the mythical is prevalent in contemporary discussions of travel and tourism (Rojek, in Rojek and Urry 1997, pp. 52–74). Hay-on-Wye's fantastical identity as a book kingdom is a good example of how the book town has created its own mythology. Echoing the argument of Barthes (1972), Rojek claims that, as a social category, '"the extra ordinary place" invites speculation, reverie, mind-voyaging and a variety of other acts of imagination' that are important for their global appeal to discerning travellers in search of specialized experiences. This can occur from inauthenticity appreciated by post-tourists—in the case of Hay—or, equally, from the authenticity sought by cultural tourists. In fact, the latter is linked to the extraordinary history of many book towns that fire the tourist imagination. For example, Montereggio in Southern Italy started its association with books in the fifteenth century with the discovery of Gutenberg's Bible fragment and its association with the nearby town of Fivizzano's origins as a printing town. From 1493, the town was a centre of bookselling, benefiting from the collapse of the silk trade in the north, which attracted available workers to become booksellers. Known as the 'shepherd booksellers', most were unable to read or write, and in order to sell books recited passages they had learned by heart, travelling long distances to do so (Campbell 2014, p. 151). As the historic centre of all this bookselling, Montereggio began hosting Italy's premier literary prize, the Premio Bancarella, in 1952 (Martin 2009). Roads in Montereggio are named after famous Italian publishers. This rich history provides an attractive drawcard for cultural tourists.

Cultural tourists and post-tourists therefore have distinct foci, but in various ways both support the Book Town Movement. Smith's (2006, p. 223) views are supportive of this argument, distinguishing cultural tourists—well-educated, earnest seekers of authentic culture and communities—from post-tourists—enjoyers of more playful tourism and leisure experiences: the new leisure tourist is far more keen to interact with simulated worlds and experiences than with real people. Therefore, the new leisure tourist may enjoy visiting a model village destination more than a real one. A book town is arguably a type of model village. Sheller and Urry (2004) thus refer to tourism destinations as 'places to play' as well as 'places *in* play'. However, 'toy' cultures such as this face risks associated with the challenge of establishing balance between extreme novelty and the ugliness that can befall places of extreme inauthenticity. The members of this group are not particularly adventurous, expecting certain levels of comfort and security when they travel, in a cosmopolitan sense. As Burns explains, 'consumerism impacts upon destinations through tourists bringing with them the urban (and urbane?) attitudes of the consumer society that they live in such as expectations of service levels, and that commodities have their price' (2001, p. 296). This points to a controversy (Shields 1991, p. 2), which lies at the meeting point of contemporary cultural change and the political economy of commodity exchange. Understandings of tourism have become fetishized so that economic activities are often opposed to important issues of social and cultural practice—taste, fashion and identity (Rojek and Urry 1997, p. 2).

Clusters of Books

Clustering is not a new phenomenon, and the convenience it provides has been valued since the earliest trading began. In this age, in which real and virtual worlds merge, book towns provide a remarkable example of the evolution of spatial geography and clustering in which face-to-face contact remains the primary success factor. Antiquarian book dealer Anthony Marshall, author of *Trafficking in Old Books* (1998) and *Fossicking for Old Books* (2004), which provide useful commentary about the secondhand book market, history and trends, argues that the effectiveness of clusters for the secondhand book market is indisputable:

> Doesn't the size of your slice depend on your preventing your competitors from grabbing a piece of yours while you attempt to grab a piece of theirs? In order for you to prosper, is it not essential that your competitors should struggle? All I can say is that it doesn't seem to work like that in our trade [secondhand books] ... Maybe it is because no two bookshops ever have the same stock. Bookshops are as individualistic as their owners. And if there is some overlap of stock, all booksellers have different ideas about price and presentation and customer service. So bookshops have a tendency to cluster. Like antique shops, you often find them in little enclaves. It makes good sense. If customers don't find what they want in one shop they can easily progress to the next, and the next. (Marshall 1998, pp. 222–3)

There is usually collaboration between enterprises in a book town, and each enterprise has its own speciality, which complements those of the others and builds a coherent book town identity as opposed to encouraging competition between individual stores—with the end-product of that merely being a street with bookshops in it (Press 2001, p. 34). This is one of a raft of approaches that have been applied to rekindle regional growth and create new opportunities for the sustainability of regional communities.

Charles Landry's (2008) work on clustering, creative quarters and activating creative assets provides an important context for this study. Landry demonstrates that clustering has proven to be important in creative places where talent, skill and support infrastructures are central to the creative economy and the creative milieu (p. xli). Particularly in urban areas, spatial clusters of activities or industry concentrations in sectors such as education, design and bio-technology provide viability and prosperity through the provision of mutual financial, technical and psychological support: 'increasing the efficiency of markets; bringing together buyers and sellers; creating overlap between adjacent disciplines or accessible centres of excellence; and stimulating competition, thereby generating "multiplier" effects, synergy, complementary interchanges and swapping of resources' (p. xli). However, Landry also stresses that the value of distinctiveness is a powerful source of creativity, using the example of Hay-on-Wye and other book towns as places that have tapped into culture as an imaginative resource to 'creat[e] something out of nothing' (p. 10).

Michael (2007) closely examines what he broadly coins 'micro-clusters' occurring in areas of rural decline, where there is 'diminution of economic opportunity and regional inequity … evident in many parts of the developed world including Australia, New Zealand and in some peripheral regions of North America and Europe including Ireland, Scandinavia and the smaller Mediterranean states' (p. xvii). Notable international clusters include cashew nuts in Brazil; chairs in Udine, Italy; the Dutch flower cluster; the Argentinean oil seed cluster and country music-based tourism in Branson, Missouri, USA (Irshad 2009, pp. 12–17). Michael's micro-cluster theory stems from what he calls a series of tangential findings in studies of niche tourism markets that include antique retailing in south-west Pennsylvania (Grado et al. 1997); antiques as a tourist market in Australia (Michael 2002) and Tony Seaton's analyses of book towns in the United Kingdom and Europe (1996a, b, 1999). He believes these collectively suggest that such markets are amenable to clustering in regional areas.

With regard to clustering in the antiques trade, Michael (2007) categorizes books within the collectibles sub-set, exploring the role played by such clusters in generating particular types of demand for travel to specific locations. The issue of clusters as trip generators is important in any assessment of visitation to book towns. Books draw people at two different levels: the main reason for visiting is to buy or collect books as a specific type of merchandise, but book browsing also provides an ancillary activity in book towns, encouraging travellers to extend their stay and therefore increase economic activity within that community. In rural areas, the clustering of bookstores within a single book town is a more appealing version of a superstore, but with fresh air, rural scenery, specialized, knowledgeable booksellers, cultural heritage and other local attractions to enhance the book shopping and collecting experience. The framework for developing micro-clusters also provides an integrated and practical alternative for public decision-makers, and explains the alternative government-assisted book town model that sprang up repeatedly across Europe from 1984 onwards. Book towns also attract small innovative publishers around the world, and having publishers working in close proximity to bookshops and book festivals is part of the cluster model that explains the success of book towns worldwide.

Networked Book Towns in Europe

Another factor in the growth and sustenance of book towns are the frameworks established to promote and support them by governments and non-governmental agencies, and the organized mutual support structures they create themselves. The early success of European book towns was a catalyst for the European Union (EU) to support research exploring the benefits of book towns to bolster rural areas. The study that led to the report *Project UR 4001: European Book Town Network* (Skogseid and Seaton 1998) was conducted between 1 July 1998 and 31 June 2000 to investigate economic aspects of creating and maintaining book towns, and concluded that book towns achieved new local growth that drove sustainability. This project grew out of interest in earlier research by Skogseid and Seaton that produced a report, *Book Town Status and User Needs Analysis* (European Union 1998). A key focus of this work was the inception and development of a virtual book town organization, named BookTownNet, the application of which became the primary outcome of the report.

In 1996, five book towns[4] had developed an organizational network (Jansen and Skogseid 2003, p. 229) known as the Book Town Network. While these book towns had each established between 12 and 36 bookshops and were attracting up to 500,000 visitors annually, they were experiencing increasing marginalization due to the rise of internet trading. Book towns soon recognized the advantages of collaborating as a global village—even selling each other's books—while at the same time maintaining a healthy level of competition. This network promoted collaboration between, and public access to, all book towns and sponsored a website—booktown.net—that provided information about book towns, including Skogseid's analyses of the economic benefits generated by book towns in terms of tourist impacts. This work led to other scholarly findings related to book towns and technology. Seaton and Alford's article in the *Journal of Information Technology and Tourism* (2001b) sought to understand the technological needs of businesses in book towns, explored how the BookTownNet website impacted on the creation of links between book towns and gathered other vital data relating to sales and tourist figures. Seaton and Alford's results were unexpected: rather than threatening traditional practices such as reading, printing and selling books, new technologies like the internet were valuable for showcasing these earlier technologies. Further, the authors recommended book towns as a prototype for cultural tourism, stating that the international potential of books as the nucleus of such cultural networks had not yet completely been fulfilled (Seaton and Alford 2001b, p. 120).

The new global economy, based on information and communications technology (ICT), has challenged the sustainability of the Book Town Movement, with its emblematic old-style bookshop image. However, it became apparent that global marketing strategies—a strength of the tourism industry—were also a valid option for SMEs. Seaton and Alford (2001a, p. 115) explain that, through strategic alliances and cooperation across different industries, small enterprises can potentially achieve marketing and publicity success as a critical mass rather than approaching the task alone. Jansen and Skogseid (2003) explored the response of book towns—consisting of small rural enterprises and communities—to the challenges posed by a new global economy and concluded that it was possible to stimulate local economies through collaboration in horizontal networks. As the book town phenomenon expanded in Europe, so did the need for enhanced communication between villages. The sharing of information and ideas through their 'indigenous network' (Jansen and Skogseid 2003, p. 234)—both between individual bookshops in the same town and between various participating towns—has enabled a wider internet profile. Although book towns were not originally intended to be a novel way to market books in the computer age, this is what has happened, with the internet creating a year-round 'bread and butter' market for booksellers. Their inventories are available on the internet or connected to web-based book-finding agencies. Book lovers who cannot travel frequently to the book towns may patronize them all year long via these mechanisms. So, as a means of distributing books and promoting knowledge about books, book towns make use of one of the most recent communication technologies to preserve one of the oldest.

At a time when there is significant change occurring in global publishing and book retailing, Jansen and Skogseid's case study highlights collaboration and the broadening of the interface between book towns and their multiple stakeholders. It suggests that any newly developed book town would benefit from promoting its unique geographical context while simultaneously engaging with other national and international book towns in search of commonality. The way the BookTownNet project targeted a specialist tourism niche market—namely 'book buyers and enthusiasts' (Seaton and Alford 2001a, p. 117)—supports Richard Booth's (1999) argument that identifying niche supporters of books and genre specializations is vital to building on the success of book towns, and that the creation of international networks providing access to people with common special interests is how book town managers and organizers can look to the future. Fostering these contacts via the internet has allowed book towns to use globalization and rapid technological development to their advantage (McShane 2002, p. 33).

The IOB and International Networks

An international community of book towns has existed in both a physical and virtual sense since 1997, and the truly global nature of the book town phenomenon is arguably one of its core strengths, sustaining existing book towns and inspiring the inception of further ones. The International Organization of Book Towns (IOB) is a support and networking organization that aims to raise public awareness of book towns, stimulate interest in them around the world and facilitate their reciprocal recognition. Booksellers and other businesses in member towns are able to exchange knowledge, skills and expertise. While the IOB specifically links book towns around the world, antiquarian booksellers have been members of an International League of Antiquarian Booksellers (ILAB) since 1948. The League had six member countries when it was established: Denmark, France, Great Britain, the Netherland, Sweden and Switzerland (Rota, in Mandelbrote 2006). The delegates' shared aim was to re-establish cross-border trust between booksellers in the aftermath of World War II (Craddock 1993). This was an important step towards developing the global market in antiquarian books that is evident today, according to Kells (2011, p. 231). Today, ILAB is one of the world's largest trade associations in any sector.[5]

The IOB claims a membership of 22 book towns worldwide,[6] while the International Book Towns Movement web page lists 20.[7] My research has uncovered 58[8]; however, the number of book towns worldwide is likely to be greater as many are unaffiliated and new book towns often take time to establish an online presence. Irrespective of exact numbers, book towns are steadily proliferating worldwide, particularly in mainland Europe. Since 2005, new European book towns have included Torup, Denmark (2006), Votikvere, Estonia (2006), Urueña, Spain (2007), Bellprat, Catalonia, Spain (2008), Tvedstrand, Norway (2008), Purgstall, Austria (2009), Esquelbecq, France (2010), Pazin, Istria, Croatia (2010), Ambierle, France (2011), Borrby, Sweden (2011), Selfoss, Iceland (2014), Ascona, Switzerland (2014), Òbidos Vila Literaria, Portugal (2015), El Pedrosa, Spain (2015), Cervera, Catalonia, Spain (2016) and Montblanc, Catalonia, Spain (2017). Since 2005, recent non-European examples have appeared in Hobart, Catskills, New York State, USA (2005), Paju, South Korea

(2006); Clunes, Victoria, Australia (2007); St Martins, New Brunswick, Canada (2007); Kampang Buku Melaka (2007) and Kedah Darul Aman (2008), both in Malaysia; Richmond, South Africa (2009); Featherston, New Zealand (2014) and Bosu-deng, Jung-gu, South Korea (between 2014 and 2016). The previous 20-year period saw 24 book towns emerge in mainland Europe and 9 elsewhere in the world, so it can reasonably be concluded that the rate of new book town development is increasing steadily. McShane (2002) remarks in his Churchill Fellowship report that in almost all cases, the primary inspiration has come from Hay-on-Wye's outstanding success—an 'if they can do it, so can we' attitude, particularly from entrepreneurial bibliophiles. Booth's imprint, Richard Booth Publications, has intermittently published the *International Book Town Gazette*, a periodical that shares news of book towns worldwide.

The IOB promotes existing book towns; offers e-commerce opportunities to the booksellers in these book towns, enabling them to offer their books to a universal public; assists book town business interests in the winter economy and stimulates the towns' use of information technology. IOB assistance enables book town communities to maintain regional and national cultural heritage, and profiles them as destinations to an international public. Another important responsibility undertaken by the IOB is organizing the International Book Town Festival every second year in a different IOB book town.[9] Seaton (1997b, p. 15) stresses the IOB's 'encouraging of international relations at the grassroots level', its significant scope to develop international networks that encourage travel between countries, thereby sharing a key objective of the European Union, and the potential benefits from joint promotions and other activities. However, the challenge to the IOB's effectiveness as an organization is that each book town is unique in the way it has been founded, in the vision of the founder/s and in its particular current and future focus.

The IOB has refereed a range of discussions about book town definitions since it was founded. Book towns that qualify as IOB members need to prove that their town is sufficiently bookish—for example, that permanent bookshops are clustered and that the community promotes itself as a book-based economy. Despite the desirability of being in the IOB, Burwood (2010) suggests that what really 'makes' a book town is the decision to proclaim itself as such, commenting that some towns—and he uses the example of Ann Arbor in Michigan in the United States—have numerous bookshops but are not IOB members, and therefore not recognized as book towns in any official capacity. Further, cultural quarters exist in cities the world over—in Jinbōchō, Tokyo, for example—many of them supporting book culture and cultural tourism. Projects and events with a book focus abound. The urban book districts, such as neighbourhoods in Buenos Aires, Concord Massachusetts, The Strand in Manhattan advertising 'eight miles of books', San Francisco and others, while sharing the creative and cultural goals of many rural book towns and enabling urban renewal, do not share the characteristics of sustainable peripheral communities and the image of a community that promotes books in the countryside, offering a counterpart to the centralized urban retail model. They are therefore excluded from being classified as book towns.

While book town accreditation is taken very seriously by members, some book towns—such as the Southern Highlands in Australia and Archer City in Texas, USA—that are listed on the Book Town Movement web page are not accredited as IOB members and are dismissive of the significance of such a membership (McShane, personal interview 2010). But, accredited or not, book towns of the kind Booth envisaged exist in non-urban settings—whether that be in a harbour town like Tvedestrand in Norway or the Swiss Alpine Village of St-Pierre-de-Clages. These locations are synonymous with books and quiet contemplation in beautiful rural surroundings.

Ideological Agendas Inspiring Book Town Formation

Ideological agendas, as well as particular economic challenges for rural communities, have also precipitated book town developments in Europe. Since 1992, the European Union has embarked on numerous endeavours to unify its member countries. One approach involves creating a series of 'cultural itineraries' (Merfeld-Langston 2007, p. 165; Smith 2003, pp. 67–8) designed to increase public awareness of Europe's history, culture and architecture. A governing body for this network of enterprises, the European Institute of Cultural Routes, was created in 1997

(European Institute of Cultural Routes 2006). Its 'Itinerary of the Book' underscores the significance of books in European cultural history and the desire to preserve them as a common heritage. Book towns have been funded as part of this process (Huckans 2005; Merfeld-Langston 2007, pp. 164–8). When considered together with the IOB's promotion of what they offer, and the parallel efforts of UNESCO since 1987, there has been considerable encouragement of book towns as a way of ensuring that Europe is more 'socially cohesive' (Merfeld-Langston 2007, p. 166; Smith 2003, p. 67) and that residents of Europe discover and appreciate their diverse yet common cultural heritage, reinforcing Europe as a 'continuous destination' (Smith 2003, p. 72).

UNESCO has focused on sustainable strategies for creative tourism, including recognition of creative policy-making around the world in rural and regional areas. The Creative Cities Network (UNESCO 2010), established in 2004, and in particular the UNESCO City of Literature programme, recognizes places of cultural and literary activity, encouraging the unlocking of the entrepreneurial and creative potential of small enterprises. Other considerations have included concern about the geographical and seasonal concentration of tourism leading to congestion, risk of accident, overwork and unemployment, and threats to both the natural and human-made environment. To counter these disadvantages, seasonality has been addressed by promoting varieties of tourism that provide an 'improved distribution of impact in time and space': social, rural and cultural tourism ('The EC and Tourism' 1988, p. 24).

These political agendas are particularly evident in France, where book towns have proliferated more extensively than anywhere else in the world. In her examination of the *villages du livre*, Merfeld-Langston discusses French pride in national book and literary culture, which is so fervent that every region in France aspires to have a book town to demonstrate a duty of honour to French books, authors and national and regional print culture. She describes books as having a 'symbolic currency' and argues that cultural capital is as vital to France as economic capital (Merfeld-Langston 2007, pp. 108–12). These factors contribute to the higher-than-usual concentration of nine book towns in France. Like other book towns, most *villages du livre* have used the book town solution as a means to revalorize their unique local and regional histories and reverse the damage caused by the drain of rural populations to cities during the nineteenth and twentieth centuries. Talented individuals have instead chosen to remain in the towns to run businesses or pursue creative pathways rather than relocate to larger metropolitan centres. The economies of book towns have been strengthened by considerable government investment. The role of the French state, through a cultural policy aimed at developing and sustaining regional distinctiveness, has been significant in creating and perpetuating significant French traditions that may otherwise be lost:

> It is no coincidence that the *villages du livre* gained momentum beginning in the 1980s, a decade marked by the decentralising trend of the Mitterand regime. In 1982, the French regions as they exist today were officially recognized as '*collectivités locales*' ... Decentralization of the 1980s also led to changes in how culture was perceived. Jack Lang, then Minister of Culture, expanded the notion to include not only 'high' forms of art ... but also popular forms of artistic expression like graffiti, *bandes dessinnées*, and popular novels such as those that might be found in book towns. (Merfeld-Langston 2007, pp. 79–82)

France's *Lire en Fête*, an event that has occurred annually since 1989, is a celebration first initiated by Lang, who developed it in partnership with the French government in order to provide entertainment and democratization, accelerate public engagement in French society and foster responsible citizenship through encouraging the development of a literate public sphere. Anti-Americanism in the interests of protecting national cultural interests also meant a re-emphasis on French television programming, excluding cultural products from free trade agreements and protecting rural environments from being overshadowed by city centres (Merfeld-Langston 2010, p. 343). Safeguarding book culture amid the threat of mass industries has been a key motivating factor in the establishment of regional book towns in France.

It is not surprising that book towns are represented as rural utopias in the literature. Utopian notions spring from discontent with one or more aspects of political, economic, religious and social circumstances, 'envisioning happier, healthier lives' (Merfeld-Langston 2007, p. 33). The book town trend, as evidenced in the *villages du livre* and other European sites, is motivated by the desire of individuals, groups or governments to create utopian communities with the aim of counteracting threats of globalization and the dominance exerted by large metropolitan centres. These ideas correlate with those of Harvey (2000), who writes of the human yearning for imagined places where people can resist the world of capital accumulation. Likewise, in *The Power of Identity* (1997, p. 60), Castells describes our world and our lives being shaped by the conflicting trends of globalization and identity, referring to one of the earliest debates in urban sociology: the loss of community resulting from increasing urbanization, and later suburbanization. Book towns—centres of communal effort and unique cultural identity—are partly a product of the social mobilization of which Castells (1997) writes, whereby people move to locations where common interests are discovered, thus creating new meaning in their lives. Local communities such as book towns, established through collective action and then preserved through collective memory, are therefore a specific source of identity. In most cases, such identities are 'defensive reactions against the impositions of global disorder and uncontrollable, fast-paced change' (Castells 1997, p. 64).

However, places such as book towns 'build havens, but not heavens', according to Castells (1997). Hay-on-Wye's embracing of a traditional way of life that rejects supermarkets and quangos comes to mind. This new idealism was a benefit of being part of the small Welsh community promoting local production and self-sufficiency amid a climate of bookselling. Castells could be referring to Hay-on-Wye when he states (p. 66): 'When the world becomes too large to be controlled, social actions aim at shrinking it back to their size and reach. When networks dissolve time and space, people anchor themselves in places and recall their historic memory.' The form of identity-building that occurs in book towns is referred to as 'resistance identity' (p. 67), where trenches of resistance are created in opposition to the ruling norm. On one hand, dominant global elites consist of identity-less individuals, or 'citizens of the world', while on the other, those refusing to accept cultural, economic and political disenfranchisement tend to be drawn to such communal identity. The establishment of cohesive peripheral territories is at the heart of the desire of local and regional governments to react and adapt to the ongoing variation of global flows. I regard book towns and other themed communities as 'communes of resistance' that defend their spaces and places against 'the placeless logic of the space of flows, characterising social domination in the Information Age. They claim their historic memory and/or affirm the permanence of their values against the dissolution of history in endless time, and the celebration of the ephemeral in the culture of real virtuality' (p. 358).

Further, the creation of book towns as authentic places in the world matches what Harvey (1996, pp. 37–9, 41–2) and Williams (1989, pp. 242–3, 249) coin 'militant particularism', indicating the political use of particularity of place as a form of political resistance against the forces of global capitalism. Book towns fit in with the worldwide trend for groups of people to build their own places and communities to live differently from 'the mass of people'. Other examples include communes, organic farms, traveller communities, urban neighbourhood groups and religious enclaves (Cresswell 2004, p. 61). Place is therefore seen as the locus of collective memory, as described by Harvey (1996, p. 306):

> 'Critical regionalism' as it is called in architecture, involving as it so often does vernacular traditions and icons of place, is considered a basis for the politics of resistance to commodity flows and monetization. 'Militant particularism' seizes upon the qualities of place, reanimates the bond between the environmental and the social, and seeks to bend the social processes constructing space-time to a radically different purpose … Imagined places, the Utopian thoughts and desires of countless peoples, have consequently played a vital role in animating politics.

The application of this theory to book towns has been critiqued by Merfeld-Langston (2007, pp. 37–8) as artificial constructions of an idealized terrain:

> Just as with other nascent utopian communities, most of the book towns which began to appear in the 1980s … have been (re)constructed culturally, physically, economically and demographically as a result of dissatisfaction with the local state of affairs. Nevertheless, in the process of transforming the towns, project initiators and administrators attempted to maintain the cultural, and especially architectural heritage already present in their communities … Moreover, they rely on the appeal of their rural locations – where it is quiet, peaceful, relaxing – and 'green' – to entice

potential visitors. The resulting atmosphere becomes a sort of bibliophile Disneyland.

The founder of Hay-on-Wye's book town venture, Richard Booth, can certainly be described as a militant particularist, and in Chap. 2 I explore the origins and history of Hay-on-Wye—the first of the book towns—highlighting the principles underlying the book town philosophy.

Notes

1. The terms 'book town', 'booktown' and 'book-town' are used interchangeably throughout the literature, although 'book town' is most prevalent.
2. Merfeld-Langston (2007) explains that other unique names, such as *villes, cités, pays du livre, de l'écrit et des métiers due livre* and *du livre et des arts graphiques,* are also used, highlighting particular features present in some French towns.
3. This acronym is generally used rather than the full descriptor 'small to medium enterprise'.
4. Hay-on-Wye, Wales; Bredevoort, the Netherlands; Fjærland, Norway; Montolieu, France and Redu, Belgium.
5. Refer to ILAB web page at http://www.ilab.org.
6. Refer to http://wwwbooktown.net. This total has increased by approximately 35% (from 14 book towns) since 2009.
7. Refer to http://www.booktown.com/InternationalBKtowns.htm. However, it needs to be noted that this site has not been updated for approximately five years.
8. This does not include the three failed book towns in the United Kingdom—Dalmellington, Scotland (1997), Blaenafon, Wales (2003) and Atherstone, England (2005).
9. The website of the International Organization of Book Towns (http://booktown.net/gi.asp) lists previous festival locations: 1998 in Bredvoort, the Netherlands; July 2000 in Mühlbeck-Friedersdorf, Germany; July 2002 in Sysmä, Finland; May 2004 in Wigtown, Scotland; June 2006 in Fjærland, Norway; May 2008 in Montereggio, Italy; September 2010 in Wünsdorf-Waldstadt, Germany; May 2012 in Kampung Buku, Malaysia; May 2014 in Tvedestrand, Norway and August 2016 in Saint-Pierre-de-Clages, Switzerland.

References

Barthes, R. (1972 [1957]). *Mythologies*. London: Paladin.

Bartmanski, D., & Woodward, I. (2015). *Vinyl: The analogue record in the digital age*. London: Bloomsbury.

Basbanes, N. A. (1995). *A gentle madness: Bibliophiles, bibliomanes, and the eternal passion for books*. New York: Henry Holt.

Birkerts, S. (1995). *The Gutenberg Elegies: The fate of reading in an electronic age*. Winchester: Faber and Faber.

Booth, R. (1999). *My kingdom of books*. Ceredigion: Y Lolfa Cyf.

Bradshaw, T., & Nichols, B. (2004). *Reading at risk: A survey of literary reading in America*. Washington, DC: National Endowment for the Arts.

Burns, P. (2001). Brief encounters: Culture, tourism and the local/global nexus. In S. Wahab & C. Cooper (Eds.), *Tourism in the age of globalization* (pp. 290–305). London: Routledge.

Burwood, N. (2010). International booktowns. *News and Trivia Archive*. http://www.anyamountofbooks.com/narchive.html. Accessed 23 Aug 2010.

Buzbee, L. (2006). *The yellow-lighted bookshop: A memoir, a history*. Saint Paul: Graywolf Press.

Campbell, J. (2014). *The bookshop book*. London: Constable and Robinson.

Carrière, J.-C., & Eco, U. (2011). *This is not the end of the book: Two great men discuss our digital future*. London: Harvill Secker.

Carter, D., & Galligan, A. (Eds.). (2007). *Making books: Contemporary Australian publishing*. Brisbane: University of Queensland Press.

Castells, M. (1997). *The power of identity: The information age: Economy, society and culture* (Vol. 1). Oxford: Blackwell.

Craddock, K. (1993, July–November). An introduction to book collecting. *Antiques and Art in Victoria*, n.p.

Cresswell, T. (2004). *Place: A short introduction*. Oxford: Blackwell.

Darnton, R. (1999, March 18). The new age of the book. *The New York Review of Books*. http://www.nybooks.com/articles/546. Accessed 30 Oct 2009.

Darnton, R. (2009). *The case for books: Past present and future*. New York: Public Affairs.

European Institute of Cultural Routes. (2006, January 18). *Cultural routes and landscapes: A common heritage of Europe*. http://www.culture-routes.lu. Accessed 10 Mar 2010.

Finkelstein, D., & McCleery, A. (Eds.). (2002). *The book history reader*. London: Routledge.

Florida, R. (2002). *The rise of the creative class: And how it's transforming work, leisure, community and everyday life*. New York: Basic Books.
Franklin, A., & Crang, M. (2001). The trouble with tourism and travel theory. *Tourist Studies, 1*(1), 5–22.
Gekowski, R. (2011, March 9). A fond farewell to secondhand bookshops. *The Guardian* [Books]. http://www.guardian.co.uk/books/booksblog/2011/mar/09/farewell-secondhand-bookshops. Accessed 12 Mar 2011.
Grado, S. C., Strauss, C. H., & Lord, B. E. (1997). Antiquing as a tourism recreational activity in south western Pennsylvania. *Journal of Travel Research, 35*(3), 52–56.
Griswold, W. (2008). *Regionalism and the reading class*. Chicago: University of Chicago Press.
Hanna, J. (2005, June 10). *Atherstone bids for new identity as England's National Book Town* [Media Release]. http://www.inprint.co.uk/thebookguide/shops/atherstone_press_release_2.1.htm. Accessed 22 May 2011.
Harvey, D. (1996). *Justice, nature and the geography of difference*. Oxford: Blackwell.
Harvey, D. (2000). *Spaces of hope*. Edinburgh: Edinburgh University Press.
Huckans, J. C. (2005, July/August). Book town revisited. *Book Source Magazine*. http://www.booksourcemagazine.com/showstory.php?sid=archive/e0507. Accessed 31 Oct 2009.
Irshad, H. (2009). *Clusters: A key to rural prosperity*. Alberta: Government of Alberta.
Jansen, A., & Skogseid, I. (2003). Book towns and the network society: New perspectives on developing rural enterprise. In S. Krishna & S. Madon (Eds.), *The digital challenge: Information technology in the development context*. Farnham: Ashgate.
Kells, S. (2011). *Rare: A life among antiquarian books*. Sydney: Folio.
Kenner, H. (1998). *The elsewhere community: A grand tour of the world, and the mind*. Sydney: Allen & Unwin.
Landry, C. (2008 [2000]). *The creative city: A toolkit for urban innovators*. London: Earthscan.
Lanham, F. (2009, January 20). Author Larry McMurtry sees the end of book culture. *Houston Chronicle*. http://www.chron.com/entertainment/article/Author-Larry-McMurtry-sees-the-end-of-book-culture-1741461.php. Accessed 31 Aug 2010.
Lindores, S. (2010, May 31). Hay festival founder is sure books' future secure. *Reuters Business and Financial News*. http://www.reuters.com/article/2010/05/31/us-britain-hayfestival-idUSTRE64U1NJ20100531?pageNumber=1. Accessed 16 Feb 2011.

Löfgren, O. (1999). *On holiday: A history of vacationing*. Berkeley: University of California Press.

Macaskill, H. (2007, March 24). The complete guide to book towns. *The Independent* [UK]. http://www.independent.co.uk/travel/uk/the-complete-guide-to-book-towns-441542.html. Accessed 22 Feb 2010.

Mandelbrote, G. (Ed.). (2006). *Out of print and into profit: A history of the rare and secondhand book trade in the twentieth century*. London: British Library and Oak Knoll Press.

Marshall, A. (1998). *Trafficking in old books*. Melbourne: Lost Domain.

Marshall, A. (2004). *Fossicking for old books*. Melbourne: Bread Street Press.

Martin, J. (2009, October 20). *Montereggio – A booktown in Italy*. Wandering Italy Blog [Weblog]. http://wanderingitaly.com/blog/article/548/montereggio-a-booktown-in-italy. Accessed 1 Sept 2010.

McCrum, R. (2006, January 15). E-read all about it. *The Observer* [UK]. http://www.guardian.co.uk/books/2006/jan/15/ebooks.technology/print. Accessed 3 Feb 2011.

McKercher, B. (2002). Towards a classification of cultural tourists. *The International Journal of Tourism Research, 4*(1), 29–38.

McShane, P. (2002). *To further Australia's understanding and involvement in the international booktown movement through a program of visits and interviews*. Winston Churchill Memorial Trust of Australia. http://www.booktown.com.au/ChurchillReport_Booktowns_2002.htm. Accessed 27 Feb 2010.

Merfeld-Langston, A. L. (2007). The villages du livre: Local identity, cultural politics and print culture in contemporary France. PhD thesis, Pennsylvania State University.

Merfeld-Langston, A. L. (2010). 'Celebrating literature to shape citizenship: France's 2007 *Lire en fête*.' *Modern and Contemporary France, 18*(3), 343–356.

Michael, E. (2002). Antiques and tourism in Australia. *Tourism Management, 23*, 117–125.

Michael, E. (2007). *Micro-clusters and networks: The growth of tourism*. Oxford: Elsevier.

Murray, S. (2009, December 10). *The book beyond the page: Book fairs, screen festivals and writers' weeks*. Monash University Seminar: Book Towns and Writer's Festivals. http://arts.monash.edu.au/blogs/events/2009/12/10/seminar-book-towns-and-writers-festivals. Accessed 14 Mar 2011.

Ong, W. J. (1982). *Orality and literacy*. New York: Routledge.

Peterson, R. A., & Kern, R. M. (1996). Changing highbrow taste: From snob to omnivore. *American Sociological Review, 61*, 900–907.

Press, S. (2001). Reading Wigtown: Place identities in a Scottish book town. MA thesis, University of Oregon.

Rojek, C., & Urry, J. (1997). *Touring cultures: Transformations of travel and theory*. London: Routledge.

Seaton, A. V. (1996a). *Book towns and rural tourism development: Hay on Wye 1961–1996*. Glasgow: University of Strathclyde.

Seaton, A. V. (1996b). *Book towns and rural tourism development: The new European book towns 1984–1996*. Glasgow: University of Strathclyde.

Seaton, A. V. (1997a, July). The book town concept: Retail specialization and rural tourism. *Insights* [British Tourist Authority/English Tourist Board].

Seaton, A. V. (1997b, April). Scandinavia, the Fatherland, and Bonnie Scotland: International book towns, Part Three. *Biblio*, pp. 12–15.

Seaton, A. V. (1999). Book towns as tourism developments in peripheral areas. *The International Journal of Tourism Research, 1*(5), 389–399.

Seaton, A. V. (2002). Tourism as a metempsychosis and metensomatosis: The personae of eternal recurrence. In G. M. S. Dann (Ed.), *The tourist as a metaphor for the social world*. Wallingford: CAB International.

Seaton, A. V. (2010, April 23–25). *Developing innovative products for Irish tourism – The McNally Tourism and Travel Archive*. Paper presented to Dromoland 2010: First Annual Tourism Policy Workshop. http://vimeo.com/11577877. Accessed 14 Mar 2011.

Seaton, A. V., & Alford, P. (2001a). The effects of globalization on tourism promotion. In S. Wahab & C. Cooper (Eds.), *Tourism in the age of globalization* (pp. 97–122). London: Routledge.

Seaton, A. V., & Alford, P. (2001b). Technology by the book: BookTownNet and SME cultural tourism networks. *Journal of Information Technology and Tourism, 4*(2), 107–123.

Selwyn, T. (Ed.). (1996). *Myths and myth-making in tourism*. Chichester: John Wiley and Sons.

Sheller, M., & Urry, J. (Eds.). (2004). *Tourism mobilities: Places to play, places in play*. London: Routledge.

Shields, R. (1991). *Places on the margin: Alternative geographies of modernity*. London: Routledge.

Skogseid, I., & Seaton, A. V. (1998). *BookTownNet – Book town status and user needs analysis* [BookTownNet Deliverable D3.1]. Stiftinga Vestlandsforsking VF-rapport 19/98.

Smith, M. (2003). *Issues in cultural tourism studies*. New York: Routledge.

Smith, M. (2006). Entertainment and new leisure tourism. In D. Buhalis & C. Costa (Eds.), *Tourism business frontiers: Consumers, products and industry* (pp. 220–227). Burlington: Elsevier Butterworth Heinemann.
Sorensen, R. (2009, April 11–12). Reading the future. *The Weekend Australian Review*.
Striphas, T. (2009). *The late age of print: Everyday book culture from consumerism to control*. New York: Columbia University Press.
Szerszyncki, B., & Urry, J. (2006). Visuality, mobility and the cosmopolitan: Inhabiting the world from afar. *The British Journal of Sociology, 57*(1), 113–131.
The E.C. and tourism: Economically and culturally important sector is vital to Europe (1988). Europe, 276: 24. ABI/INFORM Global.
UNESCO. (2010). What is the creative cities network? *UNESCO Culture*. http://portal.unesco.org/culture/en/ev.php. Accessed 13 Apr 2010.
Urry, J. (1995). *Consuming places*. London: Routledge.
Williams, R. (1989). *Resources of hope: Culture, democracy, socialism*. London: Verso.
Zaid, G. (2004). *So many books*. London: Sort of Books.

Interviews

Booth, R. M. B. E. Hay-on-Wye, Wales, 20 September 2011.
McShane, Paul. Bowral, New South Wales, Australia, 9 July 2010.
Turpin, Adrian OBE. Wigtown, Scotland, 4 September 2011; via email, 15 March 2017.

2

Hay-on-Wye: 'A Town of Travellers Who Stopped'

The market town of Hay-on-Wye, located on the border of England and Wales in the lush Upper Wye Valley, is renowned globally for its thriving micro-economy centring on antiquarian bookselling. In turn, a vibrant mix of hoteliers, restaurateurs, farmers, artists and members of the literati are able to sustain a comfortable living in the town. Hay attracts many thousands of tourists from within the United Kingdom and around the world each year, most combining a passion for books and the written word with an appreciation of the beautiful countryside surrounding the town. In this chapter, I detail the establishment of the Hay-on-Wye book town venture, explore how and why the town has successfully sustained itself for half a century and illuminate the philosophies underpinning its creation, masterminded by its founder, the eccentric entrepreneur Richard Booth.

The town's fortunes have been inextricably linked to Booth's deep-seated idealism, boundless ego and respect for a regional way of life enabling community self-sufficiency. Booth is, with justification, regarded as the person single-handedly responsible for reviving, with immense charm, this dying Welsh country town in the Powys region of Wales and leading the international Book Town Movement with enormous dedication. At the same time, he has been ridiculed for his unconventional

J. Frank, *Regenerating Regional Culture*, Sociology of the Arts,
https://doi.org/10.1007/978-3-319-65036-4_2

antics and characterized, just as persuasively, as a figure of extreme contradictions. Although, in a sense, the story of how one individual transformed a town and set in motion a global movement is an inspiring one, this chapter also explores why the central role of that one man renders Hay-on-Wye problematic as a transferable model of community renewal. Richard Booth established Hay-on-Wye as a larger-than-life, themed destination centred on book accumulation and distribution to create the fantasy elements that have perpetuated its novelty and fame over many decades. However, from the start, his emphasis was on the promotion of his book empire and the rural community of Hay-on-Wye rather than a celebration of books in the town as unique cultural items. This chapter therefore explores the idiosyncrasies of the Hay-on-Wye book town venture in order to restore the book to a central place in the success of the dozens of other book towns that emerged across the world in the decades that followed, a role that will be discussed in later chapters.

Booth: Destined for a Life in Books

The beginnings of the twentieth century's first book town can be traced to Richard George William Pitt Booth, an eccentric, Oxford-educated entrepreneur. Born into a military family in 1939, Booth is a descendant of William Pitt the Younger (Clarke 2000, p. 105). A legendary figure in the book trade, Booth inspires fierce opinions and has been described variously as 'a very curious fellow' (Collins 2003, p. 23), a man of 'idiosyncratic views and activities' (Seaton 1996b, p. 381), an 'eccentric anarchist' (Shapiro 2007a), 'a publicity engine' but 'not necessarily rational' (McShane 2002, p. 16; 2009), 'the voice of the unsettled upper classes' (Minet 1989), 'a man of blustery eloquence and speedy shifts in topic' (Chenoweth 2005), 'a deceptively vague and rumpled man' (*The Independent*, quoted in Clarke 2000, p. 105), 'an idealist and self-publicist' (*Private Eye*, quoted in Clarke 2000, p. 105), the 'King of Hay-on-Wye' and 'Emperor of the World's Second-Hand Book Towns' (Booth 1999) and 'King Richard Rubbercheque' (de Chantilly in Mandelbrote 2006, p. 132).

Booth traded a city profession—the accountancy career his parents had planned for him—for an unpredictable future in Hay-on-Wye in the

Anglo-Welsh marches. His family had lived near Hay since 1903, so he felt a strong connection to the area. 'Buying a small shop in Hay-on-Wye meant that instead of playing a minor role in a major business, I could play a major role in a minor one,' he said (Booth 1999, p. 17). In 1962, he used a small legacy to open his first secondhand bookshop, also selling antiques, in a building previously used as the town's fire station (Booth 1999, p. 68; Seaton 1996a, p. 9; 1999, p. 390), which he bought for £700 (Clarke 2000, p. 104). Collins summarizes the situation colourfully: 'He was a brash young Oxford lad, eager to do something different from his classmates. So he became a shopkeeper.' Opening a bookshop in a sleepy, declining market town appeared to be lunacy, and Booth recalls people predicting a quick downfall: 'Booth won't last three months. Nobody reads books in Hay' (Booth, personal interview 2011). However, he was to prove them profoundly wrong, providing the catalyst for a remarkable resurgence of the town's fortunes: the dramatic transformation of this decaying market town into the world's largest centre for secondhand and out-of-print books. In her history of Hay-on-Wye, Kate Clarke (2000, p. 104) states that 'trading had once more become the lifeblood of the town only this time the commodity for sale was not beef, corn or wool but books'.

Booth did not take up secondhand bookselling on a whim; it was a pastime he had enthusiastically begun as a boy. His interest in books was initially kindled by an ex-World War I guardsman, Edward Fineron, who sold books in Woking, near Booth's home in 1923. According to Booth, Fineron invested time in talking with him as a 12-year-old and prophesized that he would become a secondhand bookseller (Booth 1976, p. 7; 1999, p. 51). He never forgot Fineron's remark: 'You can be a secondhand bookseller anywhere in the world' (1999, p. 51). By the age of 14, he was a book collector. It would be wrong to think that his parents discouraged this habit. He recalls his father being so pleased that he built a specially shelved room for his books next to the kitchen. Booth's reasons for owning and reading books were not simply because of what they contained, though: 'I coveted books to read because they were beautiful objects with decorative covers and fine illustrations. Also, I hoped people would be impressed by what I owned' (1999, pp. 51–2).

Booth describes himself as being both a failure and non-conformist during his adolescence at Rugby School. After leaving the school abruptly, and in disgrace, when he was discovered cheating, Booth continued his education at 'a crammer' in Guildford. Guildford was one of the most prestigious centres for secondhand book dealing, and here he was able to further cultivate his knowledge of the book trade (Booth 1999, p. 53). At Oxford, he found another mentor, an antiques dealer named Kyril Bonfiglioli, who continued to develop Booth's interest in book dealing. Bonfiglioli was another larger-than-life figure who, like Booth's own father, a retired army officer—an ex-sergeant in the King's African Rifles—had a passion for books. Booth found him a charismatic and 'bewitching' man with an encyclopaedic knowledge of English literature (p. 64).

An Economy of Poverty

Not long after establishing himself in Hay, Booth vowed that he would make it the bookselling capital of the world, a pledge that was greeted with widespread, hearty and sceptical amusement. However, one by one, in the late 1960s and early 1970s, the local cinema, Norman castle, chapel and workhouse were filled with books—all bought 'for a song' (Booth 1999, p. 23):

> I was prepared to buy in bulk; it was the only way I could compete with the London trade and its supporting cast of runners[1] … I was not an expert or a specialist, nor was I able to manipulate the large sums of money which these establishments needed. With youthful enthusiasm, I commandeered lorry-loads of books from the paved streets of London to the muddy sheep-blocked lanes of Wales. Never before had a small Welsh town seen such large numbers of books.

Booth also combed the country, 'simply purchasing every book haphazardly that I could find' (Booth 1976, p. 9), sometimes buying entire bookshops and complete libraries belonging to Welsh Working Men's Clubs (Clarke 2000, p. 105). His vision of a secondhand book empire centred on accumulating vast numbers of out-of-print titles, previously inaccessible but now collected together in one location. His belief was—and still is—that old books never die and that no matter how unattractive a book may seem, there is always someone who will covet it (Clarke 2000, p. 106) because everyone has their own peculiar notions of value. This is the thinking behind Booth's 'Honesty Bookshop'—the 'last chance saloon' for seemingly doomed and unwanted books—described vividly by Collins (2003, p. 93):

> In a field at the bottom of the castle hill is a motley collection of rusted metal bookshelves and clapped out old hard-cover books, all left to sit in the open air. This is the end of the line for the printed word, the place where absolutely unsaleable books from Booth's stock wind up … These unfortunate volumes are not brought inside at the end of the day; they just sit out in the wind and the rain until some buyer takes pity on them and drops a few pence into the unmanned box, or until the action of sun and moisture upon the paper decomposes the books into pulp.

The honesty shelves feature prominently at the foot of the grassy hill beneath the Castle Bookshop, and during my visits I observed a constant trickle of interested travellers who, despite the intermittent rain, filed along the rows of rejected volumes, occasionally rescuing a book and dropping some coins in the box.

Booth's buying mentality reflected his views of himself as a political and social radical. When I interviewed him in 2011, he commented that 'the original vision that started book towns was that it was an economy of poverty.' He is a passionate advocate for the inexpensive book, the conviction that the right to read an affordable book is a universal one (personal interview 2011). Booth objects to the approach of companies like Amazon and other e-dealers because postage charges are usually far higher than the cost of the book itself. He said (personal interview 2011):

> If you have a few thousand publications, you can send them around the world in a container … we can send a paperback around the world … for a penny whereas with Amazon, you'll pay £2.75 for the postage even if they only sell that paperback for a penny. £2.75 is quite a high price for a poor person.

Other authorities, such as McShane (2002, p. 33), regard the book town as an extension of the traditional village marketplace—a magnet for the general populace—and this was certainly Booth's intention in Hay-on-Wye. Myers et al. (2007) examine the history of the book trade—its fairs, markets and itinerant trading patterns—identifying a clear line of commercial activity outside the formal boundaries of metropolitan book emporia (p. vii). From the Frankfurt book fairs of the sixteenth century through to the street trade in London and other provincial locations, a distinctive and colourful cast of eccentric traders have played a crucial role in the circulation of books. Travelling pedlars, hawkers and chapmen, distributing printed matter beyond the reach of conventional bookshops, are critical intermediaries in 'a complex economic system across Europe which is yet to be brought clearly into view' (p. viii) and play a part in the chain of events that led to the growth of the book trade in the non-metropolitan streets and public spaces of Britain and Europe that were the precursors of book towns as we now know them. Like those dealing in books in peripheral areas before him, Booth kept the wheels of commerce turning at a popular level through his buying and selling.

Revival of Self-Sufficiency

Respect for the rural way of life is central to Booth's complicated 'post-capitalist' philosophy and the many (real and imagined) obstacles he opposes to secure his ideal. He promotes the book town approach as an alternative way of revitalizing the rural economy rather than one that prioritizes the interests of 'officials' or government bureaucracies. Booth has a natural and splenetic distaste for quangos—the Milk Board, the Welsh Tourist Board, the Forestry Commission—which he regards as groups that 'feed off' but stand outside the local process of regeneration:

> They call them nongovernmental, but they're propped up with tax money. To build luxury hotels in farming and coal towns …The quangos are killing Hay. A town needs a reason to live. And you won't find it in the Tourist Information Centre. Or shops full of Welsh key chains and souvenir shot glasses … This town's reason to live is books. (Collins 2003, p. 63)

Booth argues that quangos destroy the rural economy of Wales by encouraging big businesses like supermarkets: 'People want the butcher, the baker and the candlestick maker, they don't want supermarkets' (in Clement 1999). When I interviewed Booth, he was vehement that the local rural economy meant exactly that, and that it didn't require subsidies because that kind of subsidization breeds a bureaucratic machine where 'the official is God'. He argued instead that protecting and encouraging the economy from within, organically, meant it would thrive: 'If you protect it, you're not going to eat anything except local bread' (personal interview 2011).

Booth's passion for protecting Hay-on-Wye's future—albeit in a way that suits his own business—is behind everything he has created. However, his methods are extreme. He has books delivered around town in a horse-drawn cart. Horse transport, he says, relieves the energy crisis and provides work for local saddlers, wheelwrights and blacksmiths, who might otherwise be unemployed. Preserving a past that is already gone—no matter what the impact of this might be on others in the town—and emphasizing the quaintness of the community suited the tourist image Booth needed to cultivate his book businesses. His vested interest ignored the fact that some people and parts of the local economy very much needed the various quangos as part of their own, non-book-related ways of making a living. Not everyone in Hay sells books. Many people still experience a normal rural economic life where, for example, the dairy industry can't function without an organization such as the Milk Board. There are people in the town who want a supermarket and other conveniences of contemporary life.

Booth's seemingly genuine support for the revival of local industries and crafts is also linked to his suspicion of the intellectual world—which is ironic, as he is an ex-Oxford scholar and since the vast numbers of books he has accumulated have afforded libraries and universities the opportunity to purchase books on obscure subject areas. Funding had been showered on universities as well as municipal and regional public libraries, and their regionally touring bookmobile libraries, over the same period. Martin Amis visited Hay-on-Wye and interviewed Booth in 1980, observing the paradox that the 'world's largest bookseller should turn out also to be one of its leading anti-intellectuals' (Amis, quoted in

Minet 1989, p. 122). In his autobiography, Booth reinforces this observation by drawing a contrast between the value of the traditional storehouses of intellectual knowledge—the universities—and the pride and integrity of the rural working class, stating that his success as a bookseller, and by inference Hay-on-Wye's success as a book centre, was grounded in the ideals of hard manual work:

> I was thrown into the society of diggers and ditches, labourers and woodmen. Rural pride enabled us to do a job others would have spurned. Pride in manual work, I believe, is the basis of any traditional rural economy. I hold a good manual worker in higher esteem than any intellectual. Working with just a few country labourers, I ended up possessing books of greater intellectual variety than all the universities in the British Isles put together. (Booth 1999, p. 21)

This stance, and his travels around Wales, led him to believe that the centralizing impulses of government-led education had undermined traditional rural cultural traditions—literary societies, historical societies, theological colleges and country house libraries had been 'sacrificed at the altar of centralised education' (Booth 1999, p. 85). Booth's methods polarized community members and commentators. He is fiercely criticized for his duplicitous role in the depredation of some Welsh working men's libraries, the closure of which he went on to declare as a tragedy, and the supply of collections to university libraries despite him pronouncing their 'deadening effect on the culture of the book' (de Chantilly, in Mandelbrote 2006). However, Clarke (2000, pp. 109–10)—who knows Booth personally as a Hay-on-Wye resident—argues that although Booth is undoubtedly eccentric, there is an honesty in his radicalism:

> His irate diatribes against the manner in which big business, the press barons, the tourist industry and bureaucracy in general spends millions of pounds a year on the destruction of rural communities have always maintained a central core of truth. His early vision of a rural revival was dismissed by many as being idealistic clap-trap yet the sentiments he expressed which seemed *avant garde* or nonsensical then are now echoed by a number of environmental groups and local government departments … It may be

> that the thrust of his argument was lost by … provocative gestures that attracted attention but possibly detracted from the serious issues being addressed, though the idea of an astute man of vision playing the fool to make a serious point is by no means new.

Booth's significance for the book town project lay in his ability to take advantage of changing dynamics in both book production and consumption, and to apply them to revive a community that had been crippled by a dramatic decline in prosperity in the post-war years. His considerable early success coincided with a time in the twentieth century when the book was extending its influence beyond what previously had been regarded as its safe constituency: the educated bourgeoisie and the middle classes. Even more significant at the time, however, was the explosion in book sales and the democratization of book consumption that was driven by the spread of the 'general-interest' book. How-to, self-help and hobby- or pastime-based books sold in their millions, as did cookbooks, horse books, travel books, sports biographies, airport novels and 'pulp fiction' more generally.

The Role of the Eccentric Entrepreneur

The role of individuals has been critical in the advancement of the Book Town Movement, and eccentric personality traits reflect the willingness of individuals to depart from conventional means of problem-solving. Although such creative individuals find it hard to operate within corporate structures, they are typically visionary, tenacious and obsessive (Landry 1996, p. 43). In a similar vein, audacity, passion and know-how are the three characteristics Merfeld-Langston (2007, p. 12) sees as necessary for entrepreneurs who pursue business and cultural objectives in book towns. Beyond these idiosyncratic traits, someone like Booth clearly displays the characteristics attributed to 'community' or 'social entrepreneurs' (Austin et al. 2006) and developers of new ventures. This view is shared by Collins (2003, p. 236), who remarks, 'Hay is a perfectly good place. And it is Richard Booth's place. Here is a man who, for better or for worse, has given his life to a town ….' Establishing a community venture can often prove to be an even more challenging task than purely commercial entrepreneurship.

More broadly, the extent and nature of entrepreneurship are increasingly acknowledged as pivotal to the economic health of countries and regions (Borsch et al. 2008, pp. 100–1). However, in the case of book towns, there is a mix of commercial, cultural and emotional objectives. Booth's entrepreneurial activity had an embedded social purpose: his work developing the Hay Town of Books facilitated a social as well as commercial infrastructure that allowed not only booksellers but a wide range of tradespeople, small business owners and artisans to engage in cooperative activities. He fostered an entrepreneurial environment in Hay, encouraging others to become booksellers and grow the book town concept. Booth (personal interview 2011) describes this as a two-way commitment, requiring 'an economy of total community input'. Successful entrepreneurs are especially well plugged into the culture, able to understand, relate and contribute to their fellows (Lavoie 1991)—a description that Clarke (2000), Collins (2003) and others would argue applies to Booth, while others like McShane (personal interview 2010) strongly believe that, rather than having the aim of bettering the town, Booth had 'money at the root of his motivations and really only ever intended that he would own all the bookshops in Hay'.

However, Booth was able to organize and reconfigure existing human and infrastructural resources in Hay and elsewhere to exploit opportunities that in turn enabled different human, social, physical and financial resources to emerge and form linkages. An entrepreneurial opportunity has the qualities of being attractive, durable and timely, while being anchored in a product or service that creates or adds value (Timmons 1997). Booth's creative intervention undoubtedly relied on Hay's picturesque rural scenery, the cultural heritage value of its under-utilized historic buildings and shops—indicators of a prosperous past—and rich local traditions. These readily melded with and enhanced his business concept centred on books. The Hay-on-Wye example, and those of other book towns around the globe, are proof that in order to succeed, a community venture such as a book town needs to be entrenched in the social context and create social capital. Alternatively—or additionally—it will make use of resources embedded in social networks of relationships (Nahapiet and Ghoshal 1998). Booth challenged the deteriorating economy and way of life in Hay, presenting the community with a new experience and identity. Because the new initiatives were built on and through familiar sites and relationships, the majority of residents adapted to them. Consequently, as Clarke (2000, p. 104) observes, 'Hay did not sink into isolation. Instead the whole economy of the town changed, and it was mainly … the inhabitants' ability to adapt to this change that ensured its survival.' In building a book town without destroying valued community conventions, Booth not only drew on but also facilitated cultural creativity. This brought many in the town into the project, but also encouraged cultural energy among people who were otherwise facing a bleak future in a town that had lost its purpose and had no sense of a shared future.

The First Book Town: A Fantasy Kingdom

Booth's unique and enduring influence, and the publicity generated by his media antics, unquestionably explain Hay's particularly rapid rise to fame and ongoing profile. His ego and larger-than-life excesses are often criticized by others, but his optimism in the face of financial vicissitudes has kept his name prominent in the media for decades. Minet (1989, p. 109) observes:

> Booth has now had a remarkable 20 years in the public eye during which he has achieved a level of penetration of the public memory which has left him all but identified with the secondhand book trade. Yet during this period, he has been unstable financially, often bitterly resented in his own trade and among his neighbours, and most amazing of all, his publicity gimmicks have been appreciated by both public and journalists simply for what they are, gimmicks. No one has really fooled anyone: the whole thing has been good, fairly clean fun throughout. At the end of it, Richard has come out an acknowledged 'great English eccentric'.

Right from the start, Booth was thinking big about the book town. For example, in 1968 Booth told Ian Cotton of *Nova Magazine*:

> I've got a staff of 13 at the moment including four cataloguers, a chauffeur and a resident gardener-handiman [sic]. Last year I bought 600,000 books. I threw away 300,000 (I have them pulped) and I sold 100,000 others. But I look forward to a visionary future. I look forward to a day when, from a book factory outside Hay, I will supply 50 specialist bookshops, all owned by me. I look forward to the day when no bookshop is complete without its own airport. (quoted in Minet 1989, p. 114)

Between 1962 and 1968, turnover of the business rose from £6000 to £100,000 per year (Minet 1989). In 1968, Booth estimates that he had 400,000 books in stock and that he was buying 600,000 titles each year (Booth, personal interview 2011). However, Minet believes that this may have been close to the economic zenith of Booth's experiment, as his fortunes were to fluctuate, sometimes plummeting dramatically over the following decades (Minet 1989, p. 112), including being declared bankrupt in 1984 (Booth 1999, p. 209). However, the returns from Booth's secondhand book business were initially positive, and his 1963 purchase of Hay Castle (Clarke 2000, p. 106) was a move that he says symbolized his attack on centralized authority and 'sealed his fate in the town forever' (Booth 1999, p. 70). The space provided by the castle, outbuildings and cobbled stables accelerated the book town project. The business was expanding rapidly: by the mid-1970s, Booth's staff had grown to 20 and a million books were housed in the town. He was listed in the *Guinness Book of Records* for having more secondhand books and more miles of shelving than anyone else worldwide (Clarke 2000, p. 108). The town quickly achieved national and international fame, partly due to the innovative book town concept, but equally due to Booth's colourful personality and the impressive, highly publicized run-ins he engineered with government bureaucracies (Seaton 1999, p. 391). The book town also appealed to other eccentrics and free thinkers. For example, England's most famous transsexual, April Ashley, lived in Hay-on-Wye for over a decade and appears in a number of Booth's publications, including *Independence for Hay* (1977), in which Ashley poses in a photograph above the caption, 'If I can change, why can't Hay?' The acquisition of the castle also generated extraordinary global publicity when, on 1 April 1977, in a proclamation to his bemused subjects, Booth declared Hay an 'independent kingdom', appointing himself king of the 'town of books'—King Richard, *Coeur du Livres*. Seaton says, 'this [publicity stunt] started as an off-the-cuff joke but was taken so seriously by local councillors and the media that Booth decided to develop the idea into a printed manifesto – *Independence for Hay*' (Booth 1999, p. 391).[2]

Leading citizens were appointed to top 'government jobs', and aristocratic titles—dukedoms, earldoms and knighthoods—were available for a price. Ambassadors were dispatched to the International Court of Justice in The Hague, and a rowing gunboat patrolled the meandering River Wye. Passports were issued and stamped for Hay-on-Wye in the town's two taverns, and the Hay National Anthem, penned by George Barker, Poet Laureate to the Independent Kingdom, was sung. Evoking the excesses of Caligula—or, if you believe some historians, the emperor's astute political criticism of his public servants—Booth also named his horse the prime minister. Three television studios and eight national newspapers covered the 'Home Rule for Hay' celebrations, and the press coverage brought thousands of new visitors.

Still selling novelty low-cost peerages to amused tourists, Hay provides a key example of the emergence of manufactured tourism experiences that rely on tourists' ironic engagement, but equally on their recognition of the value of the actual offer—in the form of the beauty of the setting, the genuinely interesting array of bookshops and books, the local produce and crafts, pubs, cafés and so on. In this sense, Hay was a pioneer in both courting and producing the phenomenon now known as post-tourism. The play between the authentic and inauthentic is inherent to an experience such as Hay-on-Wye. The relationships between book towns and a range of tourism modes will be discussed in more detail in Chaps. 3 and 4.

Local, Global and Book Sector Changes Help Build an Empire

Beyond what might be termed hyper-publicity, Booth's town of books emerged as a result of a coalescence of factors unique to the early 1960s. These included the perilous state of the secondhand book trade in the United Kingdom beyond the confines of the capital, changing modes of local, national and global transport, and specialized consumption trends that were emerging internationally and would grow to be a key in the book town's success. Booth defied the orthodoxy of the book trade, identifying a unique opportunity to make a difference in a shrinking regional industry—decentralized secondhand bookselling in Britain—and in the process masterminded a new way forward for regional tourism. In the first years of his operation in Hay-on-Wye, virtually every other bookseller of note in the country of Wales ceased trading, retired or died, and they were not replaced. The prosperous pre-war days of bookselling to the Welsh gentry had also clearly passed. However, Booth was able to turn the situation to his advantage. Despite being inexperienced in bookselling at the time, he was a 'witness to the greatest change in secondhand bookselling since Lackingdon' (Booth 1976, p. 8). James Lackingdon, whose 1797 memoir details how his supply of secondhand books beat fixed-price agreements among new booksellers, had pioneered the modern book remainder system and invented the concept of the modern book token, and—most importantly—showed how he united new with secondhand bookselling on a large scale (Booth 1976, p. 10; personal interview 2011). As well as taking advantage of the economic difficulties for some due to taxes on estates, Booth discovered that people in remote and rural areas often did not recognize the significance and value of certain books and titles that would fetch a high premium elsewhere. Thus, valuable editions would be sold to him for a pittance: 'Hay's fortunes depend in part on buying collectible books from people who don't know their value. The key issue is how do we swindle an old lady?' (Booth, in Shapiro 2007b). This behaviour from Booth may have been unscrupulous, but it is consistent with his views about redistributing books to the wider populace, enabling the democratization of knowledge.

During the 'university boom' of the 1970s, bookshops throughout the United Kingdom began to regard the individual customer as a waste of time, preferring to sell large quantities of books *en bloc* to universities and other institutions. If Booth's account is to be believed, given his obvious vehement disrespect for universities, this was part of the reason why bookshops unable to adapt to this transition closed their doors, and scores of books that didn't conform to the university market were regarded as worthless, 'leaving lots of stock for a would-be secondhand bookseller to snatch up on the cheap' (Booth, quoted in Chenoweth 2005). Minet's account of the period is more nuanced, however, attributing a whole series of factors at play in the 1960s to the decline of the secondhand book market, including retirement and property development, and suggesting that newer shops were affected by 'television, rising rents and a general fading of traditional holiday-making in the face of Mediterranean competition' (Minet 1989, p. 60). Minet believed that some of these problems were ameliorated by the growth of book fairs in London and elsewhere, to which country booksellers would radiate—particularly between 1975 and 1995.

Booth initially embraced book fairs in Hay-on-Wye and elsewhere, but by the late 1990s had come to believe that book fairs were too prolific, allowed dealers to erode the town's profits—dealers would arrive from outside the town with their books and leave afterwards with their earnings—and that increasing specialization in the book trade meant they often proved to be 'a very boring experience': he offered the example of a whole stand featuring Wisden cricket annuals (1999, pp. 269–70). However, Edmondson (personal interview 2011) argues that book fairs provide a distinct advantage to both dealers and customers because book fair dealers 'roam far and wide' to find high-quality books whereas, in a book town, books in stock remain static and the town relies on the booksellers' networks to accumulate attractive merchandise, which is challenging.

Booth argues that a book town can do a job superior to that of a national university or a public library because of container transport (personal interview 2011), which had the effect of reducing the cost of individual books. Most booksellers avoided trade in large quantities of books because of storage and transport issues. According to Minet, by operating with a 'ruthless regard for his lack of means', Booth bought in bulk and overcame the storage issue because 'property in Hay was so cheap that it could be virtually written off as a business cost' (1989, p. 110).

A global outlook was also pivotal to the success of Hay-on-Wye. Booth's infatuation with the United States, which he considered the best source for books—'cheap books in the USA were like snowflakes in a blizzard'—resulted in sprees of buying and selling, and the import of vast numbers of books to Wales:

> Booth was buying them at pennies on the dollar in the United States as old seminaries went bankrupt, as ignoramuses staffing Peabody Libraries sold off their treasures – because 'nobody reads them' – as New York institutions like Stechert-Hafner[3] shut their doors, and as little old rich ladies died and left libraries to half-literate progeny. These hauls were brought over on container ships and dumped out in countryside barns and slowly sorted by long-suffering employees, who in turn defected to found their own bookstores down the street. (Collins 2003, p. 41)

Booth planned to use the huge influx of cheap books to encourage a re-evaluation of American culture—'we would do with American books what Japanese prints had done for Oriental culture when they first arrived in Europe as the humble wrapping for china' (Booth 1999, p. 135). However, he also saw the tourism potential of stockpiling American books. In 1976, prior to Booth's falling out with the Wales Tourist Board, Hay-on-Wye received £50,000 to celebrate the bicentenary of American Independence to encourage 'camera-carrying American tourists' to prioritize Wales as a destination as well as to attract international publicity (Booth 1999, p. 135). The idea of vast quantities of books conveniently being brought to Hay and then sold relatively cheaply appealed to bibliophiles and book runners from all over the country. Booth's policy of buying entire monastery libraries or the complete collections of aristocratic estates threatened by taxes meant that little-known rare and precious titles were emerging—a treasure trove of literature—which proved a magnet to collectors for the first few decades of Hay's existence as a book town. As a result of this, McShane (2002, p. 15) observes, 'Word of mouth through the antiquarian trade backed up the popular publicity, and the legend of Hay – Town of Books was assured.'

Initially, as Booth journeyed around Britain making acquisitions, he was himself often unaware of the value of the books he found due to his own lack of experience. Never having travelled extensively abroad, he could not compare British books and the books of other nations. He soon realized that 'whatever the faults of the British Empire, its wealth meant that in the nineteenth and twentieth centuries, its books were the finest and most handsomely produced' (Booth 1976, p. 8). Focusing on building relationships with sellers, Booth rarely researched values prior to purchasing, so many treasures were bought in total ignorance (Booth

1999, p. 27). This apparent lack of discipline, however, contributed to the legendary reputation of Booth's bookshops as pilgrimage sites for collectors. Collins recounts that:

> on one side of castle hill was Booth's bookstore on Lion Street, a rambling monstrosity of half-opened shipping boxes, bindings ripped to shreds, of unguarded treasures left tossed in spiderwebbed corners … [with] its wide-armed embrace of everything you could want and everything that no-one could ever want.

He compares this with the shop of Booth's rival, Morelli,[4] where all the books were correctly priced and where there were no bargains to be had: 'There is no surer way to suck the fun out of book hunting' (Collins 2003, pp. 106–7). However, Minet (1989, p. 122) and others reflect that, in the early 1980s, books in Hay-on-Wye were of dubious quality—or what Amis describes as 'triumphantly unreadable'—which led many in the book trade to spurn Booth. Publisher Laurie Muller (personal interview 2010) concurs (Fig. 2.1):

> I have memories of Hay-on-Wye back in the 1980s. It was before they had the Hay Festival and it was purely a bookshop town … There were buildings on the outskirts … but they were basically sheds just choc-a-bloc full of remaindered books. It would have been back in 1980 because I found a whole lot of University of Queensland Press stuff that our agent had dumped there. It was quite amusing really. Booth was a buyer of remainders, with a good eye for them, and made a big deal over how he sold them. And his own place was chockers full of conventional stressed stock. Not sophisticated, and dumped there in large numbers.

The Hay Festival: Universally Acclaimed but Detested by Hay's Secondhand Booksellers

Hay-on-Wye is ideally located near a number of major centres—halfway between Bristol and Birmingham, near Cardiff, Newport and Swansea, and en route to Ireland, providing it with an advantageous geographic position. Situated in mountainous sparsely populated rural mid-Wales,

Fig. 2.1 Charismatic Hay-on-Wye book town founder Richard Booth outside his shop (c.1988) (Source: Photographer Paul Minet (used with the permission of Sheila Minet))

Hay has been able to position itself as an alternative to the metropolitan book market of London. Yet, for ten days each May/June, London draws extremely close to Hay-on-Wye. Since 1988, Hay has hosted the annual Hay Festival of Literature, which is among the largest and most important literary events in the English-speaking world. The festival draws approximately 100,000 visitors to see and hear some of the most prominent international literary figures, among them former US President Bill Clinton. His 2002 keynote speech likened the festival to a 'Woodstock of the mind'.

Initially directed by the late Norman Florence, and now by his son Peter Florence, the festival is a key cultural tourism strategy. It is estimated that it injects as much as £21.4 million annually into the local economy (Stuart 2016, para. 4).[5] It is a:

> symbiotic and sometimes uneasy blend of old and new, dust and glitz. A visitor might spend a June morning browsing 50-pence titles in the Hay Castle Honesty Bookshop and the afternoon at the festival listening to a household name field questions from an attentive, educated and challenging audience drawn from all over the UK. (Chenoweth 2005, p. 24)

The median attendee age of 41 is young for book festivals, and the 'chattering classes… people who talk and who are media savvy' are strongly represented (Florence, in Chenoweth 2005). Inspired by the impact of the festival, additional events have also been developed, driven by the local economy's need for a boost in the off-tourist season. Visitors are now drawn to Hay for a growing year-long calendar of events. McShane astutely observes that while the festival 'fed on the existing fame of Hay as the Town of Books', it is the concentrated publicity and sponsorship of this significant event that have helped to sustain and grow Hay's reputation as a book town over the past 24 years (2002, personal interview 2010). The Hay Festival has become a global not-for-profit institution that coordinates festivals and projects elsewhere in the United Kingdom and around the world. As well as the Winter Weekend in Brecon, Wales and Merthyr Rock, a rock concert also held in Wales, franchised Hay festivals occur in Xalapa, Mexico; Belfast, Northern Ireland; Budapest, Hungary; Segovia, Spain; Nairobi, Kenya; Aarah, Maldives; Kerala, India; Dhaka, Bangladesh; Cartagena, Columbia; Beirut, Lebanon; and Bogota, Columbia.[6]

The symbiosis between book towns and festivals has proved to be a very positive and mutually propelling situation; this well-managed mutuality is often central to the success of book towns. However, in Hay-on-Wye, while most businesspeople and property owners who command enormous rents during the event support the festival, the secondhand booksellers complain that it produces a 'them and us' situation. Booth's major concern, like that of many of the booksellers, is the festival's lack of relevance—being a book festival promoting new titles and celebrity authors—to a town that is renowned for the secondhand book, given that the two markets are quite distinct. Resentful of the fact the festival uses the fame of Hay to satisfy the egos and marketing strategies of various intellectuals, Booth views the festival and its horizontal promotion as an insult to the natural integrity of the secondhand book trade, where inexpensive high-quality literature will always sell, and discrimination and knowledge make the market. Others in the secondhand book sector agree with this viewpoint, including Edmondson (personal interview 2011):

> The Hay Festival has almost become independent of the book town ethos. It's so big, so professional and so commercial. Really, it just happens to be in a field outside Hay-on-Wye. Obviously, it brings people into the district and some then may do book shopping but the spin-off could be just as much achieved by having a … show in Hay-on-Wye as a literary festival. I think the London literati like getting away to the countryside … You want to focus on the town and its unique attributes rather than just being a place where you park an invasion of people, almost like a pop concert … New book commercial activity leans more towards literary festivals and Booker Prize-winning authors. It's completely different to the situation with antiquarian books. Clearly, publishers don't have a role with them.

Playden's comments were almost identical: 'Hay, the book town is about old books, antiquarian books, collectible books. Hay the book festival is in a tent on the edge of town and it's about the new novel' (personal interview 2011). Abbrasart argues that if a book town has elected to devote itself to literature—and he refers to the *villages du livre*—there is little point in the town devoting valuable space to promote contemporary literature that is available in a multitude of other locations and does not further the goals of the book town (in Merfeld-Langston 2007, p. 139).

In more recent years, Booth, another Hay bookseller, Paul Harris (2012), together with others, have accused the Hay Festival and its multimedia partners of stealing the name of Hay, declaring Hay-on-Sky to be the new economic model, one that achieves little for their small, book-respecting community. According to many antiquarian and secondhand book dealers in Hay, the worldwide ideal of a book town is not a consideration for the festival organizers. However, this tension appears to have been exacerbated in the few years since Richard Booth's semi-retirement, through a series of developments. These include the perceived lack of empathy of the new owner of Hay Castle for secondhand bookselling by some of the town's booksellers; the existence of a business partnership between the festival's sponsor, the *Daily Telegraph*, and Kindle; and, due to another partnership between the festival and Oxfam—the secondhand bookshops' major competitor—festival-goers being invited to deposit unwanted books in the Oxfam container provided, buy books from Oxfam and view a range of electronic alternatives while attending the event (Harris 2012).

Hay-on-Wye is a fascinating case study of organic book-based development, but as a book town model, until very recently it has lacked a strategic focus that embraced these wider linkages and cultural tourism opportunities. While the views of Booth, Abbrasart, Edmondson and the booksellers of Hay-on-Wye can be appreciated, they appear to be oblivious to the fact that the Hay Festival represents a massive boost to the regional economy that benefits large numbers of Powys residents. The situation is evidence of a strange lack of perspective, a resistance to progress and a form of preciousness. The booksellers in Hay-on-Wye could presumably convene their own antiquarian book festival, but their leader, Booth, has philosophically opposed the notion of festivals more broadly—and voiced a deep-seated dislike of them—for many years (Booth, personal interview 2011), justifying his position by citing a belief that history repeats itself: the end of the Roman Empire, after all, was marked by a multitude of festivals (Booth 1999, p. 259; personal interview 2011). Turpin (2009) agrees that the number of book festivals held in the United Kingdom each year is problematic:

> When Edinburgh launched a quarter of a century ago, there were four books festivals in the UK; now there are getting on for 200. From Balquhidder to Appledore, every last hamlet wants a little bit of Sebastian Faulks and Roy Hattersley. I question how sustainable this boom is, especially given the economic slowdown … it seems to me that all those book

> festivals that wish not just to survive, but to thrive, need to start asking themselves a few fundamental questions, not least 'What exactly is the purpose of a book festival?'

Yet it seems that the arrival of new blood in Hay may have resulted in a softening of the town's attitude to the Festival. The arrival of Elizabeth Haycox, an American businesswoman with experience in industries including retail, events and hospitality, has brought new ideas to Hay-on-Wye since 2010. Haycox, together with her English husband, has bought and modernized Booth's 'musty and cavernous' flagship bookshop, adding a café, cinema and yoga studio. She has also bought the golf course on the edge of town, where she lives with her family, and contributed 'the lion's share' of the purchase price for Hay Castle (Wheatley 2011, para. 2), enabling the formation of a registered charity—the Hay Castle Trust—to preserve the landmark as a historic site that provides cultural enrichment, educational opportunities and community enjoyment.[7] According to Wheatley (2011), Haycox's motivations for purchase of the castle are about preservation, attracting travelling exhibitions from the British Library and providing a central meeting place for cultural and community events. Haycox, in contrast to Booth, accredits the ongoing evolution of the town to the success of the Hay Festival, inviting the influx of ideas it brings to Hay as a marketable resource (Thomas 2014, paras. 10–12). In Chap. 3, I further explore the characteristics of literary festivals in book towns, and the ways in which they contribute to the unique identities of these peripheral places of culture.

Two Separate Worlds: New and Secondhand Books

Despite these developments and the evident resentment they have triggered among some of the booksellers in Hay-on-Wye, my broader research indicates that, in this niche of the literary marketplace, few dealers feel threatened by new technology because the antiquarian and secondhand market is an entirely different one. Bibliophiles who collect books are searching for a piece of history, and 'the first edition of a book is the closest you get to the birth of a specific idea, cultural or scientific' (DiRuggiero, quoted in Lopez de Haro 2011). As antiquarian bookseller Ed Maggs (quoted in Pitman 2007, para. 9) explains:

> as books become less of a medium for quotidian research and use, we become more aware of their rarity value. That is good for the private collector. We live in an age of great cultural elasticity. No medium is ever completely replaced … absolute scarcity helps enormously.

Of course, the vastly different ways in which books appeal to different people mean that buying for the written word is only one interest secondhand book buyers might have. Others are more interested in typography, bindings, illustrations, dust-jackets and the tell-tale evidence of a book having being read and enjoyed by others. I will discuss this further in Chap. 5. It is vital to understand this separate *market* and separate *identity* of the secondhand book.

The resilience of a book town like Hay-on-Wye and the progression of book towns opening around the world are confirmation that the secondhand book is as valuable as the new book if it is promoted, highly regarded for its particular historical and aesthetic values, and linked to international networks. Exploiting the very narrow specializations that emerged in post-World War II publishing as a means to link European, American and 'Far Eastern' book towns—Booth's particular interest—was an experiment that worked.

Specialization and globalization are intrinsically linked in the story of Hay's success. On the one hand, Booth admits that Hay-on-Wye is a locale where 'mother bookshops'—large premises or warehouses crammed with books—were established to draw crowds. Quantity irrespective of quality was prioritized as Booth strove to have the largest accumulation of books of practical use in the world (Booth 1976, p. 10). Initially, quality finds were considered a by-product of a business operating in such an ad hoc manner. However, specialist booksellers were also encouraged to help create Hay as a book mecca. For example, Minet recalls the Old Fire Station being crammed with books in Welsh, the result of Booth buying bookshops and libraries specializing in Welsh-language books and cornering this slow-selling market, which attracted local publicity (Minet

1989, p. 112). Booth also purchased a number of shops in the 1980s that were turned into specialists in prints, natural history, British topography, novels, classics and bindings. Many of these did 'not coincide, for shops as well as books passed through Richard's hands as need dictated' (pp. 116–17). Later, Booth's third wife, Hope Stuart, started a smaller specialist bookshop at Hay Castle, selling books on topics including American Indians, film, photography, transport, crafts, art and architecture. At one time, there were plans for Hay Castle to be rebuilt as the book specialist centre of the world (Booth, personal interview 2011). Gradually, other booksellers and inexperienced but enterprising bibliophiles with dreams of owning secondhand bookshops settled in Hay and opened businesses in buildings that had long been neglected in the wake of Booth's success, some of them specializing in what other dealers discarded. A number of them had previously worked for Booth and learned their trade from him, but most originated from other locations:

> Almost nobody in the town's book trade is actually from Hay. It is a town composed of refugees from London, Edinburgh, Liverpool, the States, anyplace but the Welsh countryside ... Hay is a town of travellers who stopped; it is where urbanites come to hide from their home cities and from the tentacles of big-city traders and publishers. (Collins 2003, p. 103)

McShane (2002, p. 15) calculates that, during the mid-1970s, there were 12 bookshops in Hay, with that number increasing to 18 within a decade. By 2002, when he visited, there were 39 shops operating. When I visited in September 2011, there were 26 bookshops trading in the town, although the book centre is a joint venture featuring books from 20 dealer contributors, two book-binding establishments and two businesses dealing in postal book services. Three other bookshops in nearby towns also advertised in Hay's *Secondhand and Antiquarian Booksellers, Printsellers and Bookbinders Guide 2011–2012*. In 2017, the updated version of this guide listed the number of permanent bookshops as having dropped back slightly to total 23.

While the town consists of a wide cross-section of individual proprietors with particular specializations, Booth rejects the description of a book town as a cluster of small bookshops, as it is represented by diverse sources from Tony Seaton through to Saikia's *Blue Guide to Hay-on-Wye* (2010). It is a categorization that Booth considers 'commercial rather than intellectual' and an 'undemocratic interpretation of book towns' (personal interview 2011). While resistance to this idea is important to Booth's philosophy, as I explained in Chap. 1, theory around business clustering provides important insight into book towns and is a significant aspect of their structural features. Booth believes that book towns should be described as 'rural economies that help each other in the international world' and that 'book towns are a question of the *product* not the *retailers*' (Booth, personal interview 2011). His vision is for interlinked book towns around the world where towns adopt specialist fields—whether that specialization be botany, Cold War history, Penguin paperbacks, the works of Shakespeare or golf, just to name some random examples, and where bookshops and even entire towns develop cooperative networks to maximize their exposure and develop an international clientele based on growing niche interests. The IOB is a key tool in this process of internationalization, one that Booth attentively cultivates.

Why Hay-on-Wye Can't Easily Be Replicated

While the experience of Hay-on-Wye has been emulated in almost every continent of the world except South America, in many ways, Hay is a problematic model of what a book town might achieve elsewhere. Despite Hay's success and its desirable attributes, it would be risky to accept the organic model established in Hay as a ready-made blueprint for economic success without taking into account a number of qualifying caveats (Seaton 1996a, p. 31). Difficult aspects of using Hay as a model include the 'being first factor'—Hay's novelty value as the only world book town for over 20 years. It should also be noted that Hay's development took a long time—at least 35 years. Hay-on-Wye is evidence of an evolution that has no obvious shortcuts, and the long-term nature of such a book town development would be problematic and unacceptable as an economic development trajectory for many communities in the contemporary climate. As Turpin (2009) states, 'Book towns take time to establish. Hay wasn't built in a day. Wigtown has taken a decade of hard slog to grow to its current size, something that would not have happened without some far-sighted strategic investment by Dumfries and Galloway Council.' However, Hay has also demonstrated little formal leadership in book town governance and management to offer a satisfactory model for other prospective projects. Hay's strengths, it is clear, came from the brilliant ideas of one man—Richard Booth—whose idea for a book town coincided with the need for a community to be saved: he was an individual who made a difference through forming a community of interest around secondhand books, and drawing like-minded people to both the town and the project. Booth breathed life into a village that was once all but dead, but that now attracts hundreds of readers, dealers and book collectors who frequent the town. When I visited Hay, the atmosphere was extremely festive, with banners created from book covers adorning the square and alleyways transformed into open-air bookshops. The presence of books is overwhelming, with one shop boasting 'not a book in sight' to emphasize the point. The book town idea has successfully revitalized and transformed the economic, social and cultural fabric of the town.

Booth's adoption of a global outlook and his awareness of its advantageous application in his book town project predated the sweeping globalization of later decades. His manner of approaching book town business has benefited book towns around the world which he has assisted in their establishment phase, but this is in strange contrast to Booth's lack of willingness to embrace the international profile of the Hay Festival. I attribute this to Booth's dislike of rivals such as the Florences, his business opponent Morelli and other powerful organizations that he regarded as possible usurpers of his own absolute power as the self-proclaimed 'King' of Hay-on-Wye. Irrespective of this inconsistency, Booth, in his unconventional and idiosyncratic way, created a new variety of travel experience centred on book culture in the countryside. In the next chapter, I will analyse the book town experience and its nexus with changing tourism trends including consumer concerns with quality leisure time, environmental and cultural sustainability, the growing importance of an embodied experience of place and emerging logics of desire that value travel experiences as forms of knowledge. Hay-on-Wye, and other book towns in Europe and around the globe, became destinations that encouraged slow engagement, deepening connections between people and place, and relaxation and pleasure.

Notes

1. A runner buys from one dealer and sells to another. Booth describes the full-time runner as living a 'precarious existence' (1999, p. 21). In the United States, a runner is known as a scout. McMurtry compares the book scout or hunter who scours the bookshops and stalls of the world hunting for undervalued books with the heroes of American exploration in the early Wild West (1999, pp. 155–6).
2. Booth self-published subsequent politically motivated booklets, including *An Address by the King of Hay in the Black Mountains of Wales to Russell Means, Spiritual Leader of the Lakota People in the Black Hills of the Dakotas* (1983a); *Bureaucracy in Brecon and Radnor: With Reference to a Horse Ride through Cusop Dingle* (1983b); and *Why Woolworth Will Destroy Brecon* (1983c).
3. Stechert-Hafner was a nine-storey New York City bookstore that sold its entire stock to Booth after the company was bought for its customer list, not its inventory (Rollman n.d.). Booth then transported the books back to the United Kingdom in shipping containers. The firm had previously supplied libraries worldwide and had branches in London, Frankfurt, Paris and Bogotá, but according to Booth (1999, p. 119), 'their expertise had waned after the Second World War'.
4. A London bookseller named Leon Morelli had bought up Booth's Cinema Bookshop in the 1980s, as well as factories in the area, and poached several ex-Booth employees (Seaton 1996b, p. 10; Clarke 2000, pp. 113–14).
5. Refer to http://www.aatcomment.org.uk/the-food-of-love-how-festivals-support-local-communities, where Stuart cites the event IMPACTS economic calendar calculation. This figure has increased significantly from Florence's estimation of a £4 million injection into the local economy in Booth (1999, p. 258).
6. Refer to http://hayfestival.com
7. Refer to the Hay Castle Trust website, http://haycastletrust.org/ourvision.php#ad-image-0. Trustees include Haycox (Chair), Haycox's husband Paul Greatbatch, Peter Florence (Director of the Hay Festival), Lyndy Cooke (Managing Director of Hay Festivals), a television executive, the Director for Wales of the National Trust, a fundraising specialist and an architect with expertise in the restoration of listed buildings.

References

Austin, J., et al. (2006). Social and commercial entrepreneurship: Same, different or both? *Entrepreneurship Theory and Practice, 30*(1), 1–22.

Booth, R. (Ed.) (1976). *The country life book of book collecting.* London: Hamlyn.

Booth, R. (1977). *Independence for Hay.* Cusop: Richard Booth Publications.

Booth, R. (1983a). *An address by the King of Hay in the Black Mountains of Wales to Russell means, spiritual leader of the Lakota people in the Black Hills of the Dakotas.* Cusop: Richard Booth Publications.

Booth, R. (1983b). *Bureaucracy in Brecon and Radnor: With reference to a horse ride through Cusop Dingle.* Cusop: Richard Booth Publications.

Booth, R. (1983c). *Why Woolworth will destroy Brecon.* Cusop: Richard Booth Publications.

Booth, R. (1999). *My kingdom of books.* Ceredigion: Y Lolfa Cyf.

Borsch, O. J., et al. (2008). Resource configuration and creative practices of community entrepreneurs. *Journal of Enterprising Communities: People and Places in the Global Economy, 2*(2), 100–123.

Chenoweth, E. (2005, June 27). Making Hay-on-Wye. *Publishers Weekly* [New York], pp. 24–6.

Clarke, K. (2000). *The book of Hay.* Little Logaston Woonton Almeley: Logaston Press.

Clement, B. (1999, May 4). Voting for a new Britain: King of Hay stands as a Scargillite. Unlikely ally sings Scargill's praises. *The Independent.* http://www.independent.co.uk/news/voting-for-a-new-britain-king-of-hay-stands-as-a-scargillite-unlikely-ally-sings-scargills-praises-1091383.html. Accessed 30 Oct 2009.

Collins, P. (2003). *Sixpence House: Lost in a town of books.* New York: Bloomsbury.

Harris, P. (2012). UK: Is the book town of Hay-on-Wye dying? *Sheppard's Confidential: News and Events in Antiquarian and Second-Hand Books, Ephemera, Prints and Maps,* 19 April.

Landry, C., et al. (1996). *The art of regeneration: Urban renewal through cultural activity.* London: Comedia.

Lavoie, D. (1991). The discovery and interpretation of profit opportunities, culture and the Kirznerian entrepreneur. In B. Berger (Ed.), *The culture of entrepreneurship.* San Francisco: ICS Press.

Lopez de Haro, A. (2011, April 26). Despite rapid rise of e-books, rare books aren't endangered. *Columbia News Service.* http://www.bendbulletin.com/

slideshows/1411712-151/despite-rapid-rise-of-e-books-rare-books-arent. Accessed 21 Aug 2015.

Mandelbrote, G. (Ed.). (2006). *Out of print and into profit: A history of the rare and secondhand book trade in the twentieth century*. London: British Library and Oak Knoll Press.

McMurtry, L. (1999). *Walter Benjamin at the Dairy Queen: Reflections at sixty and beyond*. New York: Simon & Schuster.

McShane, P. (2002). *To further Australia's understanding and involvement in the international booktown movement through a program of visits and interviews*. Winston Churchill Memorial Trust of Australia. http://www.booktown.com.au/ChurchillReport_Booktowns_2002.htm. Accessed 27 Feb 2010.

McShane, P. (2009, December 10). *BookTown Australia: The international book town experience – An Australian perspective*. Monash University Seminar: Book Towns and Writer's Festivals. http://arts.monash.edu.au/blogs/events/2009/12/10/seminar-book-towns-and-writers-festivals. Accessed 14 Mar 2011.

Merfeld-Langston, A. L. (2007). The *villages du livre*: Local identity, cultural politics and print culture in contemporary France. PhD thesis, Pennsylvania State University.

Minet, P. (1989). *Late booking: My first twenty-five years in the secondhand book trade*. Old Knowle: Frantic Press.

Muller, L. Brisbane, Queensland, 17 August 2010 and 7 September 2010.

Myers, R., Harris, M., & Mandelbrote, G. (2007). *Fairs, markets and the itinerant book trade*. Newcastle: Oak Knoll Press.

Nahapiet, J., & Ghoshal, S. (1998). Social capital, intellectual capital and the organizational advantage. *Academy of Management Review, 23*(2), 242–266.

Pitman, J. (2007, May 26). A paradise for bookworms. *The Spectator*. http://findarticles.com/p/articles/mi_qa3724/is_20070526/ai_n19179483. Accessed 30 July 2013.

Rollman, H. (n.d.). Richard, King of Hay. *Newfoundland and Labrador Independent*. http://www.richardkingofhay.com/articles-in-international-newspapers-and-journals.html. Accessed 19 Aug 2015.

Saikia, R. (2010). *Blue guide to Hay-on-Wye*. Taunton: Blue Guides.

Seaton, A. V. (1996a). *Book towns and rural tourism development: Hay on Wye 1961–1996*. Glasgow: University of Strathclyde.

Seaton, A. V. (1996b). Hay-on-Wye, the mouse that roared: Book towns and rural tourism. *Tourism Management, 17*(5), 379–385.

Seaton, A. V. (1999). Book towns as tourism developments in peripheral areas. *The International Journal of Tourism Research, 1*(5), 389–399.

Shapiro, M. (2007a, May 10). Making Hay out of bookstores: Welsh town's self-titled king rules over realm of bibliophiles. *SFGate*. http://articles.sfgate.com/2007-05-10/entertainment/17243084_1_river-wye-hardback-books-hay-castle. Accessed 18 Aug 2010.

Shapiro, M. (2007b, May 3). The used-book King of Hay on Wye. *Los Angeles Times* [Travel section]. http://travel.latimes.com/articles/la-trw-wye6may06. Accessed 18 Aug 2010.

Stuart, M. B. (2016, July 19). The food of love: How festivals support local communities. *AAT Comment*. http://www.aatcomment.org.uk/the-food-of-love-how-festivals-support-local-communities. Accessed 25 Mar 2017.

Thomas, H. (2014, May 29). Hay-on-Wye: A town of books or festivals? *BBC News*. http://www.bbc.com/news/uk-wales-mid-wales-27624226. Accessed 17 Mar 2017.

Timmons, J. A. (1997). Opportunity recognition. In W. D. Bygrave (Ed.), *The portable MBA in entrepreneurship* (pp. 27–53). New York: John Wiley and Sons.

Turpin, A. (2009, September 13). The missing magic. *Herald Scotland*. http://www.heraldscotland.com/comment/guest-commentary/the-missing-magic-1.919454. Accessed 11 Apr 2012.

Wheatley, J. (2011, May 26). Elizabeth Haycox, the new Queen of Hay. *The Times*.http://www.thetimes.co.uk/article/elizabeth-haycox-the-new-queen-of-hay-nq9qtmfghc8. Accessed 17 Mar 2017.

Interviews

Booth, Richard MBE. Hay-on-Wye, Wales, 20 September 2011.

Edmondson, John. Graiguenamanagh, Republic of Ireland, 17 September 2011.

McShane, Paul. Bowral, New South Wales, Australia, 9 July 2010.

Playden, Peter. Atherstone, Warwickshire, United Kingdom, 13 September 2011.

3

Slow Books: Book Towns as Third Places

Bookshops in book towns are third places, or social environments distinct from the home (first place) and office (second place). Their role as locations of civic engagement and venues for creative community interaction is pivotal to their continued success and popularity. The conviviality generated in these locations is intrinsic to community-building in book town projects, where bookshops are anchors of village life, facilitating and fostering broader, more creative interaction. While most communities have informal meeting places, what book towns and the bookshops populating them provide are places where people can escape the frenetic pace of contemporary existence and have meaningful experiences that also enhance their sense of belonging—an important societal need. Visitors to book towns enjoy accessibility and proximity in a small-town setting. They appreciate that book browsing costs nothing while festival events are relatively inexpensive and that locals congregate in the bookshops too, making the environment welcoming and comfortable. Bookshops in book towns place no priority on an individual's status in society while allowing for a sense of commonality.

The characteristic wholesomeness of bookshops in these unspoilt rural environs, with the recycled secondhand or antiquarian book at their heart, appeals to discerning travellers making ethical leisure choices.

J. Frank, *Regenerating Regional Culture*, Sociology of the Arts,
https://doi.org/10.1007/978-3-319-65036-4_3

Book towns are a counterpoint to places of 'mass' tourism, instead finding a comfortable fit within the category of slow consumption experiences. The importance of localness, sense of place and 'serious leisure' experiences in book towns connect them with the essence of the Slow Movement. Visitors to book towns invest time in activities and pastimes, including book fossicking, collecting, reading, meeting authors at events or joining people with overlapping interests to participate in workshops or festival entertainment. They often just relish wandering the streets enjoying the 'saturation' of book culture on offer and making connections with their surroundings. Those drawn to live in book towns are often seeking a more idyllic lifestyle that frees them from the trials of urban living. This chapter examines book town examples in Scotland, France, New Zealand and Australia to demonstrate the idiosyncratic ways by which visiting and local book aficionados are invited to slow down and explore their creative ambience.

Bookshops as Community Hubs

Bookstores and book towns provide opportunities for the kinds of social interaction and convivial relaxation often associated with the combination of books and coffee in particular. The modern bookshop has long been allied with the coffeehouse and café:

> In eighteenth-century Europe, when coffee and tobacco conquered the continent, the coffeehouse provided a public gathering place for writers, editors and publishers. The stimulant coffee and the sedative tobacco made sitting at a table all day a pleasant equilibrium, perfect for writing, reading, long conversations, or staring out the window. This was the Age of Enlightenment: literacy was on the rise, books were cheaper and more abundant, and bookstores were often adjacent to coffeehouses – the customers of one were the customers of another with plenty of time in both for conversation and thought. (Buzbee 2006, p. 5)

Along with cafés, coffee shops, pubs and other informal public gathering places, bookshops have been coined 'third places' (Oldenburg 1999) because they are neither home nor work—the first two places—but rather places where people can cultivate less formal acquaintances (Florida 2002, pp. 225–6). These venues all share characteristics of being local and inclusive, and therefore having the capacity to unite the community. While people have always experienced social interaction in their communities, a community's ability to facilitate this interaction appears to be more important in a highly mobile, quasi-anonymous society (Florida 2002, p. 225). While book towns often manifest themselves in tight-knit local communities, the tourist element also means that they are hosts to many disparate visitors. Bookshops serve as intellectual forums, places for 'membership' and hosts of the informal public life of our society. Bookshops are considered 'levellers', accessible to the general public and inclusive; places that embody the community's heart and social vitality, where people linger simply for the pleasures of good company and lively conversation, or to enjoy companionable silence. Third places don't set formal criteria of membership that in any way exclude people; instead, they serve to expand possibilities rather than restrict them. Human association in such places finds individuals related to one another for some objective purpose. Novelty is an important part of third places, drawing on the mix of social backgrounds of people attracted to such locales, so a third place is largely a world of its own making. There is no duty to stay in such a place beyond its ability to provide satisfaction (Oldenburg 1999, pp. 24–48). Of the bookshop filling this role, Buzbee (2006, p. 6) says:

> Ninety percent of us who buy books still get out of the house and go to the bookstore to be among the books, yes, but also to be among other book buyers, the like-minded, even if we might never say a word to them … It's a lovely combination, this solitude and gathering, almost as if the bookstore were the antidote for what it sold.

Book towns encourage a flaneuristic type of engagement with place in the spirit of Walter Benjamin who, inspired by the poetry of Charles Baudelaire, made the itinerant nineteenth-century Parisian literary type a figure of scholarly interest (Shaya 2004, para. 10). The flâneur had a key role in understanding and portraying place. In a comparable way, browsing in bookshops and fossicking in open-air book markets allow contemporary bibliophiles to be creatures of leisure, to engage in the type of curiosity that encourages thinking but also be connoisseurs of the book-filled streets of book towns. Through this behaviour, individuals become part of the living fabric of the town. I explore the flaneuristic archetype of urban, modern existence further in Chap. 5 in relation to connoisseurship of books and their collection.

Third places such as bookshops play a notable role in making a community attractive, offering opportunities for new social networks, intellectual interaction and stability as the family and workplace become less secure (Florida 2002, p. 16) and the stresses of day-to-day life intensify. Bookshops—and, I would argue, book towns—fill a void by providing a destination for acquaintance, creativity, comfort and human interaction. Importantly, Florida (2002, p. 227) states:

> An attractive place doesn't have to be a big city, but it has to be cosmopolitan – a place where anyone can find a peer group to be comfortable with and also find other groups to be stimulated by; a place seething with the interplay of cultures and ideas; a place where outsiders can quickly become insiders.

Kahn also considers an appealing location to be both tolerant of strangers and intolerant of mediocrity. She explains (1987, p. 280) that, 'amid complaints that the world has become too big or too complex, people seek out smaller social groups and wider spaces.' The interest in third places reflects an increasing demand for individual, authentic, social experiences. This trend is closely tied to the 'experience factor', now a highly marketable commodity and one that will increasingly become so as individual, social and sensory contact is replaced by virtual connection. The book as a cosmopolitan symbol is the catalyst that provides book towns with a platform for this sociability and citizenship, which resonate in our global culture where the unique and the particular are keenly sought. Books bridge an acceptance of things that are modern, urban and cultured with an embracing of the local and nostalgic, and are examples of how cosmopolitanism emerges strongly in the cultural sphere (Kendall et al. 2009, p. 3), its emergence relying on certain types of mobilities that are critical for directing people into spaces and 'transcultural interactions' that promote cosmopolitan outcomes (Urry 2007). The type of cosmopolitanism evident in book towns relies on a cultural mode of seeing and valuing difference based on moral attribution (Calhoun 2002, p. 871), and also depends on sociability with those sharing similar interests and concerns. The bookstore's relationship to the broader sphere of literary culture is important:

> Literary culture may comprise only a fraction of our society but its role is crucial. In the bookstore, the individual can meet the culture, become part of a river of creation and imagination that has flown without interruption for thousands of years. The bookstore is still the place where we may engage in the free and unrestricted congress of ideas. In the bookstore, we may be alone among others, but we are connected to others. (Buzbee 2006, p. 215)

The gathering of book enthusiasts and local inhabitants at book festivals, on bookshop tours and at events dedicated to a particular author also provides social cohesion by bringing together people who have overlapping interests (Merfeld-Langston 2007, p. 104). In the same way, book towns stimulate sociability: books can be touched, customers can interact with booksellers and bibliophiles can browse for long stretches of time. The bookstore has always been a marketplace where the ideas of a given era were exchanged, and so has played a pivotal role in the shaping of public discourse (Buzbee 2006, p. 7). The bookstore and book town are idealized by bibliophiles: they can be envisaged as theme parks for book lovers who seek the company of like-minded individuals.

Book Town Festivals: 'A Core Piece of Goodness'

Book culture at literary events in book towns can be likened to 'a kind of conversation' (Zaid 2004, p. 40): book enthusiasts cluster around authors, books, bookstores and book town activities in much the same way as they gather together to take part in a life-affirming dialogue. Furthermore, in an increasingly atomized society, the increasing incidence of literary readings is significantly due to the growing hunger for intelligent conversation (Francis 2004) and 'finding yourself' through self-development. Self-identity and visiting of book towns are intrinsically linked. Consumption of culture becomes more than a choice about our style of life and more about who we are and how we express ourselves in particular settings. Exploring the self in this way is an experience to savour: it requires an investment of time.

However, another element in the seductive allure of festivals is that they don't entirely reflect real life:

> That's why people want them. They're escapes from people's lives. So you come and you think, 'God, isn't the world a better place? I can wander round listening to interesting people talk about stuff … wouldn't the world be better if it was like this?' The festival gives you licence to get away from your normal life. Instead of being embarrassed about that and saying, 'Yes, we are creating something that is not true', we feel good about it. Our whole brochure tries to show a place where the world is not mass-produced … a place where the world is standing still. (Turpin, personal interview 2011)

During his time as festival director, Turpin has changed the image of the Wigtown Festival through presenting a programme exuding a handwritten, 'organic' quality that styles Wigtown as an idyllic small town. The festival scene where visitors and locals listen to people who have something interesting to say embodies his idea that book towns of the future will not just be about books, but rather will be places where ideas are traded.

There is nothing new about literature being described as a conversation. However, the rise of literary festivals has been described as the 'new guiding metaphor of literary culture itself' (Francis 2004). Over the last 50 years, writers' festivals have exploded in number, popularity and geographic reach (Stewart 2009; Seffrin 2006; Turpin 2011). The majority of writers' festivals today take place in peripheral locations (Stewart 2009, p. 6). This has occurred alongside the escalating trend of writers being seen as public figures—even celebrities—in contemporary life. The 'taste cultures' (Rojek 2001, p. 102) surrounding such celebrities cultivate solidarity around these individuals. The self-reflexivity of the audience at these events enables participants to recognize common bonds as well as differences between themselves and others. Such activities and the shared knowledge they impart act as a bonding mechanism (Earl 2008, p. 414), which enhances a growing sense of community. Despite the growing opportunities for e-connections between writers and their readers in blogs and on publisher sites, book town events provide opportunities for face-to-face connections that attract strong interest (Swales, personal interview 2011). Writers' festivals contribute to the wider public's engagement in issues of broader interest to society than writing alone (Starke 2000; Stewart 2009, p. 1).

Turpin (2009) describes books as 'magical objects' and the process of writing as 'mysterious', believing that book events help to fill a void left by the decline in organized religion and provide a secular forum for considering ethical concerns. It is therefore essential that book town communities understand why a festival is important to the locale where it occurs, and why it would matter if it didn't happen. Turpin (2009, personal interview 2011) and Woodford Folk Festival founder Bill Hauritz (personal interview 2011) are adamant that every festival needs to have a heart—'a core piece of goodness behind it' (Hauritz, personal interview 2011). Turpin (2009) says that 'for far too many book-fests that heart is missing, and the growing trend for festival companies to run multiple events around the country (and abroad) only adds to this sense of rootlessness and soullessness.' Contrary to ex-British Prime Minister Gordon Brown's opinion that the rise of book festivals represents a new seriousness in society, Turpin suggests that a successful book festival attracts the widest possible mix of ages and classes; promotes interaction between writers and audiences through debates and master classes; and cultivates humour rather than what he calls a 'po-faced' approach. Most importantly, a good festival should be 'rooted firmly in its locale' (2009, personal interview 2011). Equally, *people* are vital, as is an ability to embrace the local community. The lack of this quality contributes to what is perceived as a 'them and us' situation in Hay-on-Wye.

Dark Skies and Community Ownership at the Heart of the 2012 Wigtown Book Festival Programme

Set amid some of Scotland's most unspoilt landscapes on the Machars Peninsula in Galloway's extreme south-west, Wigtown Book Festival bases its programming on the nexus between ideas and books, using the distance from larger centres of population as a creative advantage and a way of focusing on local uniqueness. The festival, and the book town itself, was part of a community regeneration project that commenced in 1997:

> an attempt to find a new direction for a town that had been blighted by the closure of its two main employers, the local distillery and the creamery. Because of that, there remains a sense of ownership. In a town of just over 900 people, more than 70 work as volunteers, taking tickets, delivering programs, driving authors to and from stations and carrying out 1001 other tasks. (Turpin 2009)

The fourteenth Wigtown Book Festival in September 2012 was the largest and most ambitious yet, hosting more than 175 events over 10 days. The growing success of the event is clearly linked to the way topics are woven through the festivals that are relevant to the regional community, but that also invite broader national and international interest. To connect with audiences and participants, Wigtown festival events exude intimacy and informality, matching strong community roots to literary seriousness (Wigtown Festival Company Business Plan 2017, p. 5). Festival director Turpin's aim is to reinvent traditional formats for book festival events (Monteiro 2012) that reflect his over-arching philosophy about book towns and their role in the future. Book towns, he states, should not simply rely on collections of bookshops acting as a magnet: any model that relies on that is obsolete (Turpin, personal interview 2011; Turpin, in Rinaldi 2012). In my interview with Turpin (2011), he made it clear that his vision for the festival was to make it representative of

> a coalition of different interests … you have to let go of ideas that are about 'highbrow' and 'lowbrow'. I don't think that is a very helpful concept … you need fun stuff that's going on for free … that makes it feel like a festival … If you look at our programme, you'll find that one of the keys to making it work in ten days … is that you're essentially programming for two (not separate) but different and overlapping audiences so that the week is full of material of local interest. The people here have a huge fascination with the history of Dumfries and Galloway. You can do things which sound really obscure and they love it … I'd say any good festival and any book town should celebrate what's local.

For example, a key sub-theme of the 2012 festival programme focused on the fact that Wigtown and its surrounds are renowned for the clearest and least polluted skies in Europe. The nearby Galloway Forest Park is now the United Kingdom's first Dark Sky National Park, a commitment that requires the skies above the park to be protected from any disturbance by light. This exciting development for the region allowed Turpin to use, as a central point of interest, the way the heavens have inspired the creative imagination throughout the ages. Steve Owens, former development manager of the Galloway Forest Dark Sky Park, engrossed audiences with a presentation on the night sky and how it had inspired human creativity from the Greek myths and Stonehenge to the paintings of Van Gogh, and how light pollution threatens to destroy the views our ancestors took for granted. Those present were able to learn why the sky is dark, what people can do to keep it that way and why south-west Scotland is at the forefront of the Dark Sky Movement.

Other highlights of this strand of the programme included a stargazing supper with Marek Kukula, the public astronomer at the Royal Observatory in Greenwich. In a barn on the outskirts of Wigtown, Kukula spoke of the changing and expanding nature of space and how humankind's perception of the stars has changed throughout the centuries. He showed footage of supernovas, galaxies, planets, stars and gases that would be impossible to see with the naked eye, and invited participants to hold a small piece of meteorite he had brought for 'show and tell'. Those who attended enjoyed delicious home-baked bread and local mussels prepared by the Camper Van Chef, Martin Dorey, and stargazed through a telescope at the night sky (Bowie-Sell 2012).

The themed events commenced with an appearance by NASA project integration lead Lee Graham from the Johnson Space Centre, who spoke about the future of space exploration (Monteiro 2012). Additionally, lunar enthusiast James Atlee explained how the moon had impacted various writers, artists and even political figures across history. Scotland's Astronomer Royal, John Brown, explained the numbers that define the universe; Marina Warner and Tahir Shah discussed the enduring appeal of the *Arabian Nights* and novelist A.L. Kennedy shared her passion for *Dr. Who*. Other night sky themed events included a tribute to the late Ray Bradbury, an illustrated voyage through the universe with Stuart Clark and a drive-in movie showing of Ian Cheney's hit documentary *The City Dark* under the stars in Galloway Forest Park. Dark Skies entertainment for children included Scottish Opera's *A Northern Light* and Edinburgh Royal Observatory's inflatable Starlab Planetarium (Monteiro 2012). So not only novelists but astronomers wandered the streets of Wigtown in 2012, including Wigtown's writer-in-residence Pippa Goldschmidt, who once worked as an astronomer for Imperial College. She has since turned to writing informed by space and the stars, including her novel *The Falling Sky* (2012), which follows the journey of a female astronomer after she discovers proof rejecting the Big Bang theory.

The other significant sub-theme threaded through the programme celebrated the 2012 declaration of Wigtown as the Most Creative Small Town in Scotland. Consequently, audience creativity and participation were prioritized, with festival attendees invited not only to hear a whole host of interesting writers from Scotland and around the globe, but to bake cakes, sculpt, write a 'crowd-sourced self-help book', draw at a drop-in 'drawing gym', 'spin a yarn' using flowers and plants from local gardens, enter a talent quest, knit and weave a tapestry with Alexander McCall Smith.

The Wigtown Book Festival hosts a wide range of celebrities each year—and not only from the arts and literary sector. Yet this other wide-ranging and extraordinary expertise, together with valuable local content, is used to reinforce the relevance of the book in our lives today. Turpin (2009) questions:

> Will the nation still be in love with the literary festival a decade from now? I hope so, but I also know that the status quo has to change. This year marks the 200th anniversary of Charles Darwin's birth, an event that many of the United Kingdom's literary festivals have been celebrating. They might do well to learn from the great Victorian. Evolve or die. There's no other choice.

The Search for More Meaningful Travel Experiences

The experiences offered at the Wigtown Festival are evidence of an understanding that travel and leisure opportunities have become increasingly important for people seeking a purpose for their lives. These individuals, with idiosyncratic tastes and 'hybrid motivations and needs', extract unique meanings from a host of experiences that involve active mental or physical challenges (Gretzel et al. 2006; Weaver and Lawton 2006, p. 347). They seek highly personalized consumption opportunities that are often related to sensory and cognitive associations (Rosa and Malter 2002), which in book towns include author readings, book-related entertainment, boutique workshops and other writing activities, and immersion in serendipitous book culture with other like-minded individuals. However, this kind of experience also involves sharing authentic 'truths' of rural community life (MacCannell 2011, p. 592).

The term 'tourist' is often used as a derisive label for those who are content with inauthentic experiences, or who settle for 'mass tourism' options. Travellers, in comparison, are more likely to immerse themselves in the local culture to explore less-travelled areas where tourism doesn't necessarily drive the economy. In Erving Goffman's (1959) front–back dichotomy, travellers seek back-regions of the places they visit in their search of an intimate and authentic experience—the search for society. Rather than areas set up for tourist display, sightseeing and consumption, they will often be drawn to areas that are private, and where access is restricted: private homes and gardens, or places of gritty reality (MacCannell 1999, p. 589). This is why Turpin's (personal interview 2011) pop-up aesthetic is effective at the Wigtown Book Festival, where literary events are held in unlikely venues, and book-browsers in Hay-on-Wye and other places find it just as pleasurable to fossick in sheds full of remaindered titles as in more mainstream secondhand bookshops. Offering opportunities for this kind of authentic engagement was the thinking behind the establishment of The Open Book (Fig. 3.1)—a Wigtown

Fig. 3.1 Wigtown Book Festival artistic director Adrian Turpin (OBE) (*left*) with members of The Bookshop Band, Ben Please and Beth Porter, and two visitors to Wigtown outside The Open Book, an initiative where guests can book a period of time living above and running a bookshop (2016) (Source: Photographer Colin Tennant (used with permission of Wigtown Festival Company))

project that invites writers, artists, thinkers and book lovers to Scotland's book town to fulfil their fantasy to run a bookshop for a short period of time. Designed to attract new creative talent, and raise awareness and education about issues facing booksellers, this holiday/residency experience is a low-cost opportunity where bicycles are provided for exploring the countryside, and visitors are encouraged to blog about their experience.[1] Other unique opportunities include the festival's 'Living Book' idea, substituting the serious-minded and often anonymous interaction between an author and their hundreds of devotees with one-to-one interactions between a writer and individual readers, who 'book' a slice of time and are allowed to ask specific questions of their choosing. Amateur writers have a similar opportunity with the 'Book Doctor' when they individually discuss their work with an author visiting the festival whose identity they don't know until the session begins.

Escapism through travel is growing in significance: experiences and memories, rather than products, are sought (Smith 2006, p. 221; Derrett, in Douglas et al. 2001, p. 11). The interest is in *being* rather than *having*, or tourism as a quest to *be* as much as a quest to *see* (Seaton 2002, p. 162). In this kind of economy, experiences are considered a distinct commodity. Pine and Gilmore (1999, p. 105) describe the commerce of experience as the fourth economic activity in humankind's history after extracting commodities from the earth, producing goods and delivering services. They regard the experience economy as a tool where service providers—including airlines and banks—repackage services and present them to the consumer as experiences. Travel—of particular relevance to this new economy for its provision of themed experiences—is therefore credited with bringing people into contact with their 'true' selves (Bryman 1995; Hayes and MacLeod 2007; Löfgren 2003; Pine and Gilmore 1999)—or, as Wang (2000, p. 71) expresses it, their 'existentially authentic selves'. Travel in modern times—at least in the imagination—is an intrepid blend of the predictable and the unknown. As Rojek (1993, p. 203) states:

> The globalization of culture tinges our experience of escape with the shadow of familiarity. And yet our dreams of escape continue to entrance us and we are nagged by the feeling that our lives will be catapulted into a completely different realm by the activity of travel.

I discern a link between these ideas of authenticity and escape, and nostalgia for childhood, following Inglis, who identifies holidays and travel as opportunities people dream about in the hope of restoring the abandonment of youth. He argues (2000, pp. 4–11) that holidays prefigure utopia:

> Once away from the work-discipline where time is spent and time is money, also away from the industrial city, its dirt, and noise and fearful, nameless crowds of people, we shall restore time's losses, rediscover the magnificent freedoms of both familiarity and strangeness, natural beauty and civic ritual … attaching a permission to adults to regress to the terrific anticipation-ness of childhood and its passion to be free of all those encumbering, imperious, unignorable others …[2]

Inglis explains that people yearn for their lives to be different—happier—like in the best parts of their childhoods. This is why he argues that people are drawn to holidays that replicate images of life that escape the evils of cruelty, waste, want and exploitation: a picture of paradise (p. 8). Equally, a particular social value of the countryside is inextricably linked with uplifting childhood memories: 'both the books and the touristic experience [are] a means for individuals to identify a lost and hence progressively idealised rural past' (Squire 1994, p. 111). As rurally located places of real and imagined idealism, as places of pleasurable immersion, book towns can be regarded as rural utopias.

Travelling to book towns, often in rural and remote locations, relates to the need to create personal connections with rural and natural landscapes as a way of preserving sacred spaces in people's daily lives. Occupying these spaces symbolizes

> a metaphorical … flight from the city, a desire for emotional rather than physical distance from urban lifestyles … these contemporary … engagements with nature and the rural perpetuate an Arcadian vision … a desire for the lost places remembered and imagined, that lie beyond the city 'walls'. (Mulcock and Toussaint 2002, p. 1)

Vukonić (1996) makes the related point that leisure time in contemporary secular societies becomes 'a space for the contemplative and the creative, a unity of thought and action', but it can also be considered a counterpoint to everyday routines, a personal transition or rite of passage at a particular juncture of a person's life, or as a pilgrimage (MacCannell 1976).

Tourists seeking the essence of a place are often attracted to cultural or literary trails in book towns. A themed trail is a route of walking, cycling, riding, driving or other form of transport that draws on the natural or cultural heritage of an area to provide an educational experience that will enhance visitor enjoyment. It is usually marked on the ground or on maps, and interpretative literature is often available to guide the visitor (Silbergh et al. 1994, p. 123). The history of such trails can be traced to ancient pilgrim and trade routes, and 'informed urban walking' (Goodey 1975, pp. 29–30), as well as the picturesque tours of England and Scotland that led visitors on prescribed routes through areas with artistic and literary associations (Aitchison et al. 2002). Such trails transformed the act of walking into an acceptable recreational pastime, freeing walking long distances from former connotations of need and homelessness (Aitchison et al. 2002, p. 53). Today, these routes link literary attractions and sites with some sort of narrative, which is often thematically configured as well as physically expressed in the case of book towns.

The Southern Highlands book town in New South Wales, Australia, is distinctive for its book trail that winds through rolling hills, featuring a number of quaint rural townships. The 'BOOKtrail' relies on tourist passion for exploring the Australian countryside, indulging in invigorating walks, savouring spectacular scenery and engaging in unique literary tourism pursuits (McShane and Rosa, personal interview 2010). Like other global book towns, this nucleus of small settlements is an example of rural and regional outposts with high concentrations of booksellers, prioritizing its literary associations and presenting them in a way that encourages slow enjoyment. In particular, the historic town of Berrima thrives due to its charm as Australia's arguably best-preserved Georgian village (Gelling 2003). Bypassed by the main rail line in favour of Bowral, Mittagong and Mossvale, it has become something of a backwater, which is what delivers its uniqueness. Berrima village not only features bookshops and antique shops, which blend companionably with the books on sale, but also a professional book-binding and restoration business, The Art of Bookbinding.

An obvious highlight is Berkelouw's distinctive Book Barn just outside Berrima. The book establishment is set among farm paddocks and filled to capacity with over 300,000 secondhand books (Berkelouw, personal interview 2012). Travellers are invited to stay a day or a week, drink coffee, visit the cellar door and enjoy books beside a crackling log fire. Serious book collectors' needs are catered for in the rare and antiquarian book room five minutes' walk away, where a rare single volume can demand as much as $75,000. The opportunities to browse for books here and elsewhere on the trail are expansive, but the experience is interspersed with gems of rich literary history for the curious bibliophile, the literary tourist or the tourist seeking a meaningful or educative experience. Visits to book towns and other literary sites are points that punctuate the book collector's journey in a satisfying way, allowing slow consumption and devotion of time to book culture and the physical pleasure of bookish immersion in the countryside.

Book Towns as Ethical Travel Choices

Ethical considerations are contributing to the expanding patterns of tourist activity that benefit book towns. For some time, tourism studies have explored a range of alternatives to the perceived environmental, social and economic disadvantages of conventional mass tourism. This interest is directly related to academic and policy discourses and real-world events that occur outside the realm of tourism (Hall 2009, p. 2). Hall writes of the slow consumption approach evident in public policy and industry, including re-localization schemes such as farmers' markets and other initiatives that reinforce the potential economic, social and environmental benefits of purchasing, consuming and producing locally. He links a slow consumption approach to the notion of *décroissance*, or degrowth, that has entered the lexicon of green economics in recent years. Book towns, with the antiquarian book at their centre, support some of the tenets of degrowth in that they emphasize quality of life rather than quantity of consumption, and arguably encourage self-reflection, diversity, good citizenship and non-materialism (Flipo and

Schneider 2008, p. 318). Cultural theorist Suzi Gablik notes a growing awareness of social responsibility:

> Many people find it difficult to imagine a self that is not shaped by the concept of an isolated individual fending for herself in the marketplace. In our society, it is taken for granted that economic self-interest is a basic given of human nature. Survival-oriented behaviour gives us a kind of rationale for why it is acceptable not to feel related or compassionate towards others, and leads us to falsely regard society and the environment as objects for manipulation and exploitation … if a historically new kind of self – the ecological self – does truly emerge in our culture … the restructuring of the Cartesian self, and its rebirth as an ecological 'self-plus-other' or 'self-plus-environment' [will] thoroughly transfigure our world view (and self-view) … (1993, p. 307)

The early multiplication of book towns had a timely synergy with the Slow Movement that emerged in 1989 ('What is Slow Travel?' 2011), emphasizing 'slow consumption' (Hall 2009; Fullagar 2010; Soper 2007). Slow travel offers a rich experience focusing on locality as a destination, the characteristic flavours and textures of a region or *terroir* (Rose 1999), the importance of the unharried journey (Osbaldiston 2013, p. 13) and an avoidance of 'staged authenticity' (Dickenson and Lumsden 2010, p. 4). The focus, it is argued, should be on the vernacular, local distinctiveness and place-based knowledge:

> Going slow is a way of thinking, liking, eating and being. It is also a sophisticated response to unsophisticated, vacuous commercialism – the Slow Movement offering something that is life-affirming, rooted in a deep understanding of human needs. Slow is serious, yet it is fun too. The ideas go deep, but so do the pleasures – for slow can be seen as a bridge from panic to pleasure. (Sawday, in Bagshaw and Mills 2010, p. vi)

Pleasure is connected with consumption of pastimes that require effort and skill. This idea is perhaps pursued to its furthest extreme by Tom Hodgkinson, a British writer and editor of *The Idler*, a periodical established in 1993. Hodgkinson advocates a relaxed approach to life, enjoying each day as it unfolds rather than toiling for an imagined better future. *The Idler* campaigns against the work ethic, instead promoting liberty, autonomy and responsibility. The related Idler Academy is a bookseller, coffee house and school located in London that offers courses in ukulele, philosophy, Latin, foraging, carpentry and other subjects with the motto *libertas per cultum* or 'freedom through education' (Hodgkinson 2011).

Slow refers to a state of mind that combines leisured calm with an engagement with the local community (Gardiner 2009). This enables meaningful connections to be established with people, culture, work, bodies and minds:

> In our hedonistic age, the Slow Movement has a marketing ace up its sleeve: it peddles pleasure. The central tenet of the slow philosophy is taking the time to do things properly and thereby enjoy them more. Whatever its effect on the economic balance sheet, the slow philosophy delivers the things that really make us happy: good health, a thriving environment, strong communities and relationships, freedom from perpetual hurry. (Honoré 2004, pp. 277–9)

The opportunity for 'hedonistic infusion' is at the heart of this notion (Fullagar 2010). The physical environment, which provides solitude, silence, time and space, encourages a potent sense of wellbeing and even rejuvenation (Frederickson and Anderson 1999, p. 34; Sharpley and Jepson 2011). The prospect of browsing bookshops in an atmosphere of tranquillity is a powerful attraction for potential book town visitors, especially when there is also the prospect of discovering a bargain or precious find—the 'quiet, material pleasures' referred to by Portinari (1989) in the *Slow Food Manifesto*.

Slow experiences in book towns appeal to ethically minded individuals seeking to fix ills or fill gaps in their lives through experiencing places where there is a sense of connectedness to people, food, place and community. The unique specialty activities that book towns offer are embraced for their links with the natural, which is similarly

> reflected in a stunning diversity of cultural symbols and practices: health foods, real ale, real bread, vegetarianism, 'traditional' non-western science

> and medicine, natural childbirth, wool and cotton rather than 'man-made' fibres, antiques rather than 'man-made' reproductions, old houses rather than modern houses, jogging, swimming, cycling, walking, dancing and mountaineering rather than contrived organised leisure ... (Urry 1988, p. 42)

The slow travel paradigm offers one of a number of definite paths towards the overall goal of sustainable tourism. The Western obsession with cheap goods that have a short lifespan and a high level of turnover is being challenged through 'connected consumption' patterns that re-use goods (Schor quoted in Sassatelli 2013, p. 181). The appeal of antiquarian book-hunting and the rustic village atmosphere in which biblio-tourists holiday and explore correlates with an ethos of 'wholesomeness'. It combines with a number of other emerging theoretical trends to explain why the themed book town experience continues to provide a sustainable alternative for rural and regional communities across the world.

Part of the pressure facing the publishing sector is environmental, particularly with relation to the use of increasingly scarce natural resources. In the current climate, the sustainability of 'ungreen traffic in dead trees that lies at the root of the great paper-based empires – newspapers, magazines, direct mail and books' is constantly questioned (Brass, in McCrum 2006). Book towns and the secondhand book market appeal to a growing number of people who appreciate that the books are recycled, and this is predicted to be an escalating trend. Additionally, initiatives practised in book towns, such as book crossing and book-friendly communities, where books are encouraged to be 'set free' for interested readers to pick up or exchange, are regarded as environment-friendly initiatives that increase the collective use of books, therefore saving materials and energy otherwise directed into publishing.

While the Slow Food Movement encourages buying local produce and culinary specialties, the related idea of Slow Reading embraces the endeavours of local authors, micro-publishing of materials of local interest and community-building around local libraries and reading events (Miedema 2009, p. 4). The slow ethos significantly embraces books and reading as a means of reducing stress and increasing creativity, inspiration and motivation. New 'fast' leisure, encompassing more superficial, ephemeral and multi-dimensional pursuits such as computer games, can be contrasted with slow leisure activities like reading a novel, which allows the reader's imagination to flourish and develop (Rojek 2000, p. 42). The act of reading requires concentration and entices us to focus our attention on a single author's voice to the exclusion of everything else in contrast with faster leisure pursuits often associated with new technologies. Reading a book is also a more private activity: the reader's choices are protected from outside scrutiny, unlike in an online environment where a reading history is traceable. The idea of defining leisure by way of pace, rhythm and flow allows us to re-emphasize the position of the art of reading literature as an imaginative and liberating encounter (Robinson 2004, p. 39). Part of the leisure experience in bookshops comes from the product they sell: by their very nature, books are slow; they require time. They are written slowly, published slowly and read slowly (Buzbee 2006, p. 5). 'Books are creative acts whose only constraints are imposed by the author. As such, they are a retreat to the slow; to the thoughtful and reflective in an otherwise frenetic world' (Young 2007, p. 82).

The other-worldliness and escapism the traveller identifies in a bookstore or book town, where time seems irrelevant, can be used as a metaphor for the reading experience itself. Reading is described as being elsewhere, being absent, or in another world where the reader borrows an alternate reality: 'Readers are travellers; they move across lands belonging to someone else, like nomads poaching their way across fields they did not write, depositing its wealth … reading takes no measures against the erosion of time …' (de Certeau 1984, p. 173). Reading counteracts the distractions that erode time through making connections:

> Reading, after all, is an act of resistance in a landscape of distraction, a matter of engagement in a society that seems to want nothing more than for us to disengage. It connects us at the deepest levels; it is slow rather than fast. That is its beauty and its challenge: in a culture of instant information, it requires us to pace ourselves. What does it mean, this notion of slow reading? Most fundamentally, it returns us to a reckoning with time. (Ulin 2010, p. 150)

There is evidence that print culture affords irreplaceable forms of focused attention and contemplation that make complex communications and insights possible. Further, readers play a more active role in their communities, which benefits civic and cultural life through increased levels of volunteerism, philanthropy and political engagement (Gioia, in Bradshaw and Nichols 2004, p. vii). Slow Reading is linked to nostalgia and has been embraced by baby boomers who savour looking back on literature they enjoyed themselves. It provides them with a sense of comfort in response to rapid changes in society and to our pace of life as they search for more authentic ways of living (Sheahan-Bright, personal interview 2010). In Australia, this includes engagement with slow cultural pursuits including Slow TV, which provides free internet television coverage of interviews, debates, conversations and public lectures about key political, social and cultural issues. It provides a new format for the delivery of new ideas that stimulates interest in books and book culture ('About Slow TV' 2010). A key reason for the current popularity of all kinds of arts and literary festivals is that participants relish the

> pure luxury of taking an hour to listen to something they're interested in, and making a connection with the writer. People discover this pleasure that has previously gone unrecognized and then they seek that engagement and relaxation each year. (O'Hara, personal interview 2011)

Slow Reading, and an investment in the richness and texture of book culture, is thus about pleasure, luxury and learning: 'A lot of our life is about instant gratification. Books, like any other art form practice, are about taking time to explore, interpret, understand better, get different people's perspectives' (Derrett, personal interview 2010). Derrett also explains how the notion of the experience economy is linked to slow culture:

> I believe [slowness is] an intellectual idea … but to press the slow button is not easy. If you create the environment for them [people attending book town events] to do that, the slow food thing, the slow entertainment thing … the opportunity to do a workshop and upgrade their skills, they can switch off from whatever it is they do at home to be able to experience how

> to write a sentence, or meet Carmel Bird, or meet an editor who gives them certain advice ... There are those ways of meditating on books ... this gives people a spectrum of experience, so if they feel like having a frenzy ... they can, and if they feel like sitting quietly around a fire with mulled wine meeting a famous writer and being able to say 'I met you', they can do that too.

Gschwind (personal interview 2011) agrees that people seek experiences from travel, and thus describes the success and popularity of book towns as attributable to tourism providers and hosts in book towns psychographically understanding the things that tourists desire: intimate experiences with their environment based on their personality, values, opinions, attitudes, interests and lifestyles—whether that be in the book shopping and literary events or other opportunities relating to culture, history, cooking or physical activity. Book towns promote book culture as a means of reducing stress and increasing creativity, motivation and inspiration.

Landscape, Heritage and the Search for Lifestyle and Community Identity

One of the tenets of the Slow Movement is to preserve cultural heritage by making deep connections to people, place and culture.[3] The preservation of older, unoccupied buildings, often without the need for extensive and costly renovation, contributes to the conservation of architectural heritage in book towns around the world. The place-altering nature of this heritage is a key part of the cultural consumption that occurs in these towns. Urry (1994, p. 236), for example, writes of 'resistance through localization', which is evident in the importance that communities place on the local vernacular and character of regional architecture using local building materials, the increasing incidence of listed local buildings and the rejection of modernist architecture. Rural villages that are particularistic, localized and rich with time, Urry states, increasingly draw people to them. Likewise, the collection of essays titled *Senses of Place, Senses of Time* (Ashworth and Graham 2005) develops thinking around the relationship between heritage and an evolving sense of place. Sense of place is the product of the creative imagination of the individual and society more broadly, where a specific identity, such as a themed book town, is actively ascribed. A place gains its quality of cultural distinction and meaning partly through processes of inscription such as naming (Huigen and Meijering 2005, p. 21).

Feelings of connection and familiarity, as well as chronological layering that embodies elements from both the past and the present, are crucial elements in the evolution of place. The past is integral to individual and communal representations of identity and the meaning, purpose and value that are created (Lowenthal 1985, p. 41). Lowenthal focuses on the heritage traits that make the past beneficial to individuals and communities by providing familiarity, direction, enhancement, escape and legitimacy. Emblematic landscapes where particular artefacts (whether monuments, buildings, literary sites, semaphores or even books themselves in the case of book towns) acquire cultural status connect the present to the past in a continuous trajectory. Landscape is space, without significance until history and memory have written meanings upon it, whereupon it becomes a place. So place is therefore particularistic, emotion-laden and bound up with memory. It is human culture that makes things mean something/signify, and meanings change from one culture or period in history to another (Ashworth and Graham 2005, p. 5). Book towns are adding their own layer of meaning to this history.

Featherston: A Book Town Drawing on Its Past to Enable the Future

The Southern Hemisphere's newest book town—Featherston (Maori: Kaiwaewae) in New Zealand—is drawing on its history with World Wars I and II, and railways, as well as its scenic beauty, to establish an identity as a town that celebrates the book as an artefact. Located 63 kilometres north east of Wellington on New Zealand's north island, Featherston is part of the South Wairarapa district known for its national importance as a wine-producing area. The town sits at the foot hills of the Rimutaka Range and close to the northern shore of Lake Wairarapa (Fig. 3.2).

Fig. 3.2 Featherston, New Zealand's book town, in the scenic Wairarapa district (2017) (Source: Photographer Pete Monk)

Chair of Featherston Book Town and CEO of Booksellers New Zealand, Lincoln Gould, has lived in Featherston for 20 years. He was originally drawn to the location for its significant military past. The Featherston Military Training Camp was New Zealand's largest training camp during World War I. Between 1916 and 1918, approximately 60,000 young men trained for military service on European battlefields. The government used the camp as a German prisoner-of-war camp and military hospital in 1918–1919, and as a storage facility from 1919 until 1926 (Ministry for Culture and Heritage 2014). It was demolished in 1926; however, at the request of the United States, the site was re-established between 1942 and 1945 as a camp for Japanese prisoners-of-war in World War II. The town gained notoriety in 1943 when 122 Japanese prisoners-of-war in the camp were shot, 48 fatally, after guards believed they were about to be attacked by the prisoners (Gould personal interview 2017). A memorial to the camp was created in the mid-1970s that stands now as a symbol of reconciliation. Located just north of

Featherston, on the road to Masterton, the site features a cherry orchard and many memorial plaques, including one carrying a seventeenth-century haiku by Basho in Japanese that translates:

> Behold the summer grass
> All that remains of the dreams of warriors. (Bedford 2012, pp. 5–6)

En route from Wellington to Featherston, near the summit of the steep Rimutaka Range, there is another monument to the soldiers who marched across the hill to Trentham and then on to board the boats to go off to war. This event was re-enacted in 2015 (Mead, personal interview 2017). The range is also important because of the Fell railway, which was a valuable mode of transport during the war. The Fell Engine Museum in Featherston displays the world's only Fell Locomotive Railway Engine, an attraction for rail enthusiasts who travel to Featherston to celebrate this unique legacy.[4]

Gould describes the book town project as 'Featherston getting a signature for its history around books' and using the town's unique past as a visitor drawcard. While social memory or the ways in which communities remember the past as a collective experience are one means of examining wars (Fentress and Wickham 1994; Winter 2006), in a book town project such as this, social memory can also be identified through a study of tourist experience, or a 'reconstruction of the past in light of the present' (Coser 1992, p. 34). Physical places both hold and articulate memory as semiotic spaces, with tourists being able to read them as memory bearers. Generational change is driving the change to historically motivated tourism based on knowing and understanding the role of those involved in the World Wars. Winter (2006), for example, attributes this search for information to a 'social memory boom', especially related to people who are exploring the stories of their forebears. Visiting Featherston book town is therefore likely to be less about collective memory and honouring the dead and more about an aggregation of individual tourist experiences. Related to this issue is a subcommittee project that has been established to manage the Featherston Camp Memorial Trust. This group has commissioned a major piece of civic art by leading New Zealand sculptor Paul Dibble, well known for his *Southern Stand* sculpture (2006) in Hyde Park, London—a memorial to the war dead of New Zealand in World Wars I and II. The commissioned piece will memorialize and remember the relationship of the people of Featherston and the service camp as distinct from being a war memorial. This project aims to rectify an acknowledgement that has been 'pushed under the carpet' for decades (Mead, personal interview 2017).

Another of Featherston's distinct features is its magnificent wood-panelled and richly decorated ANZAC Hall, originally built by the community as a venue to entertain and provide for the officers and men of the camp. The hall has been restored with local government and National Heritage funding. It will be used again in the 2017 Book Festival as a space for antiquarian booksellers to display their wares for sale for the duration of the event, but also as the venue for the annual Fish and Chip Supper for 150 guests. Gould explains that this menu is chosen for its egalitarian appeal. Each year, the dinner features a guest speaker. In 2016, the speaker was film expert Sir Richard Taylor from the WETA Workshops, who is also a Featherston property owner. Taylor ran workshops for young people at the festival, which resulted in a youth mentorship within his model-making workshops. Featherston Book Town was also able to negotiate an internship for a young woman named Hope Sexton to spend a month in Clunes, Australia, prior to the Clunes Booktown Festival, and hope to send another in 2017, and eventually to reciprocate.

Gould distils the growth of the world's book towns down to one word: community. The idea of community is at the 'philosophical heart' of Featherston's thinking about the book town venture. He relates this to his experience in the book industry more broadly:

> It's about community, but so is the whole business of resilience of bookshops in the UK, Europe, America and Australia. It's about what independent bookshops provide for their community. It's about the third place – think about your home, your work and where you socialise with the community, whether it's the pub or the church or the bookshop. Joel Becker's[5] establishment of National Bookshop Day in Australia was based around the idea. It has demonstrated the resilience of bookshops. Book sales are back, growing. I have brought that idea with me into the establish-

> ment of Featherston Book Town. It's about community. Another aspect that I hope is developing is that Featherstonians will feel proud of living in 'that book town place'.

Gould describes the new feeling emerging in what had been quite a down-at-heel village as 'like a wave', with people gathering support around the book town idea. The derelict buildings that had stood empty and boarded up in the town are now proving an advantage for those seeking new business premises. The community is embracing change, and Gould and his committee involve the community wherever possible, welcoming their feedback and involvement. They see this kind of cohesiveness as essential. A good example is the Shop Windows project, where a Book Town Art Group meets before each festival to organize window displays for local businesses. There is also a Beautification Group that organizes plantings and commissions signs for the book town (Fig. 3.3).

Book Town Operations Manager Kate Mead reinforces this key point about creative community in Featherston, stating that the town has

> built a community of like-minded people that thrive on interaction with each other. There are clusters of creative activity in places like Featherston which are near the city for inspiration but also a sanctuary of rural life. Featherston provides access to other arts and craftspeople, farms, reasonably priced workshops and housing. Artists absorb the history and use it in their storytelling. The environment offers more content for their work than somewhere decidedly more rural. Cities depend on their historical precedents and the molten pot of humanity. They are frantic, energizing but debilitating at the same time, whereas Featherston offers more tranquillity and a chance to provoke work from its creative residents. (Personal interview 2017)

Internationally known as a cellist and now retired from a long-term role at Radio New Zealand, Mead has opened a coffee shop, Loco, which she is expanding into a secondhand bookshop. Her particular focus will be books of regional interest about the Wairarapa and related topics. Having started with none, by April 2017, Featherston had secured four permanent bookshops.

Fig. 3.3 Mr. Feather's Den, Featherston book town, New Zealand (2016) (Source: Photographer Pete Monk)

Book town chair Lincoln Gould's recently opened bookshop is named Messines, after the battle that occurred in 1917 just prior to the more famous Battle of Passchendaele in Belgium. Troops trained in Featherston played a prominent part in the Battle of Messines. The town of Featherston is in fact twinned with the Belgian town of Mesen. Gould's shop will specialize in military history, selling primarily secondhand books with their genesis in stock from a closed down Wellington bookshop, Capital Books (Gould, personal interview 2017). Booksellers like Gould become known for their ability to curate as well as collect, acting as a service between the location of the book and the specialist collector. Gould has found the early interest in his specialized stock astounding, especially the interest from locals interested in military subjects. However, as he explains, nearby Trentham is new Zealand's main army base. Interestingly, there are also a lot of scientists living in Featherston because of the science research facilities in the Hutt Valley. Gould describes the village as a dormitory town for those groups but also for 800–1000 people a day who board the train out of the district to work in Wellington, an hour's journey away, and the Hutt Valley. There has also been an influx of young families and Wellington commuters attracted by the town's low property prices that are lending it a new diversity.

The book town festival offers the town an emblematic event that complements other neighbouring town events themed around wine, gifts and other specializations. The annual programme includes workshops on bookbinding, letterpress and magazine-making, literary treasure trails, readings, theatre events and a Rare and Antique Book Roadshow where well-known Australian book valuer John Arnold identifies book treasures in festival attendees' bookcases (Harris 2015; personal interview, Mead 2017).

Heritage and the Lure of the Hinterland

Heritage produces and reproduces cultural and geographical meanings (Ashworth and Graham 2005, p. 5). However, heritage is also simultaneously knowledge, a cultural product and a political resource (Sack 1992). In Australia, historic heritage frequently is located in non-metropolitan regions, where the contribution of cultural tourism to economic growth is of considerable significance, as well as a policy focus. Although Australia's non-Indigenous cultural assets are only approximately 200 years old, they represent important icons and contribute to a sense of national identity. The National Tourism and Heritage

Taskforce issues paper, *Going Places: Developing Natural and Cultural Heritage Tourism in Australia* (2003), notes that the market for heritage tourism is rapidly evolving, presenting many opportunities for exploration. As well as tourist interest, people are increasingly seeking to live in places where they feel a greater connection to their community, and this often means a move from an urban to a rural lifestyle where there is the much sought-after 'character' or the aggregate of distinctive features that distinguishes one thing from another within a locale (Green 2000, p. 76).

Many book town founders and booksellers in book towns confess to being tree-changers or sea-changers,[6] idealistically seeking a more utopian lifestyle free of many of the negative aspects of metropolitan living (e.g. Schiotz, personal interview 2012; Watson, personal interview 2011). In different countries, different physical environments are seen to epitomize a slow, fulfilling life—whether this be a rural village or a sleepy seaside community. Rural book festivals and rural bookselling can be considered part of a broader mythology: that of the countryside as a counterpoint to the city. This trend can be traced back to the sixteenth century and the growth of the city of London; the countryside was heralded as the last remnant of the Golden Age, providing a nostalgic past and memories of a simpler, purer time. A less complicated life associated with the countryside was favourably contrasted with less appealing city characteristics: 'the convention of the court, the brutality of the market and the anonymity of the city' (Short 1991, p. 31). The myth has escalated with growing modernization and urbanization, increasing social tensions and looming large-scale social changes. Part of the utopian appeal of a book town, stemming from the growing global shift from rural to urban societies, has resulted in nostalgic attraction to rural lifestyles that supposedly encompass a slower pace of life and an identification with the past. Natural areas represent, and are living embodiments, of the past, contributing to a sense of continuity and identity. Nostalgia for rurality, but also for the memories and associations contained in books, is a highly sought-after commodity. Book aficionados can escape to peripheral locations to avoid the predominance of large multinational brands and other global standardizations that are perceived as unappealing.

Country life represents an unhurried lifestyle directed by the seasons, not the financial markets, where life is both authentic and more rustic—'a refuge from modernity' (Short 1991, p. 34). The countryside also plays a part in representing national identity, explained by the dual meaning of the term 'country' as both 'rural land' and 'native land'. It conjures thoughts of national peace and stability from an often mythic past, which contrast with the increasing conflict and change associated with the present. Book towns and their book festivals are considered fashionable destinations for both English and French urbanites. This pattern can be traced to the popularity of escapes from the city to castles and private country estates to enjoy country pursuits and cultural events from as early as the eighteenth century. A longing for the exotic, unspoiled landscapes that exists in the psyche of urbanites today has also had a direct impact on the development and imaging of tourism (Beeton 2005, p. 5). While selling an image is not particularly new or unique, creating a book town is a different type of commodification of place. The emergence of new uses of rural space as recreation, tourism, environmental conservation and retailing is creating different power relationships and a range of development trajectories in the countryside. Clearly, rural areas are now characterized by consumption as well as production activities.

Torup Eco-Village in Denmark and a number of the *villages du livre* provide rich and individualistic examples of living a utopian ideal in the countryside through the establishment of slow, alternative lifestyles. Torup, an eleventh-century village that was largely abandoned until a few years ago, has recreated itself as an Eco Book Village and Denmark's National Book Town. The villagers aim to live as self-sufficiently as possible in a community that adheres to a strict regime of vegetarianism, spirituality and humanity. Books form a vital part of this peaceful, spiritual environment, and the town has a lively atmosphere of open-air bookstalls and honesty bookshops (Campbell 2014, p. 141). With a focus on traditional book crafts, the commune of Montolieu near Carcassone in the South of France describes itself as a book and graphic arts village. Bookbinder Michael Braibant successfully established a Conservatoire Européen des Métieres et des Arts Graphiques in 1989, aiming to contribute to cultural development in the area, attract tourists and create jobs (Abrassart, in Merfeld-Langston 2007, p. 58). The rehabilitation of this paper mill has enabled the development of an educational resource providing writing classes and workshops in writing, printmaking, papermaking and bookbinding, designed for both adults and children (Merfeld-Langston 2009, p. 41). The town embraces slow pastimes and traditional book arts—not only bookshops but festivals, public readings and pedagogical workshops. Similarly, Fontenay-la-Joûte is located amid rolling farmland in the Lorraine district, within driving distance of Nancy, Metz and Strasbourg, and dates from the early twelfth century (Merfeld-Langston 2007, p. 60). The town's transformation was masterminded by three men—Bonnet, a sociologist; Guillaume, a politician; and Mengotti, a teacher—to enable a democratic and egalitarian means of revitalizing their rural community. The book town features a monthly Sunday book market and has created an inviting atmosphere due to the sympathetic restoration of historic houses as bookshops.

Established in Brittany in 1988, Bécherel is a geographically remote book town by the sea, boasting ancient ramparts and beautiful ecclesiastical buildings that have earned it recognition as a *Petite Cite de Charactére* (McShane 2002, p. 30). Bécherel was formerly a prosperous business centre thriving on linen and hemp production in earlier centuries, but more recently has relied economically on tanneries and dairying. However, by the 1960s the economy was failing, the population was diminishing and the town was losing its spirit. By 1983, a group of Breton women idealists led by Colette Trublet, a psychoanalyst and juvenile delinquency expert, were in search of a location where they could make a positive difference and find an antidote to metropolitan living dominated by Paris and the role of the French government in controlling important aspects of regional identity, including culture and language (Merfeld-Langston 2007, p. 52; Karel 2009). The group in France dreamed of an alternative lifestyle that would allow those involved to use their unique professional skills for the good of the community and to live a rich cultural life. Inspired by Redu in Belgium and Hay-on-Wye, 'they believed cultural and economic revival could go hand in hand in a rural community abandoned in the 1960s by a generation of job-seekers who had locked up ancestral homes and moved to the cities'

(Karel 2009), and their vision has materialized in the form of a *village du livre*—a village with 750 residents, one bakery and 15 booksellers. Many of the bookshops are housed in stately granite buildings that were one-time residences and weaving ateliers of prosperous linen merchants, with the shops clustered close together in the town's two squares and side streets.

Bécherel, like Hay-on-Wye, was undoubtedly 'inspired in part by a hippie, sixties counterculture that sought to break away from an established, centralized government norm in favour of a "back to the land" utopian approach to living and governing' (Merfeld-Langston 2007, p. 86). In more recent projects, this radicalism is less evident and newer book towns are less politically motivated, yet the respite delivered by book town lifestyles is keenly sought after. Communities like Bécherel are revered for being 'ideal' in the minds of book lovers and avid collectors.

When I asked why booksellers are attracted to book towns, Nelson (personal interview 2011) said:

> Bookselling is a lifestyle choice. Sedbergh booksellers find the country lifestyle appealing – the many local clubs and societies, wonderful scenery and walking, close proximity to both the Lake District and the Yorkshire Dales national parks, the availability of cheap real estate and low business rates.

Enjoyment of the idyllic environment and being part of a bibliophile community are major factors explaining why booksellers stay in book towns, and this may partly be related to the fact that they are newcomers and the location is a novelty. In Nelson's case, her role is stimulating and satisfying because it encompasses a variety of responsibilities additional to the management of her bookshop: organizing festivals and events, managing the town's web presence, applying for grant funding, representing the book town's interests on the Chamber of Commerce and acting as a conduit between the Sedbergh book town and governments, the public school, the media and a range of other stakeholders. Press agrees that booksellers in book towns are rarely financially motivated. Instead, they want to live in beautiful, rural surroundings and sell their books in such a setting (Press 2001, p. 74). Joyce Watson and Ian Cochrane, proprietors of The Old Bank bookshop in Wigtown, shared their story about moving to Wigtown during our interview:

> In our case, it was a moment in our life. We'd been coming here to see my parents. We are book people and we were fascinated by the concept and wondered how people could make a living. I am a librarian and Ian is a TEFL teacher – had been for 22 years. We had experienced losses of family members and experienced other changes. In 2003, we were searching for something else. I was commuting to the library for work and could see the 'writing on the wall' for libraries. I somehow wanted more control, a complete change. We opened our bookshop in September 2004 … we started from scratch, no shelves and no books! Ian went round auctions buying up thousands of books and shelved up the shop a room at a time to accommodate them. And no one knew we were actually living behind all the boxes piled up in a doorway of the shop as we hadn't anywhere to live … (personal interview 2011)

A number of booksellers with whom I spoke had moved to, or remained in, book towns for family reasons or to slow down their fast-paced lives. The book town allowed them—often well-educated people—to enjoy a valuable and desirable role in the community, whereas without the book town concept there would be nothing to draw them back to the town. In Watson's experience, people take on a venture such as running a bookshop in a book town when they have been made redundant or taken early retirement, often having had the dream of wanting to do it. However, Watson agrees with Turpin (personal interview 2017) and Seaton that buying a bookshop is not necessarily a shrewd business decision; it is about passion. She confesses that the first year was extremely challenging, and the survival of the business is testament to her family's investment, hard work and pride, but it leaves Watson and her husband with a 'great feeling of achievement'. Book town organizers and booksellers such as Watson are, in fact, guardians of cultural heritage and agents who provide access to the cultural past in villages that are repositories for objects with their own rich histories. In this sense, those who choose to make their life in book towns are like-minded. Buzbee, in questioning the bookseller's motivation, concludes, 'The answer is simple: love. You love books so much that you believe a book, any book, is an important object, nearly sacred. You also believe in the free trade of those books is key to a society's democratic nature' (2006, p. 147). Most bookseller interviewees such as Watson, Cochrane, Schiotz, Chambers, Nelson, Bakes and Sharkey are intrinsically 'book people' who would not be as content dealing in any other merchandise.

Grey Nomads: Slow Retirement

The majority of book town visitors traditionally have travelled via private transport (Seaton 1996, p. 24). Their patronage can be attributed partly to the greater mobility of the public that occurred due to private transport availability and the opportunity to explore the countryside more intimately, pleasing individual needs:

> a source of freedom, the freedom of the road which enables the car's driver to travel … along the complex road systems of Western societies … In Edwardian and later in inter-war England, an alternative machinic complex developed. This was based around the concept of the 'open road' and the slow meandering motor tour that became a highly favoured middle class pursuit. Motor touring was thought of as 'a voyage through the life and history of the land'. There was an increasing emphasis upon slower means of finding such pleasures. To tour, to stop, to drive slowly, to take the longer route, to emphasize process rather than destination, all became part of the performed act of motor touring as ownership of cars became far more widespread. (Urry 2000, p. 60)

In Australia, country bookshop patronage is a growing weekend pastime. Used bookshops are springing up and flourishing in small country towns where rents are relatively cheap, shop premises are larger and cashed-up tourists, day-trippers and weekenders are pleased to find an oasis of old books where they can while away their time and money (Marshall 2004, p. 265). However, the increased mobility of booksellers is also an important factor. Such freedom and independence allow booksellers to range far and wide in their quest to buy and dispose of books. Book fairs, book towns, suburban and country bookshops are able to flourish with mobile populations to patronize them.

While the Slow Movement is increasingly embraced by all age groups, it is especially popular among an ageing population in Australia, where growing numbers of older Australians with time on their hands—known as 'grey nomads'—are trawling regional Australia seeking meaningful connections with communities and events as well as a sense of freedom and adventure through the pursuit of a nomadic lifestyle (Onyx and Leonard 2007, p. 381). They embrace the slow philosophy, tending to refuse high-tech modes of consumption and instead supporting slow consumption (Hall 2009), as well as supporting the preservation of the environment (Dickenson et al. 2010, pp. 1–2). This trend indicates a creative approach to living:

> The availability of unobligated time experienced by many older individuals allows self-direction … The need to break out of traditional ways of seeing the world and examining new paradigms underlies Ulyssean living. Loss of the work role and seeking the challenges of new roles can help accomplish this. (McGuire et al. 1999, p. 153)

Lifelong educational pursuits, social and environmental responsibility and self-development through tourism are therefore increasingly powerful themes, driving the growth of educational tourism experiences—whether heritage tourism, cultural tourism or eco-tourism. For example, demographic trends such as ageing populations have resulted in shifting tourism patterns that signify the concept of 'the third age'—a sociological term used to describe changes in the way retired people regard themselves as a result of their greater wealth and higher living standards, allowing them to focus on personal development and greater fulfilment (Moscardo 2006, p. 31; Shoemaker 2000).

However, while presumptions about third-age travellers having abundant wealth and time to travel do not necessarily consider changing economic conditions (Moscardo 2006, p. 37), grey nomads are not 'conventional tourists'. While they often have limited financial means, they have extensive time on their hands, often spending a number of weeks in a single location with interest in developing an in-depth understanding of individual places and communities (Onyx et al.

2007). Volunteering is therefore an opportunity to contribute to the visited community, and to meet local people and other travellers.[7] Shoemaker (2000), Gschwind (personal interview 2011), Muller (personal interview 2010), Onyx et al. (2007) and others suggest that an increasing number of senior travellers, in Australia in particular, engage in part-time employment at travel destinations—a trend of potential relevance to current and future book town communities. While McShane (personal interview 2010) queries their likelihood of purchasing many books, he acknowledges their potential to engage with communities. I regard grey nomads, and other third-age travellers elsewhere in the world, as valuable to the ongoing sustainability of book towns in the future.

Bookshops and festival spaces in book towns—third places—are smaller establishments and environments where people can exchange ideas, be in contact and gather with like-minded others simply to share a bookish atmosphere or an intimate literary experience without formal endorsement from any higher authority. As instruments of social capital, book towns benefit from and reflect the concepts inherent in slow travel, embracing as they do slow books, slow reading, slow food and slow travel, and allowing leisurely immersion in distinctive regional cultures and *terroir*. They are places where the everyday is renegotiated with paradigms of serious leisure and mindfulness, where books and countryside allow meaningful consumption in a peaceful setting. They also tend to be places that rebel, to different degrees, against inauthenticity and unbridled capitalism. In that way, book towns—nurturing, nourishing and inspiring—provide an antidote to the 'evils' of city living. Significantly, bookshops and book towns, acting as third places, more broadly promote the formation of social networks and associations in creative communities. These locales are also the embodiment of growing regionalism across the world, combining real and immediate connections with globally applicable ideas. They require a dual citizenship in both the realm of ideas and the communities themselves. In this sense, they are a reaction to the relentless speed of contemporary life and carve a path to innovative, sustainable futures for peripheral areas, as Chap. 4 explores.

Notes

1. The initial phase of the Open Book Project run by Wigtown Festival Company concluded on 31 July 2015, but the project is continuing as an Airbnb holiday experience that at the time of writing was booked ahead until mid-2019 (Turpin, personal interview 2017).
2. Inglis (2000) appears to mean avoiding others in the sense of people *en masse*.
3. The Slow Movement: Making a Connection, http://www.slowmovement.com/place.php
4. The Fell Centre Rail System was used to enable specially fitted trains to negotiate the steep grade of the Rimutaka incline safely while hauling large loads (Gould, personal interview 2017).
5. Joel Becker is CEO of the Australian Booksellers Association.
6. This trend is also referred to as amenity migration or lifestyle migration (Benson and O'Reilly 2009). Regional Australia has experienced significant changes in population and employment since the early 1900s. Refer to Hugo's (1996) work on counter-urbanization and ABS (2004) data on changing Australian social trends. While Garnett and Lewis (2007, p. 29) argue that much of this evidence is anecdotal, with frequent references in the political and media spheres to a 'sea change' or 'tree change', there is now a widening body of research on this phenomenon. Refer, for example, to Kijas (2002), Murphy (2002), Osbaldiston (2010, 2012, 2013), Ragusa (2013), Burnley and Murphy (2004), Dowling (2004) and a number of reports on the challenges of coastal growth by the National Sea Change Taskforce.
7. While grey nomads can be compared with American snowbirds—older Americans who drive long distances in self-drive vehicles to winter in warmer climates—Onyx and Leonard distinguish that Australian senior travellers actively avoid being 'organized' in the way older Americans are in American holiday resorts (2005, p. 67). Their more liberated, nomadic tendencies, motivated by a desire to retire early and 'escape unpalatable bureaucratic agencies in their work life', contrast with the snowbirds simply avoiding cold winter climates.

References

About Slow TV. (2010). *The Monthly: Australian Politics, Society and Culture*. http://www.themonthly.com.au/about-slowtv. Accessed 10 Aug 2010.

Aitchison, C., MacLeod, N., & Shaw, S. (2002). *Leisure and tourism landscapes: Social and cultural geographies*. London: Routledge.

Ashworth, G. J., & Graham, B. (Eds.). (2005). *Senses of place; senses of time.* Aldershot: Ashgate.

Australian Bureau of Statistics. (2004). *Australian social trends 2004: Seachange – New coastal residents*. Cat no. 4102.0. Canberra: ABS.

Bagshaw, M., & Mills, C. (2010). *Alastair Sawday's slow North Yorkshire: Moors, dales and coast, including York*. Chalfont St Peter: Bardt.

Bedford, Y. N. (2012). The '"Peace Gardens", Featherston, South Wairarapa and the chor-farmer'. *Australian and New Zealand Environmental History Network, 5*(2). https://environmentalhistory-au-nz.org/2012/12/the-peace-gardens-featherston-south-wairarapa-and-the-chor-farmer. Accessed 20 Mar 2017.

Beeton, S. (2005). *Film-induced tourism*. Clevedon: Channel View.

Benson, M., & O'Reilly, K. (2009). *Lifestyle migration: Expectations, aspirations and experiences*. Aldershot: Ashgate.

Bowie-Sell, D. (2012, October 1). Wigtown Book Festival 2012: Marek Kukula, Martin Dorey and James Attlee. *The Telegraph*. http://www.telegraph.co.uk/culture/books/wigtown-book-festival/9578887/Wigtown-Book-Festival-2012-Marek-Kukula-Martin-Dorey-and-James-Attlee.html. Accessed 21 Nov 2012.

Bradshaw, T., & Nichols, B. (2004). *Reading at risk: A survey of literary reading in America*. Washington, DC: National Endowment for the Arts.

Bryman, A. (1995). *Disney and his worlds*. London: Routledge.

Burnley, I., & Murphy, P. (2004). *Sea change: Movement from metropolitan to Arcadian Australia*. Sydney: UNSW Press.

Buzbee, L. (2006). *The yellow-lighted bookshop: A memoir, a history*. Saint Paul: Graywolf Press.

Calhoun, C. (2002). The class consciousness of frequent travelers: Toward a critique of actually existing cosmopolitanism. *The South Atlantic Quarterly, 101*(4), 869–897.

Campbell, J. (2014). *The bookshop book*. London: Constable and Robinson.

Coser, L. (1992). Introduction: Maurice Halbwachs 1877–1945. In L. Coser (Ed.), *On collective memory* (pp. 1–34). Chicago: University of Chicago Press.

De Certeau, M. (1984). *Notes from the practice of everyday life*. Berkeley: University of California Press.

Dickenson, J., & Lumsden, L. (2010). *Slow travel and tourism*. London: Earthscan.
Dickenson, J. E., Robbins, D., & Lumsden, L. (2010). Holiday travel discourses and climate change. *Journal of Transport Geography, 18*, 482–489.
Douglas, N., Douglas, N., & Derrett, R. (Eds.). (2001). *Special interest tourism: Context and cases*. Brisbane: John Wiley & Sons.
Dowling, C. (2004). *Seachange: Australians in pursuit of the good life*. Sydney: Exisle.
Earl, B. (2008). Literary tourism: Constructions of value, celebrity and distinction. *International Journal of Cultural Studies, 11*, 401.
Fentress, J., & Wickham, C. (1994). *Social memory*. Oxford: Blackwell.
Flipo, F., & Schneider, F. (Eds.). (2008). *Proceedings of the first international conference on economic degrowth for ecological sustainability and social equity*. Paris, 18–19 April. Research & Degrowth, INT, 322p.
Florida, R. (2002). *The rise of the creative class: And how it's transforming work, leisure, community and everyday life*. New York: Basic Books.
Francis, R. (2004, November 19). Making conversation: The rise of literary festivals. *Flakmagazine*. http://www.flakmag.com/books/litfest.html. Accessed 1 Feb 2011.
Frederickson, L., & Anderson, D. (1999). A qualitative exploration of the wilderness experience as a source of spiritual inspiration. *Journal of Environmental Psychology, 19*, 21–29.
Fullagar, S. (2010). *Creating slow travel cultures: Cycle touring as an alternative hedonism*. Paper presented to Creative Communities II Conference. Griffith University, Gold Coast, 23 September.
Gablik, S. (1993). Toward an ecological self. In R. Hertz (Ed.), *Theories of contemporary art* (2nd ed.). Englewood Cliffs: Prentice Hall.
Gardiner, N. (2009). A manifesto for slow travel. *Hidden Europe Magazine, 25*, 10–14.
Garnett, A. M., & Lewis, P. E. T. (2007). Population and employment changes in regional Australia. *Economic Papers, 26*(1), 29–43.
Gelling, C. (2003). *Berrima, New South Wales*. Berrima: Berrima Courthouse Museum.
Goffman, E. (1959). *The presentation of self in everyday life*. Garden City: Doubleday.
Goodey, B. (1975). Urban trails: Origins and opportunities. *The Planner, 61*, 29–30.
Green, R. (2000). Notions of town character: A coastal community responds to change. *Australian Planner, 37*(2), 76–86.

Gretzel, U., Fesenmaier, D. R., & O'Leary, J. T. (2006). The transformation of consumer behaviour. In D. Buhalis & C. Costa (Eds.), *Tourism business frontiers: Consumers, products and industry* (pp. 9–18). Burlington: Elsevier Butterworth-Heinemann.

Hall, C. M. (2009). Degrowing tourism: Décroissance, sustainable consumption and steady-state tourism. *Anatolia: An International Journal of Tourism and Hospitality Research, 20*(1), 46–61.

Harris, C. (2015, October 15). Featherston becomes New Zealand's first booktown with new festival this weekend. *Stuff.* http://www.stuff.co.nz/dominion-post/news/73050630/featherston-becomes-new-zealands-first-booktown-with-new-festival-this-weekend. Accessed 26 June 2016.

Hayes, D., & MacLeod, N. (2007). Packaging places: Designing heritage trails using an experience economy perspective to manage visitor engagement. *Journal of Vacation Marketing, 13*(1), 45–58.

Hodgkinson, T. (2011). *The Idler.* http://idler.co.uk. Accessed 22 Oct 2011.

Honoré, C. (2004). *In praise of slowness: How a worldwide movement is challenging the cult of speed.* New York: HarperCollins.

Hugo, G. (1996). Counterurbanisation. In P. Newton & M. Bell (Eds.), *Population shift: Mobility and change in Australia* (pp. 126–146). Canberra: Australian Government Publishing Service.

Huigen, P. P. P., & Meijering, L. (2005). Making places: A story of De Venen. In G. J. Ashworth & B. Graham (Eds.), *Senses of place; senses of time.* Aldershot: Ashgate.

Inglis, F. (2000). *The delicious history of the holiday.* London: Routledge.

Kahn, B. M. (1987). *Cosmopolitan culture: The gilt-edged dream of a tolerant city.* New York: Atheneum.

Karel, E. (2009, June 30). Brittany's booktown. *France Today.*

Kendall, G., Skrbis, Z., & Woodward, I. (2009). *The sociology of cosmopolitanism.* London: Palgrave Macmillan.

Kijas, J. (2002). A place at the coast: Internal migration and the shift to the coastal-countryside. *Transformations, 2*, 1–12.

Löfgren, O. (2003). The new economy: A cultural history. *Global Networks, 3*(3), 239–254.

Lowenthal, D. (1985). *The past is a foreign country.* Cambridge: Cambridge University Press.

MacCannell, D. (1999 [1976]). *The tourist: A new theory of the leisure class.* Berkeley: University of California Press.

MacCannell, D. (2011). *The ethics of sightseeing*. Berkeley: University of California Press.

Marshall, A. (2004). *Fossicking for old books*. Melbourne: Bread Street Press.

McCrum, R. (2006, January 15). E-read all about it. *The Observer* [UK]. http://www.guardian.co.uk/books/2006/jan/15/ebooks.technology/print. Accessed 3 Feb 2011.

McGuire, F., et al. (1999). *Leisure and aging: Ulyssean living in later life*. Champaign: Sagamore.

McShane, P. (2002). *To further Australia's understanding and involvement in the international booktown movement through a program of visits and interviews*. Winston Churchill Memorial Trust of Australia. http://www.booktown.com.au/ChurchillReport_Booktowns_2002.htm. Accessed 27 Feb 2010.

Merfeld-Langston, A. L. (2007). The *villages du livre*: Local identity, cultural politics and print culture in contemporary France. PhD thesis, Pennsylvania State University.

Merfeld-Langston, A. L. (2009). Montolieu, France, village of living books. In *A compendium of clusters in less populated places: Circumstances, interventions and outcomes* (pp. 41–42). Carborro: Regional Technology Strategies.

Miedema, J. (2009). *Slow reading*. Duluth: Litwin Books.

Ministry for Culture and Heritage, New Zealand. (2014). *Featherston Camp*. https://nzhistory.govt.nz/war/featherston-camp. 18 March 2017.

Monteiro, C. (2012, September). A literary celebration in Scotland's National Book Town 28 September–7 October 2012 [Press Release]. *Wigtown Book Festival* [News and Press]. http://www.wigtownbookfestival.com/news-and-press/press-release-september-2012. Accessed 21 Nov 2012.

Moscardo, G. (2006). Third-age tourism. In D. Buhalis & C. Costa (Eds.), *Tourism business frontiers: Consumers, products and industry* (pp. 30–39). Burlington: Elsevier Butterworth Heinemann.

Mulcock, J., & Toussaint, Y. (2002). Memories and idylls: Urban reflections on lost places and inner landscapes. *Transformations, 2*, 1–16.

Murphy, P. (2002). Sea change: Re-inventing rural and regional Australia. *Transformations, 2*, 1–12.

National Tourism and Heritage Taskforce [Australia]. (2003). *Going places: Developing natural and cultural heritage tourism in Australia*. Canberra: EPHC.

Oldenburg, R. (1999). *The great, good place: Cafés, coffee shops, bars, salons and other hangouts at the heart of a community*. New York: Marlowe.

Onyx, J., & Leonard, R. (2005). Australian grey nomads and American snowbirds: Similarities and differences. *The Journal of Tourism Studies, 16*(1), 61–68.

Onyx, J., & Leonard, R. (2007). The grey nomad phenomenon: Changing the script of aging. *International Journal of Aging and Human Development, 64*(4), 381–398.

Onyx, J., Leonard, R., & Maher, A. (2007). *New partnerships: Promoting development in outback towns through voluntary programs for Grey Nomads* [Report of Bingara Field Visit – April/May 2007]. Grey Nomad Volunteering Project. Volunteering Australia.

Osbaldiston, N. (2010). Elementary forms of place in seachange. *Journal of Sociology, 46*, 239–256.

Osbaldiston, N. (Ed.). (2012). *Seeking authenticity in place, culture, and the self: The great urban escape*. London: Palgrave Macmillan.

Osbaldiston, N. (Ed.). (2013). *Culture of the slow: Social deceleration in an accelerated world*. London: Palgrave Macmillan.

Pine, B. J., & Gilmore, J. H. (1999). *The experience economy*. Cambridge, MA: Harvard Business School Press.

Portinari, F. (1989). *The slow food manifesto*. http://wwwmichaelpollan.com/article.php?id=87. Accessed 15 Jan 2014.

Press, S. (2001). *Reading Wigtown: Place identities in a Scottish book town*. MA Thesis, University of Oregon.

Ragusa, A. T. (2013). Downshifting or conspicuous consumption? A sociological examination of treechange as a manifestation of slow culture. In N. Osbaldiston (Ed.), *Culture of the slow: Social deceleration in an accelerated world*. London: Palgrave Macmillan.

Rinaldi, G. (2012, October 6). How do book towns survive in the age of the e-reader? *BBC News South Scotland*. http://www.bbc.co.uk/news/uk-scotland-south-scotland-19814700. Accessed 5 Dec 2012.

Robinson, M. (2004). Between and beyond the pages: Literature–tourism relationships. In M. Robinson & H. Andersen (Eds.), *Literature and tourism: Essays in the reading and writing of tourism* (pp. 39–79). Andover: Thomson Learning.

Rojek, C. (1993). *Ways of escape: Modern transformations in leisure and travel*. Basingstoke: Macmillan.

Rojek, C. (2000). *Leisure and culture*. Basingstoke: Macmillan.

Rojek, C. (2001). *Celebrity*. London: Reaktion Books.

Rosa, J., & Malter, A. J. (2002). E-(embodied) cognition and e-commerce: How physiological factors affect on-line sales of experiential products. *Journal of Consumer Psychology, 13*, 63–75.

Rose, N. (1999). *Powers of freedom: Reframing political thought*. Cambridge: Cambridge University Press.

Sack, R. D. (1992). *Place, modernity and the consumer's world*. Baltimore: Johns Hopkins University Press.

Sassatelli, R. (2013). Creativity takes time, critique needs space: Re-working the political investment of the consumer through pleasure. In N. Osbaldiston (Ed.), *Culture of the slow: Social deceleration in an accelerated world* (pp. 154–177). London: Palgrave Macmillan.

Seaton, A. V. (1996). *Book towns and rural tourism development: The new European book towns 1984–1996*. Glasgow: University of Strathclyde.

Seaton, A. V. (2002). Tourism as a metempsychosis and metensomatosis: The personae of eternal recurrence. In G. M. S. Dann (Ed.), *The tourist as a metaphor for the social world*. Wallingford: CAB International.

Seffrin, G. (2006). Emerging trends in contemporary festival practice: Exemplifying the modern festival through the praxis of boutique festival initiation and management at the Queensland Performing Arts Centre. PhD, QUT, Brisbane City.

Sharpley, R., & Jepson, D. (2011). Rural tourism: A spiritual journey? *Annals of Tourism Research, 38*(1), 52–71.

Shaya, G. (2004). The flâneur, the badaud, and the making of a mass public in France, circa 1860–1910. *American Historical Review, 109*(1), 41–78.

Shoemaker, S. (2000). Segmenting the mature market: 10 years later. *Journal of Travel Research, 39*, 11–26.

Short, J. R. (1991). *Imagined country: Environment, culture and society*. London: Routledge.

Silbergh, D., Fladmark, M., Henry, G., & Young, M. (1994). A strategy for theme trails. In J. M. Fladmark (Ed.), *Cultural tourism* (pp. 123–146). London: Donhead.

Smith, M. (2006). Entertainment and new leisure tourism. In D. Buhalis & C. Costa (Eds.), *Tourism business frontiers: Consumers, products and industry* (pp. 220–227). Burlington: Elsevier Butterworth Heinemann.

Soper, K. (2007). Rethinking the "good life": The citizenship dimension of consumer disaffection with consumerism. *Journal of Consumer Culture, 7*(2), 205–229.

Squire, S. J. (1994). The cultural values of literary tourism. *Annals of Tourism Research, 21*, 103–120.

Starke, R. (2000). A festival of writers: Adelaide Writers' Week 1960–2000. PhD thesis, Flinders University of South Australia.

Stewart, C. A. (2009). The culture of contemporary writers' festivals. MA (Lit Studies) thesis, QUT, Brisbane.

Turpin, A. (2009, September 13). The missing magic. *Herald Scotland*. http://www.heraldscotland.com/comment/guest-commentary/the-missing-magic-1.919454. Accessed 11 Apr 2012.

Turpin, A. (2011, September 12). Twitter, poems and Michael D. Higgins combine at the Town of Books Festival. *Md Media*. http://www.mdmedia.ie/index.php/2011/09/12/twitter-poems-and-michael-d-higgins-combine-at-the-town-of-books-festival. Accessed 5 Oct 2011.

Ulin, D. (2010). *The lost art of reading: Why books matter in a distracted time*. Seattle: Sasquatch Books.

Urry, J. (1988). Cultural change and contemporary holiday-making. *Theory, Culture and Society, 5*(35), 35–55.

Urry, J. (1994). Cultural change and contemporary tourism. *Leisure Studies, 13*(4), 233–238.

Urry, J. (2000). *Sociology beyond societies: Mobilities for the twenty-first century*. London: Routledge.

Urry, J. (2007). *Mobilities*. Cambridge: Polity Press.

Vukonić, B. (1996). *Tourism and religion*. Oxford: Pergamon Press.

Wang, N. (2000). *Tourism and modernity: A sociological analysis*. Oxford: Pergamon Press.

Weaver, D., & Lawton, L. (2006). *Tourism management* (3rd ed.). Brisbane: John Wiley and Sons.

What is Slow Travel?. (2011). *Slow Movement*. www.slowmovement.com/slow_travel. Accessed 15 Oct 2011.

Wigtown Festival Company. (2017, April 3). *Business plan 2017–2021*. Wigtown.

Winter, J. (2006). *Remembering war: The Great War between memory and history in the twentieth century*. New Haven: Yale University Press.

Young, S. (2007). *The book is dead (long live the book)*. Sydney: UNSW Press.

Zaid, G. (2004). *So many books*. London: Sort of Books.

Interviews

Berkelouw, Leo. Eumundi, Queensland, 14 August 2012.

Derrett, R. OAM. Brisbane, Queensland, 2 June 2010.

Gould, Lincoln. Wellington, New Zealand, 8 February 2017.

Gschwind, Daniel. Brisbane, Queensland, 15 July 2011.

Hauritz, B. Brisbane, Queensland, 29 November 2011.

McShane, Paul. Bowral, New South Wales, Australia, 9 July 2010.
McShane, Paul and Rosa, Steve. Mittagong, New South Wales, 8 July 2010.
Mead, Kate. Featherston, New Zealand, 8 February 2017.
Muller, Laurie. Brisbane, Queensland, 17 August 2010 and 7 September 2010.
Nelson, Carole. Sedbergh, Yorkshire, United Kingdom, 9 September 2011; phone interview, 29 March 2017.
O'Hara, Jane. Telephone Interview, Brisbane, Queensland, 9 December 2011.
Sheahan-Bright, Robyn. Gladstone, Queensland, 24 August 2010.
Schiotz, Peter. Maleny, Queensland, 4 April 2012.
Swales, Gill. Sedbergh, Yorkshire, 8 September 2011.
Turpin, Adrian OBE. Wigtown, Scotland, 4 September 2011; via email, 15 March 2017.
Watson, Joyce and Cochrane, Ian. Wigtown, Scotland, 4 September 2011.

4

Edge-of-the-Map Locations: Outposts of Sustainable Culture

The rise of book towns is intrinsically linked to strategies that deliver rural and regional sustainability.[1] Economic development is a challenge for most rural communities, and they often turn to tourism in relatively conventional forms, such as farm stay programmes, bed and breakfast (B&B) establishments and annual agricultural shows. The book town concept offers another way of bolstering rural tourism, thus keeping communities viable; it exemplifies the motivational factors Seaton (1996a, p. 28) believes are necessary to attract visitors rather than simply providing accommodation and assuming that this alone will draw people to rural areas. Like Hay-on-Wye, most book towns are located in picturesque locales or sites that have some inherent architectural interest. The majority are also in depressed or declining rural areas, and are geographically peripheral. Many had experienced retail losses, and most were struggling for new sources of employment prior to becoming book towns. These factors meant, however, that property values were cheap and rents were low (Seaton 1996b, p. 390). While most book towns had experienced economic difficulties in the years preceding their transformation, these are conditions that have proved fertile for book town projects. The Book Town Movement has sprung out of adversity rather than privilege (Booth, personal interview 2011). Expensive and prosperous towns do

J. Frank, *Regenerating Regional Culture*, Sociology of the Arts,
https://doi.org/10.1007/978-3-319-65036-4_4

not offer the inexpensive premises, display areas and storage spaces that allow booksellers and artisans to establish businesses in book towns (Berkelouw, personal interview 2012; Merfeld-Langston 2007, p. 14). Abandoned retail space in a dying rural community provides an ideal nucleus for such a scheme:

> There is a pattern to the places that have become book towns. Hay was a sleepy market town, nothing much going on there. Sedbergh was fairly quiet, not a tourist location. Blaenafon, Wigtown were places which had been absolutely decimated by recession, by economic collapse essentially. When Wigtown's dairy moved to Wales, it took 200 people with it. They were the workers … the wage earners in the town. Those low rents are determined by wider socio-economic factors that we have no control over, but that you could take advantage of if you are prepared to go to a remote location. (Playden, personal interview 2011)

High rents in metropolitan areas continue to force booksellers and entrepreneurial book lovers into more rural settings where booksellers can afford property, and where there is ample space for such businesses to flourish (Berkelouw, personal interview 2012; Marshall 2004, p. 265; McMurtry 1999, p. 179; 2008, p. 97; McShane, personal interview 2010). However, it is the very fact that book towns exist in geographically peripheral areas that makes them places of interest to tourists. Peripherality is associated with distance from the geographic centre. These marginal places—towns and regions that have been left behind in the wake of environmental, social and economic change—evoke both nostalgia and fascination. Their marginal status comes not only from their out-of-the-way locations, but also from being 'the other pole to a great cultural centre' (Shields 1991, p. 3).

Sparseness of population in these places—often small towns or villages in isolated rural or coastal locations—raises questions of economic sustainability, so these communities usually have economic structures based largely on primary industries such as farming, and tertiary industries such as tourism (Wanhill 1997, p. 48). The strong economic argument for attracting urban visitors, widely evident in Britain, has inspired strategies that aim to satisfy the demand for recreation in peripheral locations (Urry 1995, pp. 288–9). There has been a shift from policies of containment and visitor management to strategies encouraging urban dwellers to explore places 'further off the beaten track. Such places remain a labyrinth of dark corners and mystery, a rural heterotopia that allows visitors the freedom to stumble across unexpected meanings and memories' (Urry 1995, pp. 228–9). For this reason, places from nation-states to localities are commodifying and presenting themselves as 'different, as possessing singular qualities of space and culture, as being composed of essences' (Meetham 2001, p. 136). The production and consumption of narratives of space created through heritage in book towns provide the means to communicate a local identity and enable a way by which towns can present themselves as unique commodities for the global tourist system. Localness sells, and many places throughout the world aim to use this phenomenon to their advantage: 'It could be argued that the category "local" … can now be appropriated by development organizations and cultural producers to celebrate specialness, uniqueness and a "recovered" sense of authenticity' (Burnett 1998, p. 209). Regional recognition of cultural resources enables peripheral locations to recreate themselves, ensuring revival and regeneration. Evans and Shaw (2004, pp. 4–5) note that 'regeneration is both a process and an outcome. It can have physical, economic and social dimensions, and the three commonly coexist.' As a consequence of growing interest in this strategy, academic and government literature about regeneration processes that are both led by and incorporate the arts, culture and creativity is prolific in its scope and global coverage.

Historically, as illustrated by nineteenth-century European models, major events associated with books and writing were tied to the sense of artistic prestige associated with urban centres—just as the opera, the concert hall, the theatre, the museum and the art gallery were. However, increasing globalization and a degree of audience disenfranchisement (Constantoura 2001, p. 82) have invited changing cultural models of engagement that embrace rural and regional areas and their unique local cultural offerings. This transformation has triggered the development of new sites—including book towns—for artistic creation and cultural consumption. Less conventional spaces, including local landmarks, festivals, community events and online exchanges, are emerging as important hubs of creativity in rural and regional areas. Book towns provide stimulating paradigms of the way the public is engaging with rural and regional communities to embrace alternative cultural opportunities. Relatively remote rural villages like Wigtown, Sedbergh and Clunes, for example, which were not associated with high-profile events and literary activities until they rebranded themselves as book towns, have positioned themselves as up-and-coming centres for vibrant cultural activities based around books and literary culture. They have provided fertile ground for a rethinking of artistic places in contemporary culture and, in keeping with the democratization of culture that is occurring globally, provide an increasing balance between urban and rural modes of engagement that were not previously possible.

Landry (2008, p. 8) advocates distinctive cultural identities for all places, but especially those on the fringe:

> As the world of cultural resources opened out, it became clear that every city could have a unique niche and 'making something out of nothing' became totemic to anyone trying to develop or promote ugly cities, cold or hot cities or marginal places. The realization dawned that every city could be a world centre for something if it was persistent and tried hard enough – Freiburg for eco-research, New Orleans for the Blues or Hay-on-Wye for bookselling. In identifying resources, much could be learnt from the Italians' renowned for their '*feste*' or '*sagre*' which celebrate whatever resource their region is known for, from mushrooms to pasta to literature.

Culture is a powerful source of creativity in these places, and its impacts deliver the value of distinctiveness, 'so vital in a world where cities increasingly look and feel the same' (Landry 2008, p. 11). The rise of regionalism in the 1980s and 1990s drew attention to the relativity of the 'centre', overturning the association of excellence and success with solely metropolitan projects in an arts and cultural context (Frank 1996, p. 2). Equity and access in relation to funding and resources, and the distribution of cultural value between cities and regions, have since been regarded as increasingly desirable. In the case of book towns, distance from urban centres is recommended, but the desirable distance from centres of population has been a point of contention. For example, when Wigtown was selected as Scotland's National Book Town in 1997,

Booth opposed the verdict on the grounds of the town's extreme remoteness (1999, pp. 301–3). He thought the town would be unable to service a mobile economy, despite being a picturesque location with a rich history. He preferred the town of Dalmellington at the foot of the Galloway Mountains on the road north to Ayrshire, where 'the community spirit was as strong as the liquor' (Booth, personal interview 2011) and the main street contained three large ruined factories and warehouses. He considered this to be a site of grittier realism that had practical advantages, being geographically closer to Glasgow and Edinburgh, and nearer to Prestwick Airport. However, Turpin is adamant that Wigtown 'thrives because of, not in spite of, its edge-of-the-map location. Visitors, including writers, have time to talk, to drink, to spark unusual friendships, while the town's size – 980 people – makes visiting an intimate experience' (2008; personal interview 2011). However, Wigtown's geographical remoteness means it consistently needs to work on its status as a vibrant oasis of culture to survive and grow its reputation.

Founded in 2007, Booktown Richmond, as it is known, in the Karoo region of South Africa is another good example of a place that went 'from sad "nothing" town to book town' (Grant-Marshall 2012). This project began as a result of founder Darryl David's doctoral research on literary tourism, together with a partnership between fellow South African entrepreneur and bibliophile John Donaldson, who bought up almost the whole main street of the town, and Canadian bookseller Peter Baker. The initiative of these individuals is cast against a context where rural tourism in South Africa has changed significantly since the advent of political democracy in 1995. The country has embraced its considerable potential to attract tourists in search of exciting experiences in areas of unexploited natural beauty and rich cultural resources (Briedenhann and Wickens 2004, p. 189). Located between Johannesburg and Cape Town, and once a dusty Karoo town without much appeal to tourists, Richmond's book town concept has reshaped the town dramatically. It now boasts a privately run information centre, which is actually a house full of books, and restaurants with bookish themes line the main street. For example, at Baker's Supper Klub, patrons vie with books for space in the bar, lounge and dining areas. John Donald's 22-roomed Richmond Books and Prints contains more than 70,000 books on 1.85 kilometres of shelving. The bookshop is contained in several houses and converted stables, which are joined together by book-lined passageways.

Richmond, once famous for its horse-breeding and as a location for horse shows that attracted people from all over the country, now has a Horse Museum, featuring many books with an equestrian theme, as well as Boer War and equine artefacts and a large collection of antiques. This specialization is a pertinent example of how book towns appeal to global consumer diversity. The book town's signature event and literary festival, Boek Bedonnerd (Book Crazy), attracts internationally acclaimed writers and is steadily increasing its audience. The founders also take their philanthropic role seriously and have opened a library to assist with literacy in the regional community. The town's unique regional character—its difference—is emphasized to promote the book town concept.

This has also been the means to success for other book towns around the globe. The French *village du livre* of Montmorillon, located on the Gartempe River in Vienne, promotes its past as a papermaking centre. This link to the printing industry is central to its identity as a city of writing and books. It also exploits its proximity to a nearby tourist attraction, Futurescope, also known as the Numerical City, that was created in the mid-1980s near Poitiers (Merfeld-Langston 2007, pp. 70–1). Futurescope focuses on technology and visual images, while the book town promotes 'the word' and 'the image'.

Rapid economic growth in South Korea explains the renaissance in publishing that is central to the rise of Paju Book City, located just south of Seoul and fully supported by the Korean Ministry of Culture, Sport and Tourism. Not unlike Sedbergh, particular political and economic circumstances were the catalyst for this development. With the end of military rule in 1987, the previously heavily censored and regulated world of books suddenly burst the floodgates, generating dozens of small publishing houses (Grauman 2008). Newly constructed in swampy countryside, Paju is a 4 square kilometre cultural hub for the Korean publishing community that exclusively designs, creates and distributes books for 260 individual companies, with the precinct being a magnet for printers, bookbinders, papermakers, designers, copyright negotiators, distributors and writers. It is estimated to have the greatest concentration of publishers in the world, and is a ground-breaking experiment in sustainable architecture. The book city featured at the 2008 Venice Biennale as an exciting example of contemporary urban planning (Grauman 2008). In 2011, Paju hosted the Paju BookSori Festival, aimed at an international audience. Festival events celebrated the Nobel Prize for Literature, early Asian land and sea exploration on the Silk Road, comparative Asian languages, book design and world peace (Booth, personal interview 2011). Linking the future of book towns with a trade in ideas and growing their status as non-urban centres of learning (Turpin, personal interview 2011) fits well with Florida's (1995, p. 531) argument that, far from ushering in the end of geography, globalization will progress in step with the growth of regions, with globalism and regionalism part of the same transforming process.

Book Towns, Image and Tourism

Place or destination marketing is central to the way book towns use certain imagery to present themselves: in some instances, images are used as metaphors of desire. Places are increasingly being modelled as centres for consumption, an idea that is apt for deliberately created book towns. For example, Urry (1995, p. 132) states:

> Places are chosen to be gazed upon because there is an anticipation, especially through day-dreaming and fantasy, of intense pleasures, either on a different scale or involving different senses from those customarily encountered. Such anticipation is constructed and sustained through a variety of non-tourist practices such as film, newspapers, television, magazines … which construct that gaze. Such practices provide the signs in terms of which the holiday experiences are understood, so that what is then seen is interpreted in terms of these pre-given categories. The gaze is directed to features of landscape and townscape which separate them off from everyday and routine experiences.

The tourist gaze is an understanding of how the tourist behaves by the regulation of the culture. Thus, rather than being 'out of place', a person may be regulated by the gaze of others so they may embody the culture of difference. A book town and its 'out of the ordinary' characteristics allow a lingering gaze. Particularly in the case of Hay-on-Wye, the book town has been visually objectified for 50 years in endless press cuttings, television interviews and documentaries, photographs, postcards and other materials—even the making of a murder mystery film set in the small town. This repeated identification of the town through a range of materials has representation of the town almost as a simulacrum of itself in terms of this reproductive 'gaze'. The impacts of post-modernism are present in this process of image-building, where the de-differentiation and breakdown of the distinctiveness of each sphere not only result in the aestheticism of everyday life, but also a shift from 'high culture' to 'high street' (Urry 1995, pp. 149–51). Consumption is therefore less and less functional and increasingly de-differentiated from leisure, culture, retailing, education, sport and a range of pastimes: this is the tourism of everyday life. The consumption of places and their increasingly appealing localism are central to a post-modern emphasis on the allure of peripheral places. It is also significant to note that the majority of people in the area or region are now part of the market that was initially aimed at visiting outsiders. More or less everyone lives in a world rendered or reconfigured as interesting, entertaining and attractive, and this proliferation of local tourist development has altered the pattern and impact of leisure in profound ways. Conveying this identity is central to the success of local tourism initiatives such as book towns.

The notion of image, in a broad sense, has long been of interest in the study of tourism (Butler and Hall 1998, p. 115), where images of attractions, cultures and destinations are used in advertising and promotion. The way Wigtown promotes itself is a prime example of this global trend. In her thesis 'Reading Wigtown', Press (2001, p. 14) states that 'place identity' is similar to 'sense of place' in that it refers to the connection and attachment people have to a location. Humanistic geographers in the 1970s, such as Tuan (1974), led the way to an exploration of places as spaces given meaning by human feelings and the experience of living in those spaces. The shift to local, rural development that is sometimes referred to as 'bottom-up', participatory or endogenous approaches has emerged as a vital element in development policies on many scales from the European Union to Scottish Regional Councils. These institutions have responded by recognizing the uniqueness and resources of local places in the midst of increasing global connections and relations.

For example, Press (2001, p. 20) stresses that the book town has also brought outward-looking networks to Wigtown. The histories, identities and appearance of Wigtown are appropriated by the book town project so that the *place* is promoted rather than the project specifically, and tourists are led to experience the place as part of a book town visit (p. 50). Books do not feature strongly in the book town's promotional literature and, when they do, they are presented as 'sources of relation in a storybook setting, where you can "browse at leisure through an Aladdin's cave of reading material" or as an "ideal destination for a holiday with a literary twist"' (p. 52). Turpin (personal interview 2011) specifically spoke of his intention to create an organic and home-grown feel in the materials produced for the Wigtown Book Festival that would emphasize the unique, quirky but wholesome setting of the event, and distinguish it from events in major cities. Lettering and images are rustic and hand drawn. Browsing through materials describing Wigtown, it is evident that they all portray the integration of identities and appropriation of place to produce a book town identity. This observation aligns with that of Hopkins (1998, p. 141), who comments that:

> the prevalence of tourism and place promotion is both the cause and consequence of a spatially liberated, consumeristic, image-driven culture ... In a consumption-oriented society, places, like virtually all merchandise, services and experiences for sale on the market, are commodified; they are themselves consumable products: place commodities.

The book town is therefore a good example of the clear links that exist between a tourist's self-image and the destination image.

It has only been in recent years that peripheral areas have explicitly sought to develop and promote themselves in an integrated manner in order to appear attractive to tourists, investors and the community. An extensive use of image building is evident in rural community development, where there is a relationship between images and place promotion on the one hand and rural development on the other, creating a paradox in contemporary rural community development (Vik and Villa 2010).

There is a need for visibility and attention, leading to an increase in the search for impressive, striking or surprising images in rural place promotion. Ways in which places are commodified and promoted relate closely to their history, highlighting a trend that emerged at the start of the new millennium of an escalated focus on the social construction of the rural (Vik and Villa 2010, p. 158). Concurrently, representations, images and myths have become important aspects of analysis and debates regarding how to picture the rural. It might be seen as a further paradox, therefore, that rural image creation seems to be a process by which one object (a rural image) with a common identity is constructed on the basis of multiple and heterogeneous identities, meanings and interests:

> The developmental challenges that result are to transform several understandings of a place into one coherent and presentable image without destroying prospects of local mobilization, cooperation and interaction. In a rural development context, the processes of developing, extracting or choosing the community image required an approach that simultaneously encourages the activity and engagement of a large proportion of the inhabitants. (Vik and Villa 2010, p. 159)

There are differences in the responses of local residents and tourists to heritage objects and artefacts. While memory, attachment and symbolism are often most significant for a local community, the attachment of visitors to a place is likely to be to the unfamiliar, the exotic and the picturesque (Dewailly 1998, p. 128). The countryside has considerable potential for drawing tourists seeking new exciting experiences in areas of unexploited natural beauty and rich cultural resources (Briedenhann and Wickens 2004, p. 189). Rural tourism is therefore increasingly being applied in formerly marginalized rural communities that are rich in cultural heritage, in order to deliver new sustainable futures to towns whose fortunes have deteriorated.

Identity for book towns relates closely to nostalgia and memories of place, whether through the preservation of print culture (Merfeld-Langston 2007, p. 229) or the newly developed blend of the 'book town identity' with the town's original history (Press 2001, p. 82). The claim that the identity of a people is intricately related to the places they have created through altering their landscapes can therefore reasonably be applied to the blending of old and new identities in book towns:

> Each landscape is not static but can be viewed as a complex layering of meaning evolving over time. The landscape is not a fixed meaning simply conveyed to those gazing upon it. Rather, tourists and locals are both active participants in meaning making … by holding together the physical environment with the cultural expression on the land, the concept of landscape allows that the physical setting of the sites of tourism are as important as the manifestations of culture embedded in these sites. (Knudsen et al. 2008, p. 134)

The consequence of this is ongoing intervention in the construction of local identity: a constantly created and recreated sense of belonging, past, place, culture and ownership. In this way, tourism promotes growing local awareness. It is the interconnections between local and global, achieved through the encapsulation of localized meanings of place, culture and identity, that account for the particular ways in which an area's local history, landscape and culture are made available and transformed into a resource for economic and social development within a globally evolving economy and society. It can be concluded that identity, landscape and place are therefore intimately related. The tourist confronts the interaction of these elements, observing that 'identity as it is constructed in the modern world hinges on the conception of place and reification of place in the landscape' (Huff 2008, p. 34). Thus each individual derives an aspect of themselves from the interaction of landscape and place.

In a global sense, the book town has come to be regarded as a hybrid cultural phenomenon that links, crosses and connects different identities and social positions. It serves as an interface and is shared between different social worlds but understood and used differently by each of them. It can therefore be used as an example of a 'boundary object', or an entity that lies at the centre of multiple efforts to maintain a common identity across social, political and cultural sites (Star and Griesemer 1989). However, it is also important to note that a boundary object is only as strong as its capacity to accommodate local dialects (Sapsed and Salter 2004, p. 1519).

Vik and Villa (2010) present a case study of Fjærland in Norway, which shows how this book town operates as a boundary object. While Fjærland was one of the first places in Norway to develop a tourist industry, the authors explain that neither agriculture nor tourism was sufficient to maintain the viability of this village. Idyllically huddled along the waterfront, Fjærland's bookshops are housed in former barns, a stable, the old post office, a ferry terminal, an old grocery store and a boathouse (Butler 2010). Fjærland offers a postcard image of rurality with a long history of rural development, yet linked to the International Book Town Movement:

> the book town in Fjærland constitutes an image, a concept, an idea, a phenomenon that can be analysed as a boundary object. It is a relatively clear image of a beautiful, scenic little place full of bookshops of different shapes and sizes. This image, in combination with the uniqueness, surprising character and beautiful surroundings is distinct enough to be recognized … in Fjærland, in Norway and internationally. Media attention and numerous press notices confirm this … it is … 'robust enough to maintain a common identity across sites'. (Vik and Villa 2010, p. 163)

Hay-on-Wye and Fjærland are obviously quite distinct from one another. However, there is clearly a high degree of interpretative flexibility associated with the image of a book town that allows a wide range of understandings from individual to individual. The book town as a concept and image is narrow enough to be presented as having a common image and identity among people. Yet it is flexible enough to tolerate and incorporate different attitudes and approaches (Vik and Villa 2010, p. 165). Peace and quiet are central elements of the book town image. Compared with the buzz and bustle of Hay's Festival, the village of Fjærland has a sleepy feel, with snow-capped mountains and an advancing glacier fronting the water with boats gliding across it. However, despite the mayhem at festival time, Hay—like other book towns—is peaceful throughout the remainder of the year.

Potential Problems Posed by Distinctive Themed Town Identities

The ways in which book towns acquire new blended identities, or 'identity acquisition' (MacLeod 2009), is an issue I discussed with Wigtown Book Festival director Adrian Turpin (personal interview 2011) and others. This discussion disclosed the merits and problems associated with themed town strategies. While theming has long been used as an economic development strategy in rural areas in many parts of the world, it is often overlooked as an effective form of tourism. Book towns have proven this effectiveness, but other types of themed towns have also been equally popular. For example, American themed towns became popular in the 1960s as a creative antidote for economic downturn. These locations conceptualized place and regional culture in a similar way to book towns, using local heritage, history and ideas. The manipulation of space and place in this way is used in tourism to link disparate regions, shape tourist itineraries and provide multiple interpretations of the same place. The notion of the theme town relied on a number of earlier phenomena—the cultural pavilions of early twentieth-century World's Fairs, the example of ethnic districts such as Chinatowns and Little Italies, and Disneyland's idealized cultural landscapes (Frenkel and Walton 2000, pp. 562–3; Engler 1994).

While the book town project in Wigtown has fostered a heightened spirit of community and unity due to the consolidation of this enhanced town identity (MacLeod 2009, p. 143; Turpin, personal interview 2011), project leaders acknowledge that community needs must be prioritized. Book town developments face the risk of place identities being eroded unless relationships between project and place are considered, incorporating and reflecting what is important to local inhabitants or embracing identities based on enduring values (Howie 2003, p. 154). A focus on niche products and fixed identities and an over-emphasis on theming are potentially problematic and often paradoxically have the potential to create boundaries and exclude community members (Turpin, personal interview 2011; MacLeod 2003, p. 43). For example, MacLeod (p. 43) states that

> the process of essentializing and delineating a site both attract and repulse. Identities and products might intermix strongly, but may give an overall false representation of a region and its qualities ... the branding of a town brings problems of over-identification with a product, the under-representation of other qualities, and creates the risk of delimiting the identity of a town.

Derrett (personal interview 2010) and Beeton (2006, p. 61) identify the potential problem of local resources and culture being transformed into a selective heritage. In the case of book towns like Wigtown, new symbolic meanings are created so localities and regions can promote their economic success and the difference transforms the community for tourists. However, in the case of Dumfries and Galloway, the 'creeping success' of a number of clustered theme towns—Kirkcudbright Artists' Town and Castle Douglas Food Town in particular—is evidence of the region's rejection of an identity based only on high cultural definitions (MacLeod and Carrier 2010, p. 85). There are clearly grassroots efforts that reflect folk heritage and very recent memories, enabling a new cultural image for the region to emerge, including the Wickerman Festival[2] – known as 'Scotland's alternative festival', although for a complex series of reasons this was suspended in 2015. Alternate livelihoods, and local heritage, customs and memorabilia, happily accompany cultural innovations such as the book festival, live performances and other activities that are associated with traditional notions of high culture that appeal to the supposedly more educated cultural tourist. MacLeod and Carrier (2010, p. 88) state:

> [If you] add into this mix the increasing popularity of constructing grassroots heritage memorials and collections, or attractions based on indigenous culture, together with the ostensible democratization and opening up of communication channels afforded by the internet, the relationship between power, tourism and cultural heritage is becoming increasingly complex and relevant.

In the case of Wigtown, this combination of factors has enabled a reinvention of place. While the motivations for establishing Wigtown book town were primarily about delivering economic sustainability, this regional experiment in Dumfries and Galloway largely appears to have succeeded in delivering not only proven economic benefits, but also wider social and cultural enhancement. *The Economic Impact of StenaLine Wigtown Book Festival*, a study commissioned by the Wigtown Festival Company (WFC) (2009), found:

> The original concept of the book town development was to help regenerate Wigtown and its environs. Looking around the town, it is clear that there

> has been not only public but private investment in many of the town centre buildings, a significant part of which has to do with books. This is associated with the Book Town generally, but the Festival provides an important focal point and spur to action … However, the Festival brings more than just a range of narrowly defined economic benefits to the area. It provides access to some of the best writers in Scotland and the UK, and the Festival Company runs the Imagination Library which provides free books for under-fives in the Machars area and currently has an uptake rate of almost two thirds of all those eligible. Those are part of the quality of life, strengthening the community and making Dumfries and Galloway a more attractive place to live. Its ability to provide a lifestyle that attracts residents from many different age groups and walks of life is one of the most distinctive features of Dumfries and Galloway, and the role the region plays in Scotland's civil society.[3]

In a more recent communication, Turpin (2017) explained that Wigtown has moved from an event model to a year-round model for several reasons. In particular, this change was in response to the ongoing difficulty for an arts and cultural organization in maintaining its funding base when most activity was corralled into just ten days each year. It was also in keeping with a local council/Creative Scotland contract to manage literature development for the region. There was the feeling that for the book town to prosper, it needed to more fully become a hub that exerted influence beyond its immediate area. This change was also about recognizing the beneficial role played by the book town in working with young people, and delivering increased effectiveness for projects that require operation over longer timescales. Turpin now describes the WFC as a year-round literature development organization whose largest project is the Wigtown Book Festival. Yet a year-round organization also faces its own distinct challenges, and the 'shift in focus has been a gradual process, requiring a period of adjustment' for staff and stakeholders (WFC Business Plan 2017–2021, p. 3). Another particular challenge is how to sustain itself around the year. Resilience will be a key focus into the future as cuts to public funding to the arts in Scotland are widely expected from approximately 2018, and the repercussions from Brexit are predicted to create economic uncertainty (Turpin, personal interview 2017). Wigtown began addressing these issues through participation in an EU Leader project that commenced in 2016. This project funding has been made available to pilot possible models for activities outside the main festival timeframe, including a science weekend, creative writing courses, the running of an introduction to social media course, history weekends and other mini-festivals. The aim is to weave these kinds of events into a year-round mix that will bring the book town closer to Turpin's aspirational notion of what a book town can be—a place of culture, knowledge and inspiration whenever it is visited. The project will also allow Turpin and his team to examine structural issues for the book town around branding, marketing and social media.

Community members and other stakeholders agree that, although the book town project is not supported by the entire community, the project has benefits that have resulted in increased social capital[4] (Turpin, personal interviews 2011, 2017; Yates, personal interview 2011; Watson, personal interview 2011). The Wigtown Book Festival in particular requires close cooperation between stakeholder groups, the establishment of numerous formal and informal networks, and the involvement of publishers, local businesses and artists (Turpin, personal interviews 2011, 2017).[5] Links and networks have been forged that are advantageous for purposes not immediately associated with the original objective, and the introduction of new blood into the community in the guise of in-comers and new ideas and lifestyles has added creative energy to the community.

Non-Book Lovers: The Multiplier Effect as Appeasement

Sustainable tourism is a 'form of economic development that is designed to improve the quality of life in the host community' (WTO 1995), with quality of life understood as the physical and social attractiveness of a place, which can influence people to live, work or play in, or visit, an area. The changing nature of regional areas poses fundamental challenges for residents, business operators, community leaders and governments concerned with maintaining economically strong, environmentally sustainable and socially vibrant regional communities. Decentralized, service-based industries such as tourism offer the potential to diversify regional economic activity in the face of the changing global economy (Prosser 2001). Book towns provide an identity for small communities by achieving increased social cohesion and increasing cultural capital (Gretzel et al. 2006, p. 14; Merfeld-Langston 2007, p. 112). However, there is clearly a question concerning the extent to which a whole region or town's population is likely to identify with a book town initiative per se. At stake is the multiplier effect. Tourism dollars are new dollars injected into regional economies that have a multiplier effect in the local economy, where they are spent and re-spent by employers and employees. From a local government perspective, tourism therefore has the potential to diversify and support the local economy by encouraging the establishment of new businesses and attracting people into the area.

A benefit of book town tourism is that it can be built using largely existing infrastructure as well as offering a more ecologically sustainable form of development. In a positive sense, increased cohesion arises from improved economic security, and therefore the sustainability of other social meeting places such as the football club, the local pub and other widely used community establishments. That is, bookshops in and of themselves will not necessarily contribute a great deal to a sense of identity for the whole existing community, but the sustainability of other institutions will. As the book town project flourishes, new and expanded services and facilities that serve both visitors and local community members are likely to emerge—for example, galleries, transport, visitor services, restaurants, retail shops and entertainment opportunities. The diversity of book town audiences broadens in response to this expansion. The repopulation of rural areas brought about by book towns therefore increases and sustains community ventures, and potentially builds inclusive social capital.

Where possible, it is advantageous that book town projects are community led and responsive to community interests. Turpin (personal interview 2011) explains that 'leaps of imagination' come from outsiders to the community in many cases, as when a town's modus operandi is deeply culturally ingrained, it is difficult to change things. A successful book town project is unlikely to emerge from a solely local model, instead requiring a 'mixed economy' consisting of both enthusiastic community members from the local area and new blood. Turpin warns that community engagement should negate elitism and imposition, instead demonstrating awareness to local sensitivities and the wariness that inevitably exists for people from outside.

The repopulation of rural areas through book town projects also helps communities to become active rather than passive. Ploughman (2006) investigated why some Queensland country towns thrive while others languish. His research indicates that towns demonstrating resilience, optimism and growth are those where innovative newcomers inject a diversity of ideas and experience. More specifically, prosperity hinges on having young, creative citizens who tolerate difference, are well travelled and well educated, and allow a turnover of civic and leadership roles. His study is similar to another by Isserman et al. (2009) in a North-American context. Diversification of the resident population in turn encourages changing value systems (Huang and Stewart 1996, p. 28) and stimulates fresh thinking and different solutions to problems. Clunes book town in Victoria, Australia, is a key example of how a blend of newly arrived citizens—many of them self-confessed tree-changers—and longer term residents has resulted in a varied mix of ideas and diverse inputs that have benefited the town as a whole and strengthened its shared commitment to continuing survival (Campbell, quoted in Pryor 2008).

What emerges from the literature (e.g. Beeton 2006; Craik 2001, p. 123) and through discussions with book town stakeholders (McShane, personal interview 2010; Nioa, personal interview 2010; Turpin, personal interview 2011) is the importance of local communities having a genuine degree of ownership over and input into cultural tourism ventures in order to achieve cultural sustainability. It is vital that local people have a voice, enabling them to communicate the social value of their place, or present messages to tourists that provide an important point of interest and empathy for local communities (Cole 2006). If communities are motivated and supported to represent their position in the tourism hierarchy as significant, this social valuing can enable spiritual or traditional connections between the past and present, empowering disempowered groups. The social valuing of place therefore challenges hegemonic constructions of the tourist space (Wearing et al. 2010). Rural tourism development—particularly in a destination that has been ethnically homogenous, such as Wigtown—shifts the basis of solidarity from a shared cultural background to a shared image of community. This increased pluralism is the catalyst for the creation of a dynamic of working together to develop the community's image and encouraging shared identification (Turpin, personal interview 2011).

However, it is also important to note that the nexus between place and community is not defined solely by residency. People living elsewhere may also be part of a community with a strong linkage—a community of interest. This cohort can include frequent visitors, second home owners, ex-residents, ethnic groups, people with family connections and those with strong special interests—whether steam train enthusiasts, quiltmakers or book lovers. In some cases, it is possible for these individuals to have a stronger interest in the place than some members of the local community. Huang and Stewart (1996, p. 29) conclude that tourism development in rural communities has psychological impacts on residents' perceptions of their town. They suggest that outsider–insider bonds are maintained through a shared culture and that the expectations of tourists encourage residents to fill roles that befit an ideal image of the community. It is the everyday efforts of residents to accommodate tourists' expectations that encourage the blend of all residents to behave in accordance with an ideal town image, binding everyone together. These ideas were also expressed by Derrett (personal interview 2010), who spoke of the importance of host communities creating positive experiences for visitors through communicating 'positive vibes'.

This argument relates to Florida's (2002, p. 223) point that regional economic growth is driven by the location choices of creative people—those he describes as the holders of creative capital who favour locations that are diverse, tolerant and open to new ideas. Creative people are the pivotal type of human capital that is intrinsic to regional economic growth. This argument centres on the specific theory of the importance of place, where 'place is becoming the central organizing unit of our economy and society, taking on a role that used to be played by the large corporation' (p. 224). It follows that the diverse individuals who seek out livelihoods in book towns—refugees from metropolitan centres in many cases, as discussed in Chap. 2—undoubtedly contribute oxygen to ideas and options that create a sense of empowerment for the local population as well as enhancing the intrinsic charm of rural book town locations and their inhabitants. While it can be argued that rural people live in different epistemic realities (Kneafsey 2000), inclusiveness, broad mobilization, and multi-level cooperation are vital to successful rural development projects such as book towns (Turpin, personal interview 2011; Nelson, personal interview 2011; Borsch et al. 2008). It is evident from some of the book town projects I observed that it is not unusual for people from different backgrounds and social worlds to work on joint projects and communicate effectively to achieve mutual goals, despite eccentricities and booksellers' preferences for working individually, which has led to setbacks in some book towns.

Successful book towns celebrate and embrace the 'outside' and 'non-artistic' elements of their community bases. They draw on the resources of community organizations—local residents and amateurs—as well as highly specialized professionals who add creative potential to these locales (Nelson, personal interview 2011; Turpin, personal interview 2011). In many cases, book towns have strong connections to regional cultural activities, and symbolic places and traditions. They encourage community participation, which is often related to a gradually growing cultural diversity associated with increasing mobility. Book town founders and festival directors are at the forefront of building synergies and pathways between regional areas and urban identities, high art and low art, participation and performance, curation and interactivity with tourists and residents alike. This process of recontextualizing has been successful in attracting new audiences to these events and profiling the areas as tourist destinations. This change in orientation is what draws tourists to book towns, and it is leading to sustainable futures for towns that would otherwise likely have diminished. The terrain of thinking about regional development that emphasizes the significance of market forces in the global economy has therefore contributed not only to an economic restructuring of rural areas but to substantial cultural realignment as well. Cultural renewal is readily used as a catalyst for economic and social sustainability (Gibson and Connell 2011, pp. xv–xvi, 10), and the book towns of Clunes in rural Victoria in Australia and Sedbergh in Cumbria, England, are examples of successful book town initiatives that demonstrate these characteristics.

The Clunes Booktown Festival: Event Tourism and Regional Sustainability

Clunes is an historic gold town 36 kilometres north of Ballarat in Victoria, Australia.[6] The annual Clunes Booktown Festival draws approximately 18,000 people from Victoria and interstate to this town of approximately 1600 inhabitants[7]; these visitors are attracted to the concept of marrying a vast array of books with heritage buildings in a rural setting while mingling among a like-minded bibliophile community (Kennedy 2010, p. 6). Supporters may be like-minded, but they represent a wide range of age groups and occupations, and there is evidence of a widening geographic spread of visitors. This event 'attracts patrons from backgrounds as varied as the books on offer, from engineers to administrators, tradespeople to teachers, signalling the widespread appeal of the event' (Kennedy 2011, p. 214). Perhaps this broad appeal is enhanced because the event has developed into a 'festival of the book' as opposed to a writers festival or a book fair. In 2016, the weekend festival featured 55 booksellers and more than 40 speakers (Saffer 2016).

Back to Booktown, as the event was known before being rebranded in 2013 as Clunes Booktown Festival, was designed as a means to generate rural renewal in Clunes through book-based cultural tourism. Prior to the establishment of Clunes as a book town, visual artist Patrick Jones[8] had created a Booklovers' Trail in the region which attracted book lovers on weekend getaways to bookshops in the towns of Bendigo, Castlemaine, Campbell's Creek, Kyneton, Daylesford, Woodend, Ballarat, Buninyong and Trentham. It had been inspired by Hay-on-Wye's success (Jones, quoted in McFadyen 2005). Promoted as a journey of discovery, the trail offered an alternative introduction to the region. The organizers of the Clunes Booktown Festival have further built on the idea of discovery—originally the discovery of gold, but now a focus on books, ideas and learning—to promote Clunes as a place that celebrates a strong interest in the written word. Another factor that helped contribute to the development of Clunes as a book town was Hepburn Shire Council's interest in a suite of Sunday markets in Clunes, Creswick, Talbot and Avoca—with each town holding a market on one Sunday of each month. At that time, Villages of the Old Goldfields Inc. (consisting of representatives from all four towns) had an interest in rural renewal and economic development issues, kick-starting and maximizing the key features of the towns. During the same period, Tess Brady, the book town's first artistic director, was involved with the Words in Winter festival programme,[9] centred in Daylesford, with satellite programmes in Hepburn Shire and was interested in extending the cultural theme further. In 2007, prompted by severe economic decline in Clunes as a result of a decade of drought and resultant low community morale, Brady and three other 'tree changers' joined forces to create the book town idea for Clunes (Brady 2012, 2).

Led by Creative Clunes Inc., the parent body of the festival and its associated activities, which was established in 2007 after the first book town event, Clunes today features eight permanent bookshops as well as another four businesses that carry books together with other commodities and one online trader (Fig. 4.1).[10] Clunes has been an accredited member of the International Organization of Book Towns since April 2012, following a visit to the World Book Town Symposium in South Korea by a number of book town organizers. This visit coincided with their attendance at Paju Booksori, Asia's largest book fair, which attracts over 100,000 people. Recent developments have included the establishment of writers talks on the third Sunday of each month, known as Booktown on Sunday, the appointment of a CEO and new artistic direc-

Fig. 4.1 Fraser Street, Clunes, Australia—book lovers enjoying refreshments (2016) (Source: Photographer Carol Saffer)

tor, and an invitation from the OECD to present a case study of Clunes Book Town for its *2017 Tourism and the Creative Economy Report*[11] as an example of small-town rural renewal. Clunes has also been appointed to host the 2018 International Book Town Conference (Johnstone, in Saffer 2016).

This ongoing advancement and success have been made possible through government assistance and the energies of community volunteers. Prior to these developments, Clunes received a funding grant of $2.7 million in 2012 from the Victorian government to develop the town's museum and a tourist information centre, and was selected as a hub in one of nine Victorian locations to receive state-funded assistance as part of the Advancing Country Towns (ACT) project (Brady 2012, p. 12). Financial support will continue from 2017 to 2020 while Clunes is the recipient of a $240,000 funding grant from Creative Victoria.[12]

Clunes has secured patronage from three levels of government—a success that is arguably a result of the growing pool of social capital in Clunes. The book town project is the driver for the wider integrated sustainable development occurring in the town. Success stories like Clunes help address a number of key social, economic and cultural issues. In Australia, as in other nations, a number of regional problems have surfaced over recent decades that have demanded the attention of policymakers and generated calls by regional interests for ameliorative action by governments. These problems include the sudden economic shocks caused by downturns in 'one industry towns' as a result of economic restructuring; the continued emptying of the inland; the ongoing domination of state economies by their capital cities; increasing disparities within and between regions across a wide range of social and economic indicators; and environmental pressures and high unemployment in rapidly growing coastal regions (Collits 2000).

Geoffrey Blainey (1983) identified the 'tyranny of distance' as having exerted a profound impact on the human occupation of Australia, and this view is no less applicable to the development of rural tourism. However, the potential of tourism to contribute to rural community development provided a principal focus and rationale for the National Rural Tourism Strategy formulated in the mid-1990s (Killion, in Douglas et al. 2001, p. 171). This led to an increased focus on regional tourism, and the planning and development of projects. The Foundation for Rural and Regional Renewal (FRRR)[13] was also established as partnership between philanthropy, governments and business to stimulate rural and regional renewal in Australia, tackling a broad range of issues faced by rural and regional communities, including the funding of and support for innovative new business ventures and support in times of natural disaster, such as floods, cyclones, drought and bushfires. These bodies have cast light on issues impacting on regional communities. La Trobe University also hosted The Sustainability of Australia's Country Towns: The Third National Country Towns Conference in Bendigo (2010), resulting in the publication of *The Sustainability of Australia's Country Towns: Renewal, Renaissance, Resilience* (Martin and Budge 2011), part of a burgeoning academic interest in rural and regional sustainability in Australia.

Festivals have played a particularly significant role in rural renewal over the last decade. Tourism, festivals and other cultural events have become the economic mainstay of a number of regional towns, operating alongside agriculture and other primary production to sustain the social and economic health of rural Australia (Gibson et al., quoted in Kennedy 2011, p. 6). Event tourism based on cultural activities is a key differentiator for tourism in Victoria in particular, where over 60 regional tourism events and festivals occur each year (Lade and Jackson 2004, p. 1). While festivals temporarily change the identity of rural and regional communities, they can also strengthen their original identity by eliciting a strong appreciation from visitors for their heritage character and appeal. In Wigtown, Graiguenamanagh, Featherston, Clunes and many European book towns, the signature event or festival is synonymous with the book town's identity and origins.

Clunes is an example of a town that has used an innovative path to navigate a sustainable way forward through the use of theme-placed branding. The use of place-branding as a strategy for rural development is described by Storey (in Halseth et al. 2010, p. 158) as 'the employment of elements of the local by rural places as they endeavour to reimagine themselves in order to deal with broader processes of rural change and restructuring'. Place-branding is steadily emerging as an instrument for development by leveraging the unique attributes of country towns. Back to Booktown was developed as a branding exercise to advance the community's wider cultural enterprise activity in response to threats such as population loss, agricultural decline and drought (Kennedy 2010, p. 6). One of the challenges for a rural development project such as Clunes is creating a sufficiently differentiated rural tourism product that has the drawing power to not only attract visitors from urban settings, but also steer them away from competing rural destinations. In the case of Clunes, this competition includes other historic towns such as Maldon and Castlemaine, the recreation of mining days at Sovereign Hill, and the vineyards, art galleries and scenic landscapes of adjoining districts. In this sense, as Sorensen (1990, quoted in Butler and Hall 1998) comments, 'development processes [in Australian rural townships] will … continue to exhibit a Darwinian flavour'.

Organizers of the Clunes Booktown Festival claim that the event provides an annual $4 million boost to the region (Kennedy 2010, p. 19), with accommodation and restaurants booked out in neighbouring towns a year in advance of the event. The organizing committee has built on Seaton's (1999, pp. 394–5) criteria to ensure the success of the project. Links between the town and a number of well-known Australian films, including the *Mad Max* series (commencing in 1979) and *Ned Kelly* (2003), are also significant. Links to cultural heritage are vital: bookshops now occupy some of the grand old buildings of the gold rush era, which previously stood empty, creating a nostalgic atmosphere with old-world charm. The nostalgia is also enhanced by other associated activities that occur at the Clunes Booktown Festival, including Punch and Judy shows, horse and cart rides, scrabble tournaments, a Children's Book Town, brass bands, local wine tastings and a range of literary events. Positive attributes, such as the town's wide heritage street, an accredited museum, a buoyant local agricultural show and the location of a rural campus of Wesley College where Year 9 students spend a term in the limits of the township, also contribute to its success. Visiting parents and attendees at college events seek weekend entertainment, so enjoy bookshops, wine tastings and the calendar of literary activities.

Clunes' geographical location has proved critical to its success. The town's built, natural and social fabric, and its proximity to regional centres and the city of Melbourne have increasingly attracted a number of tree-changers to the town (Kennedy 2011, p. 211). The association with

Melbourne is pivotal to Clunes's growing reputation: 'It is this relationship of being the country location, the weekend escape, the holiday house for Melbourne, which we are building upon' (Brady 2012, p. 11). Fifty-four per cent of the book town's visitors from 2012 were from Melbourne ('Review Clunes Book Town' 2012, quoted in Brady 2012, p. 8). Interest in Clunes has been heightened by Melbourne's status as a UNESCO City of Literature and the establishment of the Wheeler Centre for Books, Writing and Ideas, as well as the promotion of the Clunes project through these urban avenues.[14]

Tourism has an important role outside the metropolis. The motivations of rural tourists can be linked to the dominance of urbanization in Australia and the search for a 'rural idyll' that is a key feature of Australia's art, literature, film and television. The search for the roots of long-standing folkways remains a powerful motive for domestic visitors in particular (Killion, in Douglas et al. 2001, p. 170). Arguably, book towns have also been successful in Clunes and in the New South Wales Southern Highlands as a result of the 'embedded Anglo-hearth bias in Antipodean spatial reasoning' (O'Neill and McGuirk 2007). The imperial legacy of Britain and the resultant colonial history have impacted on how Australians engage with culture and the 'unsettled settledness' of Australian society that continues to be played out within the contemporary landscape (Gelder and Jacobs 1998). The Clunes event has therefore been described by Brady (2011) and others as the annual transformation of this heritage village into a 'European-style book town', with book traders in rare, out-of-print and small-press new titles setting up shop in the heritage buildings.

The Clunes book town project centred on change from the start. Brady regarded herself not only as a writer in the community, but as a change agent and a risk-taker, as well as someone who 'dreams of the impossible', and believed the organizers needed to 'be a little crazy, have a lot of courage, be able to imagine the seemingly impossible, and just give-it-a-go' (Brady 2011). Rather than relying simply on the talents of book lovers, a project such as this thrives if a mix of people proficient in skills such as local government liaison, community issues, marketing, media and promotions, business and the arts can take part in leading it. A significant part of the early book town's development was centred on lifting the community's morale and 'firing their imagination', but there was also an element of chance that permeated the event from the beginning (Brady 2011). Innovation and 'creating something out of nothing', as recommended by Landry (2008), have therefore saved the town of Clunes from the ravages of decline, drought and population drain.

Sedbergh: A Sustainable Centre of Excellence for Literature

Again with a markedly cultural emphasis, the Sedbergh book town project in Cumbria, England, started after the 2001 Foot and Mouth Disease outbreak as a desperate economic rescue initiative orchestrated by a group of residents involved in the local Chamber of Commerce, 'not in self-interest but by the whole town in a concerted effort to revive it' (Holman 2006). At this time, there was a widespread realization of the vulnerability of rural communities that were dependent on farming. Considerable time was invested in planning for the initiative's success, including appointing Tony Seaton as a consultant to advise on the book town journey and applying his carefully researched success criteria. The project initiators applied for funding from the National Government for rural regeneration in Cumbria and received £44,000, which contributed to the appointment of a full-time manager, Carole Nelson, the opening of a tourist office that has itself become a cooperative bookshop specializing in material on popular local outdoor pursuits including hill walking and the establishment of a board and start-up book town company (Nelson, personal interview 2011).

Between 2002 and 2012, the town repeatedly applied for and received funding from the National Lottery, which supports culture and the arts in Britain, and the English Arts Council because, as well as providing economic benefits, Sedbergh is focused on cultural enhancement—specifically, cultural education. Nelson (personal interview 2011) argues strongly for the book town as an important cultural achievement in Sedbergh and stresses the focus on cultural tourism in ongoing plans for the town. Of all the book towns I visited, Sedbergh distinguished itself as the locale that has most valued the role played by arts and culture in sustainability and regeneration. Sedbergh's book town project is an example of Landry et al.'s (1996) argument that use of the arts relies on the importance of seeing local people as the principal asset through which renewal can be achieved, with the authors advocating participatory arts programmes that are flexible and responsive to local needs. Arts and cultural festivals and events enhance social cohesion by bringing communities together, helping to build private and public sector partnerships and assisting communities to develop the organizational skills to help themselves.

An old weaving and market town with a castle mound and venerable bowed buildings lining a cobbled main street, Sedbergh is a very self-contained little place, situated in the Yorkshire Dales National Park at the confluence of four river valleys: the Lune, the Rawthey, the Clough and the Dee. Surrounding the town are hills rising to 600 metres that create breathtaking scenery. The town itself sits at the foot of the Howgill Fells, likened to a herd of sleeping elephants by ardent fell walker Alfred Wainwright (Nelson, personal interview 2011), yet it is only 5 miles (8 kilometres) from the M6 motorway. Steeped in history, Sedbergh lies on both the ancient route of the Roman Road from Chester to Carlisle and on the cross-Pennine walking route between Kendal and Richmond. Thus, while the location is considered peripheral, within approximately 2 hours' drive (approximately 150 kilometres), there is a population of over 6 million people at the disposal of a well-promoted book town initiative.[15]

Carole Nelson (personal interview 2011), the astute proprietor of The Sleepy Elephant bookshop and emporium, which features textiles and books on textiles, needlework, art and design, literature and children's books, was previously book town manager from 2007 to 2010. She explained that most visitors arrive in Sedbergh by private transport; however, she recommends—as does McClarence (2009)—journeying by train. This offers an experience on the Settle/Carlisle line, one of the scenic wonders of the British railway; arrival at Dent, England's highest station and the ensuing drive into town from the station, 'wind[ing] through narrow lanes, edging past tractors and Land Rovers, through cobbled village streets of whitewashed cottages' (McClarence 2009). Prior to Sedbergh's reincarnation as a book town, its only claims to fame were the hill walking attractions of the Cumbrian countryside (an activity destroyed by Foot and Mouth), Hadrian's Wall, its importance in the beginning of the Quaker Movement and its very old and distinguished public school, founded in the early sixteenth century. These generated some local business, but constant competition with shopping malls in larger nearby towns had diverted much of Sedbergh's commercial life away. With an ageing rural community and an increasing number of empty shops, the book town project brought new life and livelihoods to the village:

> This [project] has been good for the town. It's brought more people in, which supports and safeguards the future of the shops that really matter – the butcher, the grocer, hardware shop, post office and the like – but it also allows us to celebrate the glory of books. The sort of books people buy in book towns aren't your throwaway airport novellas, but important ones that you are prepared to keep, read to your children and which eventually become old friends. (Nelson, in Bagshaw and Mills 2010, p. 17)

However, since 2012, Sedbergh has experienced a number of difficulties not initially encountered when the book town was originally established. Although the Foot and Mouth crisis first sparked the idea, Sedbergh book town had a buoyant few years as a result of the Blair government's 'give-away agenda' that enabled the Committee to fund an impressive programme of literary events. Nelson (personal interview 2017) explains that 'as ever, culture doesn't make money, so funding is vitally important'. Between 2008, when Britain experienced a banking crisis, and 2011, Britain was concerned with raising billions of pounds to fund the 2012 London Olympics, and much of the Arts Council's funding from the National Lottery was directed towards the Olympic cause. As a result of the economic downtown, other avenues of funding were also unfruitful at this time. During the same period, Sedbergh's Book Town board experienced a year of terrible health problems, with four members diagnosed with life-threatening illnesses. The board decided to cancel events and effectively 'tread water' until it was once again possible to access core funding and find a nucleus of new board members.

Until 2012, Sedbergh mounted an impressive programme of literary and musical events each year, including a number of major festivals. One of these was an ideas festival called The Write Idea, which in 2010 and 2011 featured poetry events including readings and writing workshops, and in 2012 focused on the prose forms of story-making and narrative writing, offering 'a chance for people to meet the top thinkers in a particular subject and express themselves in a public forum … it's about incubating ideas, not selling things' (Nelson, in McClarence 2009). Until funding challenges inhibited programming, the Festival of Books and Drama took place annually in mid-September and featured talks and book launches by writers, with their books on sale across Sedbergh bookshops. Each year, the festival adopted a particular theme. The book town is actively aware that small country locations have fewer experiences of diversity than urban centres, and 'inclusion' was the 2007 motif of the Festival of Books and Drama. It featured events to include children with special needs, ethnic minorities and ex-asylum seekers, and embraced literature of the world as well as that of a local nature, demonstrating broad content and culture (Business Plan 2008, p. 18). The 2009 theme was 'travel and adventure'—appropriate, given the outdoor pursuits for which the vicinity is known. To promote education and breadth of programming for this event, which involved both professional and amateur writers, published members of the Wandering Educators[16] organization were invited to publicize their new books and take part through a book launch or illustrated presentation (Voights 2008). Other events included an annual music festival that in 2012 focused on the Queen's Diamond Jubilee; the Sedbergh Folkfest and a range of seminars and workshops throughout the year. In 2008, Sedbergh's itinerary was so diverse as to include a Romance Weekend on Valentine's Day to celebrate the Mills and Boon Centenary Exhibition; a historic re-enactment weekend focusing on the Napoleonic Wars; an event titled Literary Mayhem that featured workshops from travel writing to swordplay in Shakespeare's plays; a Jane Eyre talk and film presented by the Bronte Society and a Cumbrian Fringe Festival showcasing the best of Cumbrian writers and performers (Nelson, personal interview 2011).

This artistic and cultural focus in Sedbergh has been achieved through the work of the Sedbergh Book Town Literary Trust, a registered educational charity that was established in 2007. The Trust exists to ensure that

Sedbergh excels as a book town worthy of national status and that it is renowned as a centre of excellence for literature development and the written word. Sedbergh promotes events that demonstrate excellence through performance as well as ensuring a programme that emphasizes the 'imaginative education', which celebrates, in partnership with other providers of literary education and complementary attractions, the region's distinguished literary identities. Partnership with Sedbergh School—patron of the Festival of Ideas—is also significant. In this way, the Trust provides participative opportunities for all ages and ability groups, optimizing activities that may lead to published works or professional performances (Nelson, personal interview 2017). Sedbergh Literary Trust's embrace of arts and cultural events demonstrates its close working allegiance with the Arts Council Northwest's *raison d'être*, and the book town's efforts to fit within the national arts strategy:

> Essentially the Book Town project is a *provider of live literature*, *of the artefacts of literature* through the book shops and a *literary educator* with an opportunity, through its events and activity, to engage with a considerable and inclusive audience.[17]

'Live literature' is defined as the performance of literature. It seeks to embrace and involve a public audience in the performance of, or interaction with, composed words and writing (Business Plan 2008, p. 16). The Arts Council of Great Britain considers that literature has at its heart the communion between writer and reader, and that it is the book and this private interaction that give literature its power. However, as literature continues to evolve, technology and new forms of distribution, as well as live literature, are creating new ways of engaging with writers and the living word. For increasing numbers of people, the live literature event—once essentially a vehicle for promoting and selling books—is now an arts experience in its own right. Funding is therefore prioritized to organizations that are artistically creative and entrepreneurial, and priority at this time was given to develop a network of creative producers and venues offering an experience that was both artistically imaginative and professionally enticing (Business Plan 2008, p. 17). The Trust therefore prioritized events that offered visitors the opportunity to experience celebrities in an unexpected setting and to find out what a live literature event was about.

The burgeoning series of events in Sedbergh 'added another string to the bow' of the dozen or so existing, and mostly specialist, booksellers in the town. The decision of the residents when they established the Sedbergh Book Town Committee in 2003 was to develop a community of businesses involved in the many phases of writing, selling publishing and designing books and other publications. An existing base of book-related businesses, including a book producer and several booksellers, had previously been located in Sedbergh,[18] and anxious businesspeople and other interested parties looked to Hay-on-Wye's earlier success as the inspiration for how they could draw visitors back to the area's dramatic countryside and support the survival of vital town centre amenities. As well as visitors, the book town concept attracted more booksellers. These included Mark and Evelyn Westwood, who moved Westwood Books to two floors of the repurposed Sedbergh cinema from their original base in Hay-on-Wye after 30 years there. In May 2006, Sedbergh was officially recognized as England's book town when it was welcomed into the International Organization of Book Towns (IOB), joining the other UK book towns of Hay-on-Wye (Wales) and Wigtown (Scotland). This followed financial assistance from Rural Regeneration Cumbria (now Cumbria Vision),[19] which funded a feasibility study, a business plan for the project and the registering of a company limited by guarantee—Sedbergh Book Town Limited—as well establishing a cooperative and social venture, the Dales and Lakes Book Centre and Tourist Office, and a promotional programme in 2005 that included a book town newsletter, television web segment titled *Get to Know Sedbergh* and YouTube presence (Business Plan 2008, pp. 4–13). Soon after this, Sedbergh Book Town Company was awarded funding to support the growth of the book town as a major component of the Cultural Industries Sub-Strategy, part of the Culture Cumbria Cultural Development Strategy (Rebanks 2010) (Fig. 4.2).

However, Nelson has more recently explained that another malign influence for book businesses since 2011–2012 had been the rise of the Kindle and other similar devices. Previously, outside every bookshop there had been paperbacks on sale that had formed a small but important

Fig. 4.2 England's book town of Sedbergh tucked beneath the Howgill Fells (2017) (Source: Photographer Hugh McMillan)

department for most booksellers. Nelson and others discovered that, particularly in the case of novels, previous customers became enticed by e-readers offering instant purchases and many free downloads for older works, which led to a drastic decrease in paperback sales. In store, dealers became accustomed to sightseers opining, 'You don't need to buy a book anymore as you can get it online' or being asked 'Do people still buy books?' While the town has now passed through this period of newfangledness with e-readers, and book buying is experiencing a resurgence, this was a problematic time for bookshop owners in Sedbergh. While the town is now encountering new challenges as a result of Brexit and a period of unknown economic consequences that will make life difficult for the arts sector, Sedbergh has, positively, just welcomed a writers retreat business and is planning a programme of new events to commence in 2017–2018, and Nelson remains quite optimistic about the book town's fortunes.

There are still eight excellent bookshops in Sedbergh, and Nelson says it is important to understand that nostalgia plays a significant part in what is sold in the town, with pre-1950 titles very popular, and children's titles by authors including Rowling, Blyton, Jennings, Elinor Brent-Dyer's 'Chalet School' series and W.E. Johns' 'Biggles' books collected avidly, in many cases for adults to re-read. They are drawn to the specialist bookshop experience and the skills of design, typesetting and use of materials that make books artefacts that last. Books embedded into a book town experience are still why people visit Sedbergh Book Town. McClarence (2009) captures the feelings of both authenticity and serendipity I experienced when I visited Sedbergh in September 2011:

> the bookshops stretch down the straggling main street: general stockists, transport and industry specialists, topography, children's books, music just around the corner … Happily, the bookshops don't obtrude among the butchers and bakers and shops selling linseed oil and night lights, dog biscuits and corn-on-the-cob holders. Sedbergh is still a characterful, unpretentious working town, with posters for lost sheepdogs and the Royal British Legion Annual Dinner and 'Shamus Plays for You at the Red Lion'.

As well as the novel appeal of being a centre for books and literature, the village is, importantly, a real, functioning rural community, which also has enormous appeal in a variety of ways. It is the blend of bookish immersion, the narrow cobbled laneways, the views to the beauty of the countryside and the genuine charm of other village activities and characteristics that deliver a unique visitor experience.

Regional Centres of Culture, or Just Places That Sell Books?

Significant to any examination of book towns, tourism and sustainability is the argument that regionalism provides a critical framework for understanding literary culture. As explained in Chap. 1, new global/local dynamics indicate that it is possible to be cosmopolitan in a micro-community and that increased communication, technology and connectivity mean book towns can be urbane like cities and maintain networks that sustain them both financially and socially. It helps to envisage the potential value of book towns if we think of their regional location as showing not 'ignorance of the world beyond … but the assertion of distinctiveness in relation to the outside world' (Meinig, in Griswold 2008, p. 14). Regional identities can be defined as the specific meanings (including feelings and images) that are attached to a region by individuals who experience the region subjectively. For example, Griswold (2008, p. 175) describes particularly well the way in which certain New Yorkers fashion their leisure time around pursuits and pleasures involving books, art, coffee shops and travel in regional areas, saying it 'offers the reading class a cultural mooring to anchor and orient them in a tumultuous world'. She comments that this combination of features is so ubiquitous as to be unremarkable—even unseen. This thinking can perhaps be linked to Giddens' (quoted in Kendall et al. 2009, p. 34) claim that humans share a desire for certainty and ontological security in a world of risk, uncertainty and unpredictability where their existence is one fulfilled by multiple and meaningful attachments and a personally rewarding sense of belonging. Griswold emphasizes that 'reading-class cosmopolitans "do localism" as a way of confirming and deepening one of the identity dimensions which they have selected for themselves', and further points out that regionalism resonates with their wished-for identities by offering the pleasure of roots to the rootless (2008, pp. 167–173). Griswold describes the urge for a connection with regional locations as a 'collective necessity' and summarizes regionalism in art as a 'sharply distinctive and celebratory depiction of the culture of place' (2008, pp. 3–9).

Regionalism aggressively promotes its own cultural expression and is flourishing as a result of globalization and information technology, not despite them. Cultural regionalism and regional literature are thriving in the United States due to the distinctions that regions make between themselves and larger cultural centres (Griswold 2008, pp. 1–13). Similar observations have been made in France, where regional literature is considered to be the most privileged category of secondhand and antiquarian books in the *villages du livre*, including books about the particular region, its literature and its language, and titles by regional authors. These books are deemed most collectible, most sought after by tourists and a significant means by which regions can promote their unique cultural and geographical offerings (Merfeld-Langston 2007, p. 274). For example, Montolieu celebrates Occitan poetry, Bécherel hosts Breton language courses and a number of its book establishments have Breton names. Emphasis is placed on supporting contemporary regional authors, and in turn enlisting their endorsement, and writers endorse the book town projects. Lorraine fiction writer Elise Fischer, for example, has for many years actively engaged with Fontenay-la-Joûte's cultural programme and now resides in the village that inspired her French/English novella set there, *Meurtre au Village der Livre* (Merfeld-Langston 2014, p. 130). Bookshops in all the book towns I visited also contained large sections of literature relating to local history, geography and culture.

Book towns reflect a growing interest in regionalism with relation to print culture and creative writing. Regional creative writing demonstrates that there is a 'a strong, highly localized identity reinforced by geography' (Green 2010), and the acknowledgement of culture—particularly with regard to storytelling and writing—as a premise for regional identity provides a valuable means of articulating the links between people and their environment (Trotter 2001, p. 336). Creative narrative more broadly contributes to the tourist experience, where it cultivates sympathetic imagination, thereby enabling greater understanding and empathy (Chappel and Brown 2006, p. 1767). Regional writing is important as an outlet for the deep expression of local knowledge where geographical and literary landscapes are fused together and creative literature is a 'reservoir of cultural understanding … replete with intimate and revealing perspectives on the relationships between people and place' (Robinson and Anderson 2004, p. 3). Wigtown Book Festival's annual poetry competition, for example, has a category for writing in Scots language, and since the festival's adoption of responsibility to encourage literature across the region of Dumfries and Galloway, it has appointed, in both 2015 and 2016, 'animateurs' to support activities in both Scots language and Gaelic—minority languages in the modern era, although once widespread throughout Scotland. In 2013, the Wigtown Book Festival commissioned local poet and writer Hugh McMillan (2014) to document tales and stories of the Dumfries and Galloway region, exploring history, lore and myth as well as characters and anecdotes that reflect contemporary times; the book was a response to a key text of Galloway ethnography, John Mactaggart's scholarly and humorous *The Scottish Gallovidian Encyclopaedia*, first published in 1824. This work was launched at the Wigtown Book Festival in 2014. In McMillan's (2013) words, book town projects such as this reflect the fact that 'where people inhabit a landscape, they create a landscape of the mind'.

My earlier research examining regionalism in the arts recognizes the diversity and significance of regional arts practice and highlights regionalism in that context as drawing attention to the relativity of the centre (Frank 1996, pp. 2–13). Griswold (2008, p. 158) also argues that 'regionalism thrives on distinction from the cultural center'. A number of ideas that I explored at that time are applicable to the decentralized book town model and the particular regional statement expressed by book town founders and their followers through the establishment of rural and regional book projects. Advocacy for regionalism in the late 1980s and early 1990s (Kleinart 1991, p. 17) emerged out of the historical processes of decolonization in nations like Australia, highlighting a concern for the self-determination of Indigenous people, an acknowledgement of migration and a reinterpretation of national identity. Yet the ideals of regionalism were being contradicted by reality: the regional artist at that time was aware that the art world was mediated through city-focused networks and central bureaucracies. To state that their work reflected regional difference was to contravene the prevailing criteria for excellence (Green 1992, p. 38; Williams 1989, p. 37). In the same way, the emergence of book towns and other comparable initiatives are examples of a revitalized regionalism in remote communities—and even whole countries—that traditionally have had their cultural lives shaped by a regionalist position in relation to monolithic centres and repositories of national and international culture in a book-related and literary sense.

Geographical remoteness in Australia increasingly is considered a distinct advantage for cultural industries development (Eltham 2009). Donald Horne (2002, p. 4), for example, promotes Australian regional hubs as a way of bolstering culture:

> It seems to me ... that one place to look [for greater richness of cultural experience] might be 'the regions'. They're smaller, more comprehensible –

> and, as between them, remarkably diverse … The idea of 'regional centres' – in all their diversity – is a much more valuable way of looking to the future than nostalgia about a stereotype called 'the bush'. And it's here that extending vision from 'the arts' to 'cultural life' might be most valuable, especially if people in 'the regions' began to consider more their own particularity and tell their own stories – by whatever means – big or small – so that they themselves have something to think about – and also giving visitors something to think about.

Economic Research Service (ERS) research in North America confirms that the arts and associated projects are concentrating there in less populated areas throughout the country, including small, rural counties. Likewise, the emergence of these non-traditional arts magnets—especially since 1990—demonstrates the ability of some rural areas to attract creative talent and shows that this is connected to the growing number of initiatives promoting rural cultural tourism (Wojan and McGranahan 2007). Both inherited features (such as climate, the natural environment and population) and created features (such as book town developments with their amenities, arts events, entertainment and restaurants) therefore make regions attractive. As Florida (1995, p. 528) states:

> Regions are becoming focal points for knowledge creation and learning in the new age of global, knowledge-intensive capitalism as they in effect become learning regions. These learning regions function as collectors and repositories of knowledge, ideas and learning.

In the case of Malaysia, the impetus for developing book towns is unquestionably to make the country a centre for knowledge and excellence in the fields of education and culture. Kampung Buku Langkawi was the first book village to appear in South-East Asia in 1997, on the tropical island of Langkawi. However, the Book Village Foundation Malaysia was established earlier in 1994, with founding members including prominent Malaysians such as Sanusi Junid, a former Cabinet minister. The organization aims to promote reading as a way of life, especially among families and youth, and endeavours to ensure that reading materials are available to all members of society. The organization has since established a second book town in the historical city of Melaka with additional support from the Melaka state government. This particular village aims to create a niche for itself as a reference and resource centre for book and reading materials concerning local and national life to promote interest in and awareness of Melaka, and supporting authors originating in the region. These books and documents—particularly focused on history, tourism, culture, fiction and biography—are housed in the Anjung Karyawan Melaka, or Melaka Literature Corner, with the majority donated by publishers, government agencies and writers who appreciate the organization's vision and objectives.[20] In 2012, Langkawi Book Town hosted the International Book Town Festival and conference, drawing book town founders and booksellers from around the globe to witness their unique application of the concept.[21]

However, not all interviewees agreed that book towns were cultural and learning projects. Roberts (personal interview 2011), Playden (personal interview 2011) and Chambers (personal interview 2011) see bookshops and book towns simply as a manifestation of another—quite specific—retail activity. Playden considers bookselling is 'somewhat removed' from the arts:

> I don't see what we were doing as in any way related … to the arts and culture economy … It is just straight retailing. For it to be considered cultural tourism, that would mean the bureaucracy would have to start considering people who sell books for a living the same way they consider theatre producers, painters and musicians and I'm not sure they ever will because we're not the same kind of people and it's not the same kind of business. We're not producing the arts and culture. We're simply selling something which somebody else has produced. (personal interview 2011)

Regarding Graiguenamanagh's Town of Books Festival in Ireland, book town founder Brian Roberts does not see a book town project as cultural in the same way that Landry (2008) does, despite the remarkable cultural heritage potential and the distinctiveness he is aiming to achieve. Referring to the town's signature book event, the Town of Books Festival, Roberts says:

> I always fight to say this is not a literary event at all. It's a collectors' fair … I'm a book collector … I buy books for reference so I see them as collectors' items and reference books. I probably wouldn't go to a literary festival. I don't see Graiguenamanagh as a literary town at all. (personal interview 2011)

While Nelson unquestionably sees the Sedbergh book town project as fitting within an arts and cultural context, she says popular culture is the key target area, claiming that:

> If we were to do 'learned highbrow stuff' we wouldn't get anyone to come to our events. You need to know your audience. You need your locals. There is nothing like the animosity of someone who doesn't like books. They feel their intelligence is being criticised. You need your community with you. (personal interview 2017)

Turpin (personal interview 2017) agrees. 'Local impact is essential,' he says. However, he distinguishes book towns and book festivals from other sub-sets of the arts and cultural industries, stating:

> Book festivals are part of the cultural industries but we are a parasitic part. We might be a nice parasitic part … It will produce events, but it's not producing artistic or cultural material. Lots of festivals and book towns will have writers in residence and specific writing projects with schools, but it's not the same as if I was working for a theatre company. We would be putting on shows and we would be directly delivering a cultural product. You could argue that some of the events are cultural artefacts but they're at one remove back. The actual cultural artefact is the book. So we have to be realistic about it and say 'we're part of the entertainment industry. We … produce an experience … (Turpin, personal interview 2017)

Derrett (personal interview 2011) believes books, book towns and publishing are all part of an 'absolutely critical' sub-set of the arts 'because it underpins lots of other arts practice. Books are creative. It's about reflecting on our culture.' Muller (personal interview 2010) and Sheahan-Bright (personal interview 2010) also identify an arts and cultural context as an essential component of book towns, a fact illustrated by other types of businesses commonly seen alongside bookshops like galleries, museums and art photography studios, and the presence of a range of activities centred on creative writing, such as workshops, residencies and readings, and other features inspired by literary interest, including book trails and writers' houses. Similarly, Schiotz (personal interview 2012) believes that any arts and cultural activity taking place in a community creates an atmosphere conducive to secondhand books.

As they 'ride the rapids' in the face of relentless global change, rural and regional communities have embraced book town projects as means of survival through cooperative effort and the rebuilding of social capital—albeit in the often non-conformist ways in which bookish people approach such a task. Unique regional experiences are central to why book towns have asserted themselves around the world, and this corresponds with the ideas of Florida (2002), Landry (2008) and others. More broadly, successful rural and regional book town projects have prospered by identifying and strengthening the very characteristics that distinguish them from other places, and this has attracted and retained talented individuals and their creative enterprises. However, this success is also dependent on addressing prejudices in rural communities about the ability to sustain book-based projects to enable the regeneration of rural places. As hubs of cultural tourism, and to an extent post-tourism, book towns and their associated events and festivals stand as beacons of innovation and distinct models of how to promote local distinctiveness and originality that excite the imaginations of bibliophiles. Book towns have struck a chord with lovers of the written word, who are willing to travel across the region, the nation or the world to visit them.

It is the unique nature of the book itself that is fundamental to the way Clunes, Sedbergh and other book towns have been embraced around the world. Chapter 5 examines the role that books, as items of material culture, play in the success and popularity of the Book Town Movement. Books are the documentation of a culture (Derrett, personal interview 2010), but they are also part of every literate person's *biographia literaria*, or literary life story, to use the words of Coleridge, as Sutherland (2009) and others state. Books make us who we are. Chapter 5 explores the nature of books as items of cultural commodification, both deconstructing their ongoing cultural relevance and significance and investigating why books—their collection, celebration and use as a springboard for greater intellectual communion and human interaction, which is what book towns do—matter increasingly in the digital age.

Notes

1. Paasi (1991, p. 249) describes a region as a 'socio-spatial unit with a longer historical duration, a representation of "higher-scale" history into which inhabitants are socialized as part of the reproduction of the society. Region is thus essentially a social and cultural category with an explicit collective dimension representing institutional practices sedimented in the history of the region … It is mediated into daily life and is produced and reproduced in multitudinous social practices through communications and symbols, which can be common to all individuals in a region, though the meanings associated with them will always be construed personally on the basis of specific life situations and biographies. Individuals come and go; regions remain and are transformed.'
2. Refer to The Wickerman Festival, http://www.thewickermanfestival.co.uk
3. Over the five years prior to this report, the number of people attending Wigtown Book Festival events increased from 2300 in 2003 to 12,400 in 2008. This represented an increase in attendance of over 400% (Refer to *The Economic Impact of StenaLine Wigtown Book Festival 2008*, a report prepared for Wigtown Festival Company by Cogent Strategies International Limited 2009, p. 9). Since that time, growth has escalated further. For example, Wigtown Book Festival's attendance grew 18% between 2014 and 2016, with a total attendance in 2016 of approximately 25,000, with approximately 11,250 unique visitors. The festival created £2.1 million for the Dumfries and Galloway economy, and the event had a 23:1 return on public investment (Wigtown Festival Company Business Plan 2017–2021, p. 5; Turpin, personal interview 2017).
4. The term 'social capital' has attained currency most notably through the works of Bourdieu (1984, 1986) and Putnam (1995, 2000). In his studies of Italian communities, Putnam's over-arching finding is that any increase or decrease in the level of social capital in a community leads to a corresponding decline in the quality of life within that community.

Social capital and strong communities are therefore closely linked. A strong community is one with high levels of coordination and cooperation for reciprocal and mutual benefit where there are lively civic engagement and effective collective action (Putnam 2000). Social capital is the 'grease that allows the community to wheel to advance smoothly' (Putnam 2000) and is essentially the development of a network of trust within a community (Cuers and Hewston 2006).

5. MacLeod (2009, p. 143) lists examples of groups created with relation to the theme town developments, including Wigtown Book Town Company, Kirkcudbright Forum, Kirkcudbright 2000, CDFTI, The District of Wigtown Chamber of Commerce, Wigtown Book Festival Company and Glorious Galloway: http://www.gloriousgalloway.com. He also refers to international links established with the French towns of Pont Aven and Bécherel, and the fact that Wigtown hosted the 2003 festival for the IOB.
6. Refer to http://www.booktown.clunes.org
7. The 2011 Census recorded a population of 1373, an increase of approximately one-quarter since the 2006 Census record of 1026: http://www.victorianplaces.com.au/clunes
8. The Jones family managed Reverie Books in Trentham for many years (McFadyen 2005).
9. Refer to http://wordsinwinter.com/event
10. Refer to http://www.clunesbooktown.com.au/bookshop-directory-2
11. Refer to http://www.oecd.org/publications/tourism-and-the-creative-economy-9789264207875-en.htm
12. Refer to http://clunesbooktown.com.au/creative-victoria-grant-success
13. Refer to Foundation for Rural and Regional Renewal, http://www.frrr.org.au
14. Refer to https://www.wheelercentre.com/about-us
15. A two-hour catchment includes major conurbations of Greater Manchester, Leeds/Bradford and Merseyside (Nelson, personal interview 2011).
16. WanderingEducators.com is an international community of travelling educators, and a resource for discovering extraordinary travel destinations, fascinating people, and global artists and photographers, among many published articles. As well, WanderingEducators.com is the largest source of travel guide reviews on the internet. Refer to http://www.wanderingeducators.com/learn-more.html

17. Sedbergh Book Town Limited and Sedbergh Book Town Literary Trust, *Growing and Thriving Joint Business Plan 2008–2011*, pp. 16–17. Sedbergh: Sedbergh Book Town Limited.
18. For example, R.F.G. Hollett, a well-known antiquarian bookshop, had been located in Sedbergh for over 40 years (Nelson, personal interview 2011).

    Cumbria Vision is the dynamic strategic organization charged with leading the economic regeneration of Cumbria. It published the Cumbria Economic Plan in September 2007, which focuses on the development of key sectors in the county's economy that have the potential for sustained growth, including digital, cultural and creative industries: see http://www.copeland.gov.uk/attachments/cumbria-economic-plan-2007
19. Refer to Book Village Foundation Malaysia: http://www.bookvillagemalaysia.com/
20. Refer to 'IOB – International Organisation of Book Towns', Booktown. Net: World of Books, http://www.booktown.net/gi.asp, 5 March 2009.

References

Bagshaw, M., & Mills, C. (2010). *Alastair Sawday's slow North Yorkshire: Moors, dales and coast, including York*. Chalfont St Peter: Bardt.

Beeton, S. (2006). *Community development through tourism*. Melbourne: Landlinks Press.

Blainey, G. (1983). *The tyranny of distance: How distance shaped Australia's history*. Melbourne: Sun Books.

Booth, R. (1999). *My kingdom of books*. Ceredigion: Y Lolfa Cyf.

Borsch, O. J., et al. (2008). Resource configuration and creative practices of community entrepreneurs. *Journal of Enterprising Communities: People and Places in the Global Economy, 2*(2), 100–123.

Bourdieu, P. (1984). *Distinction: A social critique of the judgement of taste*. Cambridge, MA: Harvard University Press.

Bourdieu, P. (1986). *The forms of capital*. http://www.marxists.org/reference/subject/philosophy/works/fr/bourdieu-forms-capital.htm. Accessed 25 Nov 2010.

Brady, T. (2011, March). *Clunes Back to Booktown and the writer*. Victorian Writers Centre. http://www.snodger.com.au/tessbrady/images/pdfs/Writer-in-community-VWC.pdf. Accessed 20 June 2012.

Brady, T. (2012, September). Clunes address. *Paju Booksori: World Booktown Symposium*. https://clunesbooktown.com.au/ Accessed 10 July 2013.

Briedenhann, J., & Wickens, E. (2004). Rural tourism: Meeting the challenges of the new South Africa. *The International Journal of Tourism Research, 6*(3), 189–203.

Burnett, K. A. (1998). Local heroics: Reflecting on incomers and local rural development discourses in Scotland. *Sociologica Ruralis, 38*(2), 204–224.

Butler, B. D. (2010, 17 June). What's your favourite book town? *Travel Between the Pages: The Intersection of Travel, Books & Art*. http://travelbetweenthepages.com/2010/06/17/whats-your-favorite-book-town. Accessed 18 Aug 2010.

Butler, R. W., & Hall, C. M. (1998). Image and re-imaging of rural areas. In R. Butler, C. M. Hall, & J. Jenkins (Eds.), *Tourism and recreation in rural areas* (pp. 115–122). Chichester: John Wiley and Sons.

Chappel, S., & Brown, L. (2006). Literary tourism beyond the city. In P. Whitelaw & B. O'Mahony (Eds.), *CAUTHE: To the city and beyond* (pp. 1764–1773). Melbourne: Victoria University School of Hospitality and Tourism.

Cogent Strategies International Limited. (2009). *The economic impact of StenaLine Wigtown Book Festival 2008: A report for the Wigtown Festival Company*. Glasgow: Cogent Straegies International Limited.

Cole, S. (2006). Cultural tourism, community participation and empowerment. In *Cultural tourism in a changing world: Politics, participation and (re)presentation* (pp. 89–103). Clevedon: Channel View.

Collits, P. (2000). *Small town decline and survival: Trends, success factors and policy issues*. Paper presented to Future of Australia's Country Towns. LaTrobe University, Bendigo. http://www.regional.org.au/au/countrytowns/global/collits.htm. Accessed 31 Aug 2010.

Constantoura, P. (2001). *Australians and the arts*. Sydney: Federation Press.

Craik, J. (2001). Cultural tourism. In N. Douglas, N. Douglas, & R. Derrett (Eds.), *Special interest tourism: Context and cases* (pp. 113–139). Brisbane: John Wiley & Sons.

Cuers, S., & Hewston, J. (Eds.). (2006). *Strong communities handbook: In what ways can urban and regional planning contribute towards high levels of social capital and community strengths in new and re-developing communities?* Brisbane: Queensland University of Technology.

Dewailly, J.-M. (1998). Images of heritage in rural regions. In R. Butler, C. M. Hall, & J. Jenkins (Eds.), *Tourism and recreation in rural areas* (pp. 123–137). Chichester: John Wiley and Sons.

Douglas, N., Douglas, N., & Derrett, R. (Eds.). (2001). *Special interest tourism: Context and cases*. Brisbane: John Wiley & Sons.

Eltham, K. (2009, January 7). Where the bloody hell are you? *Electric alphabet: Writing and publishing in the digital near-future* [Weblog]. http://electricalphabet.wordpress.com/2009/01/07/where-the-bloody-hell-are-you. Accessed 31 Aug 2010.

Engler, M. (1994). Theme towns: The pitfalls and alternative of image making. *Small Town, 25*(1), 4–7.

Evans, G., & Shaw, P. (2004). *The contribution of culture to regeneration in the UK: A review of evidence*. A Report to the Department for Culture, Media and Sport. London: DCMS.

Florida, R. (1995). Toward the learning region. *Futures, 27*(5), 527–536.

Florida, R. (2002). *The rise of the creative class: And how it's transforming work, leisure, community and everyday life*. New York: Basic Books.

Frank, J. (1996). Does regionalism have an impact on the arts practice of a community? MBus (Arts Mgt), Queensland University of Technology.

Frenkel, S., & Walton, J. (2000). Bavarian Leavenworth and the symbolic economy of a theme town. *Geographical Review, 90*(4), 559–584.

Gelder, K., & Jacobs, J. M. (1998). *Uncanny Australia: Sacredness and identity in a postcolonial nation*. Melbourne: Melbourne University Press.

Gibson, C., & Connell, J. (Eds.). (2011). *Festival places: Revitalising rural Australia*. Bristol: Channel View.

Grant-Marshall, S. (2012, November 23). From sad "nothing" town to book town. *BDLive.com*. http://www.bdlive.co.za/life/travel/2012/11/23/from-sad-nothing-town-to-book-town. Accessed 25 Jan 2013.

Grauman, B. (2008, October 29). Words, mountains, architecture form unique city of books. *Bloomberg*. http://www.bloomberg.com/apps/news?pid=newsarchive&sid=aNrGkzc99VXU&refer=home. Accessed 18 Nov 2010.

Green, C. (1992). Unofficial world: Postcolonialism and the metropolis. *Art and Text, 43*(38–41), 96–97.

Green, S. (2010). "The rainbow bridge": Writing and teaching in a regional context. *Text, 14*(1). http://www.textjournal.com.au. Accessed 7 Apr 2011.

Gretzel, U., Fesenmaier, D. R., & O'Leary, J. T. (2006). The transformation of consumer behaviour. In D. Buhalis & C. Costa (Eds.), *Tourism business frontiers: Consumers, products and industry* (pp. 9–18). Burlington: Elsevier Butterworth-Heinemann.

Griswold, W. (2008). *Regionalism and the reading class*. Chicago: University of Chicago Press.

Halseth, G., Market, S., & Bruce, D. (2010). *The next rural economies*. Wallingford: CABI.

Holman, T. (2006, June 30). Out and about in book town: Sedburgh in Cumbria has been designated England's first official book town. *The Bookseller*, p. 30.

Hopkins, J. (1998). Commodifying the countryside: Marketing myths of rurality. In R. Butler, C. M. Hall, & J. Jenkins (Eds.), *Tourism and recreation in rural areas* (pp. 139–156). Chichester: John Wiley and Sons.

Horne, D. (2002). *Keynote address: The arts, the regions and the economy*. Paper presented to Groundswell: Regional Arts Surging Forward. Regional Arts Australia National Conference, Albury Wodonga.

Howie, F. (2003). *Managing the tourist destination*. London: Continuum.

Huang, Y.-H., & Stewart, W. P. (1996). Rural tourism development: Shifting basis of community solidarity. *Journal of Travel Research, 34*(4), 26–32.

Huff, S. (2008). Identity and landscape: The reification of place in Strasbourg, France. In D. C. Knudsen et al. (Eds.), *Landscape, tourism and meaning*. Bloomington: Ashgate.

Isserman, A. M., Fesser, E., & Warren, D. E. (2009). Why some rural places prosper and others do not. *International Regional Science Review, 32*, 300–342.

Kendall, G., Skrbis, Z., & Woodward, I. (2009). *The sociology of cosmopolitanism*. London: Palgrave Macmillan.

Kennedy, M. (2003, March 10). Books could help town to turn over new leaf. *The Guardian*. http://www.guardian.co.uk/uk/2003/mar/10/books.artsnewstemporary. Accessed 30 June 2010.

Kennedy, M. (2010). *Research audit: Clunes back to booktown 2010*. Bendigo: La Trobe University Planning and Development Program. http://www.booktown.clunes.org/documents/latrobe.pdf. Accessed 20 June 2012.

Kennedy, M. (2011). Binding a sustainable future: Book towns, themed place-branding and rural renewal. A case study of Clunes' "*Back to Booktown*". In J. Martin & T. Budge (Eds.), *The sustainability of Australia's country towns: Renewal, renaissance, resilience* (pp. 207–226). Ballarat: VURRN Press.

Kleinart, S. (1991). Towards regionalism. *Eyeline: East Coast Contemporary Visual Arts, 14*, 17.

Kneafsey, M. (2000). Tourism, place identities and social relations in the European rural periphery. *European Urban and Regional Studies, 7*(1), 35–50.

Knudsen, D. C., et al. (Eds.). (2008). *Landscape, tourism and meaning*. Bloomington: Ashgate.

Lade, C., & Jackson, J. (2004). Key success factors in regional festivals: Some Australian experiences. *Event Management, 9*, 1–11.
Landry, C. (2008 [2000]). *The creative city: A toolkit for urban innovators*. London: Earthscan.
Landry, C., et al. (1996). *The art of regeneration: Urban renewal through cultural activity*. London: Comedia.
MacLeod, D. V. L. (2003). Culture and the construction of a niche market destination. In D. V. L. Macleod (Ed.), *Niche tourism in question: Interdisciplinary perspectives on problems and possibilities*. Glasgow: University of Glasgow Press.
MacLeod, D. V. L. (2009). Scottish theme towns: Have new identities enhanced development? *Journal of Tourism and Cultural Change, 7*(2), 133–145.
MacLeod, D. V. L., & Carrier, G. (2010). Tourism, power and culture. In D. V. L. MacLeod & J. G. Carrier (Eds.), *Tourism, power and culture: Anthropological insights* (pp. 64–89). Bristol: Channel View.
Marshall, A. (2004). *Fossicking for old books*. Melbourne: Bread Street Press.
Martin, J., & Budge, T. (Eds.). (2011). *The sustainability of Australia's country towns: Renewal, renaissance, resilience*. Ballarat: Victorian Universities Regional Research Network Press.
McClarence, S. (2009, May 17). The little town taking a leaf out of Hay's book. *The Observer* [UK]. http://www.guardian.co.uk/travel/2009/may/17/sedbergh-book-town-cumbria. Accessed 3 Apr 2011.
McFadyen, W. (2005, June 25). Walking many a country aisle. *The Age* [Melbourne]. http://www.theage.com.au/news/victoria/walking-many-a-country-aisle/2005/06/23/1119321846994.html. Accessed 22 May 2011.
McMillan, H. (2013, October 2). The lore (of Galloway) and you. *Wigtown Book Festival*. http://wigtownbookfestival.com/blog/the-lore-of-galloway-and-you/7. Accessed 10 Dec 2013.
McMillan, H. (2014). *McMillan's Gallovidean encyclopaedia*. Wigtown: Wigtown Festival Company.
McMurtry, L. (1999). *Walter Benjamin at the Dairy Queen: Reflections at sixty and beyond*. New York: Simon & Schuster.
McMurtry, L. (2008). *Books: A memoir*. New York: Simon & Schuster.
Meetham, K. (2001). *Tourism in global society: Place, culture, consumption*. Basingstoke: Palgrave.
Merfeld-Langston, A. L. (2007). The *villages du livre*: Local identity, cultural politics and print culture in contemporary France. PhD thesis, Pennsylvania State University.

Merfeld-Langston, A. L. (2014). Judging a book town by its cover: Marketing French *villages du livre*. In P. Wallen & P. Young (Eds.), *Place and locality in modern France* (pp. 125–137). London: Bloomsbury.

O'Neill, P., & McGuirk, P. (2007, June 15–17). Towards an antipodean theory of space. In B. Mitchell, et al. (Eds.), *Proceedings of the ARCRNSISS methodology, tools and techniques and spatial theory paradigm forums workshop* (pp. 207–216). University of Newcastle, Australia. Melbourne: RMIT Publishing.

Paasi, A. (1991). Deconstructing regions: Notes on the scales of spatial life. *Environment and Planning A, 23*, 239–256.

Ploughman, I. (2006). Innovation in rural Queensland: Why some towns thrive while others languish. http://www.plowman.com.au/Innovation_in_rural_Queensland.pdf. Accessed 22 Feb 2006.

Press, S. (2001). Reading Wigtown: Place identities in a Scottish book town. MA thesis, University of Oregon.

Prosser, G. (2001). Rural tourism. In N. Douglas, N. Douglas, & R. Derrett (Eds.), *Special interest tourism: Context and cases* (pp. 165–185). Brisbane: John Wiley & Sons.

Pryor, C. (2008, May 2). Country viewpoint – Robert Campbell, Clunes, Victoria. *ABC Rural.* http://www.abc.nat.au/rural/telegraph/content/2006/s2233658.htm. Accessed 20 June 2011.

Putnam, R. (1995). Bowling alone: America's declining social capital. *Journal of Democracy, 6*(1), 65–78.

Putnam, R. (2000). *Bowling alone: The collapse and revival of American community*. New York: Simon & Schuster.

Rebanks, J. (2010, December 5). *Culture Cumbria: A review of the current position and future potential.* Rebanks Consulting Limited. http://rebanksconsulting.com/resources/Culture%20Cumbria.pdf. Accessed 8 Oct 2011.

Robinson, M., & Andersen, H. (2004). Reading between the lines: Literature and the creation of touristic spaces. In M. Robinson & H. Andersen (Eds.), *Literature and tourism: Essays in the reading and writing of tourism* (pp. 1–38). Andover: Thomson Learning.

Saffer, C. (2016, May 6). OECD wants to take a leaf out of Booktown. *Mojo.* http://mojonews.com.au/oecd-wants-to-take-a-leaf-out-of-booktown. Accessed 22 Mar 2017.

Sapsed, J., & Salter, A. (2004). Postcards from the edge: Local communities, global programs and boundary objects. *Organization Studies, 25*, 1515–1534.

Seaton, A. V. (1996a). *Book towns and rural tourism development: Hay on Wye 1961–1996*. Glasgow: University of Strathclyde.
Seaton, A. V. (1996b). Hay-on-Wye, the mouse that roared: Book towns and rural tourism. *Tourism Management, 17*(5), 379–385.
Seaton, A. V. (1999). Book towns as tourism developments in peripheral areas. *The International Journal of Tourism Research, 1*(5), 389–399.
Sedbergh Book Town Limited and Sedbergh Book Town Literary Trust. (2008). *Growing and thriving joint business plan 2008–2011*. Sedbergh: Sedbergh Book Town Limited.
Shields, R. (1991). *Places on the margin: Alternative geographies of modernity*. London: Routledge.
Star, S., & Griesemer, J. (1989). Institutional ecology, "translations" and boundary objects. *Social Studies of Science, 19*(3), 387–420.
Sutherland, J. (2009, January 26). Interview with Ramona Koval, 'Magic Moments: Life Changing Encounters with Books, Music and Film'. *The Book Show,* ABC Radio National. http://www.abc.net.au/rn/bookshow/stories/2009/2770765.htm. Accessed 14 Apr 2011.
Trotter, R. (2001). Regions, regionalism and cultural development. In D. Carter & T. Bennett (Eds.), *Culture in Australia: Policies, publics and programs* (pp. 334–335). Melbourne: Cambridge University Press.
Tuan, Y. (1974). *Topophilia: A study of environmental perception, attitudes and values*. Englewood Cliffs: Prentice Hall.
Turpin, A. (2008, September 21). Putting the big in Wigtown. *Scotland on Sunday*. http://scotlandonsunday.scotsman.com/sos-review/Putting-the-big-in-Wigtown.4512771.jp. Accessed 18 Aug 2010.
Urry, J. (1995). *Consuming places*. London: Routledge.
Vik, J., & Villa, M. (2010). Books, branding and boundary objects: On the use of image in rural development. *Sociologia Ruralis, 50*(2), 156–170.
Voights, J. (2008). Sedbergh's book town: Festival of books and drama. *Wandering Educators*. http://www.wanderingeducators.com/books-film/books/sedberghs-book-town-festival-books-and-drama.html. Accessed 10 June 2011.
Wanhill, S. (1997). Peripheral area tourism: A European perspective. *Progress in Tourism and Hospitality Research, 3*, 47–70.
Wearing, S., Stephenson, D., & Young, T. (2010). *Tourist cultures: Identity, place and the traveller*. London: Sage.
Wigtown Festival Company. (2017, April 3). *Business plan 2017–2021*. Wigtown.
Williams, R. (1989). Metropolitan perceptions and the emergence of modernism. In *The politics of modernism: Against the new conformists*. London: Verso.

Wojan, T., & McGranahan, D. (2007). *Creative class codes*. Washington, DC: USDA. http://www.ers.usda.gov/data-products/creative-class-county-codes.aspx. Accessed 15 July 2012.

World Tourism Organization. (1995). *Global tourism forecasts to the year 2000 and beyond: Europe*. Madrid: World Tourism Organization.

Interviews

Berkelouw, Leo. Eumundi, Queensland, 14 August 2012.

Booth, Richard MBE. Hay-on-Wye, Wales, 20 September 2011.

Chambers, Joanna. Abergavenny, Wales, 20 September 2011.

Derrett, Ros OAM. Brisbane, Queensland, 2 June 2010.

McShane, Paul. Bowral, New South Wales, Australia, 9 July 2010.

Muller, Laurie. Brisbane, Queensland, 17 August 2010 and 7 September 2010.

Nelson, Carole. Sedbergh, Yorkshire, United Kingdom, 9 September 2011; phone interview, 29 March 2017.

Nioa, Anne. Maryborough, Queensland, 4 September 2010.

Playden, Peter. Atherstone, Warwickshire, United Kingdom, 13 September 2011.

Roberts, Brian. Graiguenamanagh, Republic of Ireland, 17 September 2011; phone interview, 28 March 2017.

Sheahan-Bright, Robyn. Gladstone, Queensland, 24 August 2010.

Schiotz, Peter. Maleny, Queensland, 4 April 2012.

Turpin, Adrian OBE. Wigtown, Scotland, 4 September 2011; via email, 15 March 2017.

Watson, Joyce and Cochrane, Ian. Wigtown, Scotland, 4 September 2011.

Yates, Carolyn. Wigtown, Scotland, 4 September 2011.

5

Sacred Objects and Magic Encyclopaedias: Books in Book Towns

This chapter highlights the totemic role of the book itself as the symbol and material catalyst for the spread and success of book towns. It also contrasts the tangible materiality of books with the infinite possibilities of digital culture in an age that, for many bibliophiles, marks a painful transition from an industrial to a post-industrial world. Books in book towns create shrines to the historical and cultural rootedness of print culture that, to varying degrees, relate to the particularistic local histories and economies of the towns involved. Books are examined as unique commodities and as objects of desire that awaken and enliven the past in pleasurable ways, inspiring travel by book-loving pilgrims and curious passers-by. At the heart of this anticipation and desire is the importance of collecting and owning books. Specialization of book interests and the cult of book collecting are examined, as is the question of how, through capturing the interest of bibliophiles, these drive the book town phenomenon.

While the founding of Hay-on-Wye as a book town was driven by the goal of accumulating books in large numbers in order to create a novelty kingdom, the emphasis in later book towns has shifted towards a commitment to celebrating books and literary culture with, at its core, the

J. Frank, *Regenerating Regional Culture*, Sociology of the Arts,
https://doi.org/10.1007/978-3-319-65036-4_5

intrinsic uniqueness and beauty of the book. Book towns marshal literary elites, publishing companies and their associated targeted publicity machines to germinate events and build profiles of attraction. In this way, local place-based profiles and particularities interact with broader networks of mobility and exchange. The chapter thus also seeks to explain the important connections between old books and the multibillion-dollar new book industry, where the ever-shortening lifespan of new books, together with shifts in buying trends, provides opportunities for the growth of secondhand book markets as books, despite a plethora of digital alternatives, become material souvenirs of the reading experience. The reverence for the actuality of books demonstrated in book towns has been a central tenet of the particular philosophies of book town leaders. Nöel Anselot in Redu and Larry McMurtry in Archer City, Texas, are both avid book collectors and protectors of accumulated collections as well as authors in their own right. The containment of knowledge and opportunity for learning that books in vast numbers represent was fundamental to McMurtry's Archer City venture, established to leave a book-inspired legacy for the town and the wider region. The rise of book towns as havens of innovation, creativity and sites of increasing cultural significance can be attributed to the aura surrounding books, and the symbolic juncture they mark between the past and the future.

McMurtryville: An Oasis of Books in Texas

The book town that stands out as perhaps the most unlikely and unusual of the eccentric single-founder models is Archer City, Texas, the brainchild of Pulitzer Prize-winning author, screenwriter, academic, book scout and book town devotee Larry McMurtry. Archer City has a population of approximately 2000 and is located half an hour's drive south of Wichita Falls and about two hours' drive north of Dallas-Fort Worth. It is situated in the 'Texas Panhandle'—the vast, empty prairie country of west Texas, north of the Brazos River, ancient lands of the Comanche. Bookselling now features, amid ranching and oil, as a minor industry in the region. The book town was created when McMurtry, emerging from a bout of depression after major surgery, dreamed of owning a huge bookstore like the ones he trawled through as a young book scout, hunting for rare finds on behalf of established dealers, 'a repository of literature and knowledge that will be a legacy for his home town and indeed for modern America' (McShane 2002, p. 10). McMurtry recalls:

> I began to realise that with real estate as it is now in urban centres, the only way you could have a giant bookstore is to have it in a small town ... I just love the possibilities of really big used bookstores – vast repositories of knowledge – and the only hope of preserving them for another generation is to build one in a small town. (in Horowitz 1997, para. 19)

Until 2012, four separate buildings—once empty storefronts—housed the Booked Up Inc. empire, though McMurtry has since auctioned off part of his collection. He downsized his Booked Up empire in August 2012 after collecting books for 55 years, auctioning 300,000 books. However, Archer City still contains his main bookstore, containing between 150,000 and 200,000 books,[1] and his own private collection of 28,000 books (Lindenberger 2012), and McMurty's commitment to books and writing continues to make Archer City a place of pilgrimage for writers seeking inspiration. Locals believe it is McMurtry's lucrative writing career that has made such an ambitious venture feasible in the face of difficult times for others in the US book trade (Fig. 5.1).

There are parallels between Richard Booth and Larry McMurtry. While McMurtry didn't have Booth's non-conformist showmanship, he did have the grand—perhaps quixotic—objective of stocking a million books in a tiny town; was disillusioned by the notion of a book town drawing large numbers of tourists; had complete control over the book town venture as its single founder as well as sufficient renown as a writer to generate publicity for the venture and wished to revive a town for which he felt affection. McMurtry's interest in books and his abilities as a bookseller and book collector were also at odds with his family's cowboy heritage. He did not fit the traditional Texan rancher mould, just as Booth was at

Fig. 5.1 Larry McMurty's 'Booked Up' bookstore, Archer City, Texas, USA (2014) (Source: Photographer Tui Snider)

odds with his family's expectations that he would become a London accountant:

> Unfit for ranch work because of my indifference to cattle … I went instead into the antiquarian book trade, becoming in effect a book rancher, herding books into larger and larger ranches (I now have filled a whole town with them, my equivalent of the King Ranch.) I couldn't find the right cow but I could find the right books, extricating them from the once dense thickets of America's antiquarian bookshops. (McMurtry 1999, p. 54)

For almost 30 years, the lack of books in Archer County and West Texas was the kink in McMurtry's relationship with his home town, but the pull to return was strong and he solved the problem by taking the books to Archer City and instantly transforming the place, establishing Booked Up in several large, empty, inexpensive buildings. Like Booth in his castle, McMurtry also purchased the 'town's most imposing house' and presided over the community, despite many locals being 'indifferent ... to my bookshops' (McMurtry 1999, p. 119). Describing his obsession as life-changing, McMurtry says, 'I was involved in the art of escape: the escape from the cowboy life, the life of men and horses, into the culture of books. In fact, I *read* my way out of that culture' (p. 94).

Archer City's isolation and inability to attract other booksellers have been problematic (Huckans 2005), although McMurtry wanted to convert local buildings into a collective to attract other bookshop proprietors (Jones 1997). While the town is charming in its own way, with its American main street and a typical Midwestern town square with handsome stone courthouse, there is little else to attract other booksellers to the town (Jones 1997). Other Archer City enthusiasts have participated in projects to revitalize the town and put it on the map as an oasis of culture in the middle of the plains. For example, the town's historic hotel, The Spur, has been restored and is open for business, and the previously crumbling Royal Theater, immortalized in *The Last Picture Show*, which was filmed on location in Archer City, has been rebuilt, allowing the town to become a centre for the performing arts.[2] Archer City also promotes itself as a seminar town and creative writing retreat, and attracts site visits by creative writing and journalism students with bookish enthusiasms (McMurtry 2009b, pp. 70, 85). However, much like Booth, McMurtry is disinterested in book fairs and festivals in Archer City (Jones 1998). The town is a living metaphor for McMurtry's purism: a book town for serious collectors rather than a magnet to attract busloads of mainstream tourists:

> Archer City is intended as a place of pilgrimage for the true bibliophile or at least the serious book-buyer. The long drive to get there, the lack of amenities or other diversions in Archer City, and the almost invisible signage are all hurdles for the casual tourist ... he showed little enthusiasm for the notion of linking Archer City to other book towns. (McShane 2002, pp. 10–11)

However, McMurtry is at variance with Booth in that he keeps only quality books in his stores, spending long days purging his shelves to maintain the calibre of his stock (Roberts 2009, p. 4). The preservation of quality literature is therefore central to McMurtry's book town establishment philosophy. The status of the book as a significant realm of memory is enhanced and the book town emphasized as a place of literary and cultural heritage.

Books as Unique Commodities

So why do bibliophiles like McMurtry and the book pilgrims who travel to Archer City and other book towns amass books, often throughout their whole lives? There are a number of explanations that build to a broader understanding of why book towns and antiquarian book buying remain so popular and well supported. First, the association of books with their readers is unlike any other relationship between objects and their users (Manguel 1997, p. 214), whether it be light bulbs, CDs, cars or other mass merchandise:

> Books, as storehouses of ideas and as a perceived means to human betterment have long been viewed as a kind of 'sacred product'. The value of books would seem to lie, first and foremost, in their capacity for moral, aesthetic and intellectual development, and only secondarily – if at all – in the marketplace. What makes a 'good' book good – or rather, what makes books good – is their purported ability to transcend vulgar economic considerations for the sake of these loftier goals. (Miller 2006, p. 19)

Books are not only valuable for the information or entertainment they provide, but are important cultural artefacts—even objects of devotion. As commonplace as books may seem, the cultural magic that they work transforms them from industrially produced consumer items into 'sacred products' (Striphas 2009, p. 19). The physical beauty of a well-designed book signifies the history of the book as an artisan product, and in some cases renders a book irreplaceable. Merfeld-Langston (2007, p. 6) remarks that 'no miracle of digitization will lessen the aesthetic value of a Medieval illuminated manuscript or a Grolier binding.'[3] Besides encouraging appreciation of literature, many book towns—particularly those in Europe—emphasize the importance of traditional arts associated with books and their production, such as calligraphy and hand-colouring, and highlight the intrinsic artistic qualities of books, especially handcrafted paper or bindings. To use the example mentioned earlier, in the French *village du livre* of Montolieu, established in 1990, bookbinder and energetic book town enthusiast Michel Braibant established a printing museum as the centrepiece of the village. In addition to its exhibition of old printing presses, the museum conducts an education programme for students with workshops in the art of the book, demonstrating practices such as printing, calligraphy, typography, papermaking and bookbinding (McShane 2002, p. 26). Book towns such as this are educative and allow their communities to address the inherent artistic value of books, their sumptuous beauty and the laborious endeavour and skill involved in producing a book by hand.

Books are revered as repositories of cultural history, not only through their texts and illustrations, but also because, through provenance and use, they have become complex artefacts. In France, where governments consider the book as *un product pas comme les autres*—a product unlike any other—the book is not simply considered an object of leisure, knowledge or commerce, but a *patrimoine écrit*, or written patrimony, that has earned special recognition (Merfeld-Langston 2010, p. 348). *Patrimoine* is a concept related to French pride and history, denoting a rich legacy inherited from generations of ancestors. The prominence of literary festivals and book towns in France is closely linked to books and citizenship, where literature and literacy are not just regarded as useful per se, but as a vital component in building citizens who are knowledgeable and capable of exercising an informed and responsible role in society and abroad.

The important place of books and literature in French culture is evidenced by the naming of many streets after well-known writers or literary characters, the existence of numerous prestigious literary prizes, the media's keen interest in literary topics and the influence of the nation's writers in political and social issues. Reading is regarded as an essential component of democracy. Most distinct regions of France have their own book town, and the majority of French regional governments regard it as imperative to create a book town as a 'badge of honour'. Books connect France and its past, perhaps as a reminder of the nation's former standing as a major power. Bookstores have the social and cultural role of 'irrigating the country with books' (Merfeld-Langston 2010, p. 351) or delivering the required sustenance that is derived from all things literary.

Straight-Grained Morocco and Sprinkled Calf: The Cult of Book Collecting

Collectibles such as antiquarian books may be regarded as objects of desire, whose 'lives are not going to be used up, for they will be kept in a state of suspended animation or even restored and then laid down for posterity. They will be regularly fondled and admired like fat, pampered cats' (Franklin 2008, p. 8). These objects, according to Adrian Franklin,[4] then enter a circuit of exchange—not between users and consumers but between enthusiasts, who treasure them as sacred objects, allowing the items to commence a new life in the hands of the serious collector. A book that is left on a shelf is a dead thing perhaps, 'but it is also a chrysalis, an inanimate object packed with the potential to burst into new life' (Hill 2009, p. 2). In *Unpacking My Library*, Benjamin (2007, p. 60) reflects that, 'There is, in the life of a collector … a relationship to objects which does not emphasize their functional, utilitarian value – that is, their usefulness – but studies and loves them as the scene, the stage, of their fate.' Further,

> the period, the region, the craftsmanship, the former ownership – for a true collector, the whole background of an item adds up to a magic encyclopaedia whose quintessence is the fate of his [sic] object. In this circumscribed area then, it may be surmised how the great physiognomists – and collectors are the physiognomists of the world of objects – turn into interpreters of fate. (Benjamin 2008, p. 104)

Antiquarian books are perhaps more intriguing for the serious collector because of their histories and provenance, the labyrinth of prior ownership that brings them to the hands of their new owner. Fadiman (1998, pp. 118–19) enjoys the sensation of 'being a small link in a long chain of book owners', one of the reasons for this being that, in a secondhand bookstore, each volume is one of a kind, 'neither replaceable from a publisher's warehouse nor visually identical to its original siblings, which have accredited individuality with every change of ownership'. A variety of things can happen to a book to make it more special and desirable. Similarly, in their biblio-memoir *Used and Rare*, Lawrence and Nancy Goldstone (1997, p. 74) describe how they were drawn to collecting once they realized that 'books had stories associated with them that had nothing to do with the stories inside them ... we began appreciating there was a history and a world of ideas embodied by the books themselves'. When we collect secondhand books and read them, we are taking a role as part of a community of readers within a long history of reading. The physical characteristics of books themselves reveal aspects of these histories: they fall open at interesting places; they have covers and design that bring us face to face with unfamiliar aesthetics.

Part of the attraction of collecting is its accessibility and the egalitarian nature of the pastime. Apart from subjects such as historical periods, geographical regions, cooking, sport, people's lives or detective novels, books can be collected for their original dust jackets or their bindings, and for being autographed, first editions or copies that once belonged to a particular identity. Some books are collected for their book plates—small memorial labels on the inside front cover of books representing an aspect of the owner's life or family lineage. Other new areas of book-related collecting include paper engineering, bookmarks and bookends (Kells 2011, p. 293).

Unlike the contemporary shopping mall, high street or department store, which have all become 'utterly boring and predictable' and 'the same for each city and every country' (Franklin 2008, pp. 8–9), buying collectibles introduces an element of serendipity to shopping: a collectible item will not only place itself in your path, but it will be more affordable. The art of collecting reveals our connections with the material world. In contemporary society, consumers are driven and governed more by desire than by satisfaction, so that the adrenalin rush we experience when consuming things tends to be fuelled by anticipation rather than the satisfaction of acquiring the item. It is in the *wanting* that the true passion, excitement and pleasure lie for the collector (Franklin 2008). Part of this satisfaction centres on the current nostalgia—particularly among the middle classes—for a romanticized past that these items re-embody. Collecting is also connected with desire and longing for community, while association with the particularism of books is a way of expressing a cosmopolitan identity, made more sophisticated by association with other times and places: 'Every new search is a voyage to the Indies, a quest for buried treasure, a journey to the end of the rainbow' (Starrett, in Fadiman 1998, p. 118).

This emphasis on anticipation mirrors patterns of consumerism more broadly, suggesting that covert day-dreaming and expectation are processes central to modern consumerism (Campbell 1987, p. 94). Individuals don't necessarily seek satisfaction from the products themselves, but from anticipation and imaginative pleasure-seeking. Motivation for consumption is not simply materialistic; rather, consumers seek to experience in reality 'the pleasurable dramas they have already experienced in their imagination ... there is a dialectic of novelty and insatiability at the heart of contemporary consumerism' (Urry 2002, p. 13).

Books, Ownership and Self

The 'chase for books' is a key reason why people visit book towns. The book collector may be described as a kind of detective who thrives on the search for desired titles in rare-book dealers' catalogues and bookshelves, at auctions, in secondhand bookshops, at library sales or flea markets, and in antique shops. A number of writers have explored the mysterious and intimate relationship to ownership that is inherent in book collecting, as distinct from borrowing books, incidental ownership and the accumulation of books for reading (Benjamin 2007, pp. 59–68; McMurtry 1999, p. 119; Manguel 1996, p. 214). Personal ownership, rather than borrowing, is vital to book collectors such as McMurtry, who states (1999, p. 19):

> From the beginning, I sought to acquire books. I could, I suppose, have secured a card from the public library in Wichita Falls, but I didn't want

> books I had to bring back. I wanted books to keep, books that I could consider – think about for a few days before I read them … From the first I was attracted to the look and feel of books – I liked to enter what Walter Benjamin called the aura of reading, which involved mental preparation and was a way, I guess, of savouring the experience ahead. This time of anticipation is one of the pleasures of having a personal library.

At times, collectors even attribute feelings to books. They can be motivated to buy a book to save it from its lonely and abandoned situation and to give a book its 'freedom' (Benjamin 2007, p. 61), thus allowing the 'rebirth' to which Franklin (2008), Hill (2009) and others refer.

Australian secondhand bookseller Peter Schiotz (personal interview, 2012) says he encounters two varieties of customer: the reader who buys something quickly, and the buyer who is a collector. For the second group, ownership is essential: 'If you collect first editions of James Joyce, you don't want a picture of the first edition. You *want* the first edition,' he says. Bibliophiles offer all manner of reasons why it is essential to actually own books, including 'voluptuous greed', the sight and comfort of crowded bookcases and even 'jealousy of the past' (Manguel 1997, pp. 237–8). 'The pleasure of holding the book itself: savouring the type, the binding, the book's feel and heft' adds to the pleasure of wanting and owning a book (McMurtry 2008, p. 47). Laurie Muller (personal interview, 2010) speaks of the emotional resonance and attachment he feels to the books he owns: to part with them would be too great a wrench. John-Paul Sartre in *Words* (1964) describes his grandfather's library as a place that instils comfort, wellbeing and a clear sense of identity, while publisher and author Susan Hill (2009, p. 202) speaks of the reassurance of sharing your house with overwhelming numbers of volumes:

> The books have somehow shrunken back into the shelves. Into themselves, like old people hunched into jackets that are too big for them, sleeves that are too long. They seem to be singing. All through the house, the books are murmuring, turning over in sleep like pebbles on the shoreline as the tide recedes. But when I reach the stone-flagged hall and stand for a moment, listening, everything falls silent. I hear the comforting, inhabited, friendly silence of a house full of books.

A sense of 'coming home', or identity affirmation, that is engendered by the establishment of book towns enables greater certainty, prosperity and hope that may be romantic but is not illusory. Fictional utopias such as Atlantis feature on a semaphore in the book town of Fontenoy-lau-Joûte, France, but the towns themselves are built on more solid foundations, and no longer in danger of disappearing (Merfeld-Langston 2007, p. 37). The search for familiarity and comfort is quite possibly the underlying reason why a majority of people visit book towns—whether it manifests in the way a book looks, feels or smells, or the memories it invokes. As book consumers, we are nostalgic for bygone eras that conjure up the good things we have lost. Carole Nelson, proprietor of The Sleepy Elephant Bookshop and Emporium in Sedbergh (personal interview, 2011), states:

> People fancy things. It's the chance. It's the luck. We always use the simile that its treasure hunting and usually the treasures people are hunting for are a memory from childhood, or adolescence or from a relation, something that meant a lot to them. Because the memory had to do with a book and the book's gone, they're always trying to find that book again, and they wander all over the country in bookshops looking for that book. They like the chase, but book collecting's a very gentle thing.

Other bookseller interviewees also reported that their clients often sought familiar book jackets to enable them to relive their childhoods—visually as well as experientially.

Every reader's bookshelf is different. A collection of books uniquely defines or 'makes' the person,[5] and the uniqueness of each reader is reflected in their personal library or 'intellectual genome' (Zaid 2004, p. 11). Hill (2009, p. 2) reflects:

> What a strange person I must be. But if the books I have read have helped to form me, then probably no-one else who ever lived has read exactly the same books, all the same books and only the same books, as me. So just as my genes and the soul within me make me uniquely me, so I am the unique sum of the books I have read. I am my literary DNA.

The origins of this idea of literary DNA can be traced back to Samuel Taylor Coleridge's *Biographia Literaria*, where he describes his evolution as a human being. In one of a series of biographical letters written to his friend Thomas Poole in 1797, Coleridge wrote (in Sutherland 2009, p. iv):

> At six years old I remember to have read Belisarius, Robinson Crusoe, and Phillip Quarll, and then I found the Arabian Nights' Entertainments, one [erotic] tale of which ... made so deep an impression on me (I had read it in the evening while my mother was mending stockings) that I was haunted by spectres whenever I was in the dark, and I distinctly remember the anxious and fearful eagerness with which I used to watch the window in which the books lay, and whenever the sun lay upon them, I would seize it, carry it by the wall, and bask, and read.

Sutherland comments on this vignette, in which the poet remembers his mother darning the socks and the sun falling on the books in the window bay, likening the book to a time machine that takes the reader back to the moment a book was read (Sutherland 2009). Similarly, Melbourne antiquarian book dealer Anthony Marshall (2004, p. 281) claims that 'sifting through your book collection is like seeing your whole life in flashback; so many memories and associations'.

The reasons for building a large collection of books are almost as varied as the people who collect them. 'With thought, patience and discrimination, book passion becomes the signature of a person's character,' states Basbanes in *A Gentle Madness: Bibliophiles, Bibliomanes and the Eternal Passion for Books* (1995), his richly anecdotal celebration of book collecting. Manguel (1997, p. 237) delights in

> knowing that I'm surrounded by a sort of inventory of my life, with intimations of my future. I like discovering in almost forgotten volumes, traces of the reader I once was – scribbles, bus tickets, scraps of paper with mysterious names and numbers, the occasional date and place on a book's flyleaf which takes me back to a certain café, and a distant hotel room, a faraway summer so long ago.

Australian journalist Phillip Adams (2012, p. 38) recollects a life that has run in parallel with the books he has collected: 'Sometimes I remember the very bookshop I bought them in – often the second-hand shops I haunted as a child ... We've grown old together ... Books are … the bricks with which you've built your brain.' Walker (2010, p. 21), meanwhile, attributes a lifetime's book passion to overcoming serious illness and developing the inner strength to overcome life's obstacles:

> make an honest platform of story in your mind, like a raft, using the sound timber of everything you've loved and read. As with any raft, it may sometimes feel unsteady; it may falter under the weight it must carry, and, over time, it will need repair. It may not withstand the sea for all eternity, but nor does it need to – it needs to last a lifespan, nothing more. For the time that it does hold together, you can stand on it like Robinson Crusoe and look back at the site of your own shipwreck, and you can say to yourself, as he did, grateful for being able to say it, 'I am here, not there.'

The overriding compulsion that governs the actions and attitudes of individuals is therefore the pursuit of a desired identity. In this way, Ulin (2010, p. 11) talks of books providing both an escape and an enhanced sense of self: 'What I was after … was not merely an escape but also a point of entry, a passport or a series of passports, not to an older version of myself but to a different version – to the person I wanted to become.' Reading becomes an extension of self, with Fadiman (1998, pp. ix–x) in *Ex Libris* thus stressing that the model of readers as simply consumers omits 'how we maintain our connections with our old books, the ones we have lived with for years, the ones whose textures and colours and smells have become as familiar to us as our children's skin'. Our sense of the past and the part played in our lives by books is historical and cultural, but also familial. Books are intrinsically linked to individual or family mythology. In cases where children are read to and where books are part of the family's daily routine, a mythology arises from the early books that shape the child's imagination. Characters become companions, embedded in family anecdotes that 'people a child's inner landscape' (Hill 2009, p. 195). A book collection, moreover, is inseparable from its creator. As Walter Benjamin identifies, the phenomenon of a collection loses its meaning as it is detached from its personal owner (2007, p. 67).

Old Books and Their Capacity to Reawaken the Past

Through recent studies of objects and materiality, it is evident there are significant 'sociologies of sensory formations' (Bartmanski and Woodward 2015, p. xxii) that link objects with the nostalgia of earlier times. Organic objects in the digital world retain the possibility of intimate connection. The sensual appeal of old books, for example, provides a richly evocative experience that should not be overlooked, as Classen (2012), Kurschus (2015, p. 56) and Rodger (2008) argue. The smell of a book may stimulate our senses—whether it be the book's newness, mustiness or its aroma of leather. Scientific studies have determined that the distinctive smell of old books is due to the gradual decay of hundreds of volatile organic compounds that make up components of books in paper, ink and adhesives. When the chemicals are released, there are traces of almond, vanilla, sweet flowers and 'grassy notes' created by chemicals including benzaldehyde, vanillin and ethyl benzene, respectively, combined with an underlying mustiness that varies as a result of a book's past and present environment (Strlic et al. 2009, p. 8617). This unmistakeable smell is as much a part of the book as its contents. While new books also have a distinctive aroma, it is not as developed. The creation of a perfume named Paper Passion, which was presented at the Design Fair in Milan, certifies the chemical appeal of the smell of books (Kurschus 2015, p. 57). As Bartmanski and Woodward (2015) claim about vinyl records, antiquarian books espouse a materialism that is warm, humane, magical and sensual, providing evidence that progress is not perfectly linear. Likewise, it is despite rather than because of digitalization that antiquarian books continue to make sense and provide relevance. It is not possible to remove human agency from an old book's physical and cultural evolution: the human element linking people and technology prompts the ongoing yearning for tactile engagement with the book in paper form. Antiquarian books are regarded in certain circles as sacred formats and enduring icons of material culture. Their rich history, authenticity and positioning in relation to digital mediums make them central to the sustainability of the Book Town Movement.

The excitement of discovery is also a key feature of book collecting. For example, Benjamin (2007, pp. 59–61) describes his disposition as he unpacks his books after they have been stored for a period of time as 'not an elegiac mood but, rather, one of anticipation which these books arouse in a genuine collector', and explains that unpacking them is like rediscovering them all over again. He speaks about collecting in an active sense, rather than about the resulting collection; it is the *act* of collecting that excites him. The childlike elements of collecting, the 'magical', 'whimsical' and 'renewing experience', comparable to the discovery a child feels when touching and naming items, or creating with paint and paper, are an important part of Benjamin's experience as a bibliophile. Gathering the last item in a specific collection is like recreating a unique and precious juxtaposition of artefacts, and might be likened to completing a mosaic or puzzle. Benjamin (1999, p. 205) refers to this process as a kind of 'enchantment': 'to enclose the particular item within a magic circle where, as a last shudder runs through it (the shudder of being acquired) it turns to stone'. The watchful dreaminess of Benjamin's writings, as they meander through the bourgeois experience of nineteenth-century history, conveys the special power and even magical significance of books that, in part, have faded with the industrial age. The Book Town Movement, in a comparable way, provides an avenue for the preservation of traditional print culture and a reawakening of the past in this current age of new technology and globalization.

The idea of the reawakening of books and other objects from the past is central to Benjamin's *The Arcades Project* (1999) where, taken up into the collector's own time, space and 'divinatory gaze', a light is thrown on what has previously been, and the item is 'actualized' or reawakened from the past into the present moment—'reborn' and 'recognized':

> In the dusty cluttered corridors of the arcades, where street and interior are one, historical time is broken up into kaleidoscopic distractions and momentary come-ons, myriad displays of ephemera, thresholds for the passage of what Gérard de Nerval (in *Aurélia*) calls 'the ghosts of material things'. Here, at a distance from what is normally meant by 'progress', is the ur-historical, collective redemption of lost time, of the times embedded in the space of things. (Eiland and McLaughlin, in Benjamin 1999, p. xii)

Possession of objects is linked to their tactility, but the collecting of them is also related to what Benjamin (1999, p. 883) calls 'practical memory, and … all the profane manifestations of "what has been" … We construct here an alarm clock that rouses the kitsch of the previous century to "assembly".' Old books thus awaken us and help us remember: they deliver a 'reversal from the world of dreaming to the world of waking' (p. 884). To understand the rich vein of our history, he suggests, we should consult the 'refuse' and 'detritus' of our past, which relies on chance, depending on the serendipitous methods of collectors rather than historians (Eiland and McLaughlin, in Benjamin 1999, p. ix). Benjamin also flags that books are different from all other collectibles: the bibliophile is a unique species of collector who does not entirely withdraw the treasures from their functional context (p. 207).

Benjamin's *The Arcades Project* is testimony to him being *un rat de biblioteque*—mostly he would pass the day in libraries or read feverishly in his room late into the night (Clark 2000). He savoured Paris because it was both up to date and old-fashioned, with the two conditions coexisting street by street or shop by shop. It was possible for Benjamin to take a detour through the streets of 1860s Paris each morning on his way to work: a cultural experience loosely comparable with the inexhaustible blend of old and new found in a book town like Hay-on-Wye, and dozens of towns like it around the world.

A habit of randomness is another characteristic of the bibliophile and avid collector, which is surprising because large collections of books frequently are associated with Dewey library systems and other means of systematizing books into painstaking order. Benjamin, however, reflects on the 'accustomed confusion' of his books: 'every passion borders on the chaotic, but the collector's passion borders on the chaos of memories,' he confesses; and he asks, 'For what else is this collection but a disorder to which habit has accommodated itself to such an extent that it can appear as order?' (Benjamin 1999, p. 60). This 'randomness' is on display in the many secondhand and antiquarian bookshops in book towns I visited as part of this study. In his Hay-on-Wye memoir, *Sixpence House*, Paul

Collins (2003, p. 147) describes working among the haphazardly stacked bookshelves of Booth's Bookshop in Lion Street:

> I am stymied by the piles of books blocking the shelves I need to get to and finally just cram books down behind the mounds of books, hoping they'll miraculously land on the right shelf ... This place is meant to be chaotic. It cannot be anything else, as it exceeds the patience of ten men.

Likewise, Minet (1989, 115) recounts a disorder in Hay-on-Wye that has become simply 'the way things are done':

> Wandering around Hay the other day, I was struck by the identity that the place has acquired as almost a Ghormenghast of books. One comes across distant bays and corridors of books in which some eager employee has slaved to complete some catalogue, or heap books up on some subject, or even file long-forgotten orders, only to be transferred elsewhere or depart for the outside world, leaving the sum of his endeavours to gather dust, until some remote successor disassembles his work to repeat the operation elsewhere. Only when some more adventurous than usual bookseller or librarian such as myself ventures in, lost, perhaps, on the way to some known section, does the pattern get temporarily broken.

McMurtry (2011) advises that when establishing a secondhand bookstore, it is important to leave stacks of books in piles on the floor as the book collector will gravitate to these rather than to ordered shelves. While there is some alphabetization throughout Booked Up in Archer City, he doesn't believe in too much order. According to signs posted about the town, books are organized 'Erratically/Impressionistically/Whimsically/Open to Interpretation', and therefore *Moby Dick* could feasibly be located in American Fiction, Animals, Nautical, Fishing and Hunting, or Travel (Clark 2009). From my observation of people in the rabbit warrens that comprise many secondhand bookshops in book towns, it is apparent that the disarray created by teetering stacks of volumes on the floor and piled on chairs makes the experience of book browsing more like a treasure hunt, and therefore far more appealing. As well as the conflict between order and disorder, the bibliophile is likely to face the internal conflict between excessive purchasing and the cost of doing so, described by Zaid (2004, p. 11) as the conversation between 'the excesses of graphomania and the excesses of commerce, between the sprawl of chaos and the concentration of the market'.

The very materiality of the book is therefore central to any debate about the viability of books and book towns, and why books are collected. Steffens (2009, p. vii) describes books as having a quality of permanence, suggesting that they can be compared with buildings: 'There is a responsibility if you are to design something that is meant to last that brings the book close to architecture, because architecture is meant to last, and before it comes to form it comes to function.' The book as a historic artefact is at least as old as any other human construction, and definitely the most common. More books survive from every period of the world's history than all other items of antiquity grouped together (Barker 2001, p. 179). Collins (2003, pp. 205–6) also uses the metaphor of architecture to describe large numbers of books housed together: 'To see any library, any bookstore, any archive, is like seeing a city: you are viewing buildings constructed atop the unknown and unknowable cities that once were and might have been.' Book collections, often housed in magnificent libraries, have drawn people to particular geographic locations and changed lives throughout the centuries:

> Writing and the books that contain those writings have exerted a talismanic effect on humankind for millennia. From even before classical times and the construction of the Library of Alexandria, and then later with the growth of the monastic libraries and the establishment of the university towns of northern Italy and western Europe, great collections of books have drawn mankind to them. (McShane 2002, p. 4)

Books amassed together in places such as large libraries or well-stocked bookshops can evoke the hallowed experience of visiting a church or cathedral. Jacques de Decker[6] uses the image of a *cathedrale de livres* to describe the book town of Redu. Merfeld-Langston (2007, pp. 136–8) believes this metaphor is revealing because, just as cathedrals are sacred places that house holy relics (books, here) and welcome the faithful devotees who come to worship, so in book towns the faithful range from the pilgrim or tourist to the dedicated bibliophile with varying degrees of devotion. Book towns provide a sanctuary for their visitors, but are also the result of immense achievement requiring patience, dedication and vision by their creators. Book towns are far more than simple clusters of bookshops: they are dynamic communities centring on the appreciation—and even the worship—of books and the historical arts associated with crafting books by hand.

While the notion of the book town and its applicability to current political, social, cultural and economic thinking ensures its contemporary relevance, contemporary book towns share a connection with other locations throughout history where large numbers of texts have been accumulated and housed together. The Mauritanian town of Chinguetti, once a key settlement along the trade route of the Sahara Desert and an intellectual centre the origins of which extend back to the eighth century, was arguably the first town of books. This township had a vast collection of 40,000 manuscripts—many of them scientific and Koranic texts—dating back hundreds of years, brought there by merchants and pilgrims en route to Mecca. UNESCO has chosen Chinguetti as a world heritage site along with three of its neighbouring villages. Chinguetti is twinned with French book town Fontenoy-la-Joûte (Merfeld-Langston 2007, p. 2). Another early example is Timbucktu in Mali which, as well as being a legendary and exotic location, was once a significant centre of learning. Following the building of a number of mosques and madrasas in the fifteenth century, it gradually accumulated one of the finest collections of scholarly manuscripts in existence. These ancient documents are now preserved in the Ahmed Baba Institute, thanks to the philanthropic support of Bill Gates and others (Saikia 2010, p. 88). In 2007, Timbuktu was twinned with Hay-on-Wye, in recognition of this earlier book town precedent.

For as long as there have been books, collectors have sought value where there appears to be none, culling historic items from piles of refuse to the benefit of society, and performing 'an inestimable service to literature' (Burton, in Basbanes 1995, p. 17). Through their accumulation of antiquarian and secondhand books, book towns play their own role in the process of cultural filtering. McMurtry regards the countless thousands of books he has gathered together in Archer City, Texas, as

> a kind of anthology of bookshops past – remnants of twenty-two [defunct] bookshops now reside there … I still believe that books are the fuel of genius. Leaving a million or so in Archer City is as good a legacy as I can think of for that region and indeed, for the West. (1999, p. 179)

The large collections of books that are in totality in book towns may be regarded as significant legacies that their eccentric founders, governments or collective creators have inspired and engineered to pay tribute to both the literary past and the creative future of their regions.

Old Books Were Once New Books

To some extent, the future of book towns is reliant on current trends in new book publishing (Berkelouw, personal interview, 2012) that, on the surface, appear promising for the secondhand and rare book sector. A recent resurgence in sales of collectable hard-cover titles as well as digital books at the expense of paperbacks reflects a shift in consumer behaviour (Kean 2012). E-books may actually create more demand for the paper versions, and for an enduring version of that reading experience (Osmond, in Sorensen 2009; Sheahan-Bright, personal interview, 2011). Secondhand bookstores also benefit from the fact that new books only 'last' for 90 days, meaning that if you seek to locate a backlist title, you are unlikely to find it in a shop selling new books; therefore, millions of readable books are only available through the secondhand market (Muller, personal interview, 2010). Cost is another important factor, and knowledgeable secondhand and antiquarian dealers are often located at the highly profitable end of the market where they can sell a book for a considerably higher price than they bought it for. However, despite these advantages, Gekowski (2011), Marshall (2004), McMurtry (2008) and others predict that the secondhand book sub-sector, at least in the city, is under considerable long-term threat. Marshall, a Melbourne antiquarian bookshop proprietor, laments:

> People still read but for many – especially younger people – the book is a disposable item, a perishable, consumable commodity, an encumbrance

> even. Buy it, read it, toss it. And the days of settled families, living out their lives in one rambling house, are gone. People travel, they get divorced, they move house, they change jobs and partners, they tend to live in small apartments or units. This is not an environment to encourage book hoarding. It may be a temporary hiccough; or it may not be. (Marshall 2004, p. 266)

In all the book towns I visited, antiquarian and secondhand books predominated, but they coexisted with new bookshops that provided buying opportunities for those seeking newly released titles. Berkelouw Books, Australia's largest antiquarian and rare book business, for example, has 'taken the plunge' and is now also selling new books. This was a necessary step for the business because in places like Bowral in the Southern Highlands of New South Wales and Eumundi in Queensland's Sunshine Coast hinterland, people want to buy the book that's being talked about and reviewed (Berkelouw, personal interview, 2012). However, the new book sector is fraught with challenges, and in Australia profitability is shrinking due to parallel importing in particular—a result of the variable global economy, which Australian governments have failed to overturn.[7] Books and their survival are important to the future of secondhand books, and the falling by the wayside of the bigger book chains has provided a valuable boost to independent bookshops in Australia.[8] Bookshopping as a destination experience is not quite as popular as it once was in the experience of businesses like Berkelouw, due to conflicting demands on people's time and because books are considered non-essential items. Leo Berkelouw therefore spends more time directly contacting book collectors about items of potential interest than assuming collectors will come to his shops on their own initiative (Berkelouw, personal interview, 2012).

To analyse the importance of the book as a unique commodity at the heart of the book town phenomenon, a study of the viability of all aspects of books, publicity and engagement with print culture is relevant. In Australia, the independent bookshop sector's performance has been comparatively robust over more than a decade,[9] today representing approximately 27% of the market (Small Press Network 2016), up from 20% in 2011 (Akerman 2011, p. 3). In 2011, this compared favourably with both the United States and United Kingdom, where there was approximately 10% market share. However, between 2009 and 2016, while the number of independent bookstores in the United States increased by 27%, filling the gap of the demise of Borders and other superstores, the reverse occurred in the United Kingdom and the Republic of Ireland, where numbers plummeted by 25%. This downward spiral has now stopped, partly as a result of independent bookstores diversifying and adapting, and there are indications of a recovery in physical book sales, something that has surprised those in the mainstream media who had repeatedly predicted the imminent death of the book.[10] Australia's relative stability can be explained partly by the ongoing role of the independent bookshop in our cultural fabric as a place of discovery, and because many customers still seek a face-to-face experience:

> One thing the Book Depository or Amazon can't provide is the experience of a physical, community-based bookshop: it's committed staff, whose vocation bookselling is; the community of writers and readers that forms around it; and the genuine commitment to the life of words that represents. (Shaw 2011)

The enduring strength of the independent bookstore is the human experience it offers, and the environment for conversation a true book lover will initiate with either the bookseller or other customers in the store—an experience not available online or in large chain stores without experienced staff. Browsing is a social activity—physicality and tactility are essential for a vibrant place. In the appropriate geographical situation, bookshop culture is important to both social and cultural aspects of the community:

> Bookstores thrive in towns that foster education and the arts, that treasure their history, that don't turn their noses up at things that are quirky or different. People who live in these communities crave intellectual stimulation, and they see their independent bookshops as being at the centre of that need – a place to lose yourself in a good book (or is that find yourself?), to meet friends, to share ideas, to discuss current events. Sure, they may not have as many books as a two-storey corporate franchise, but they have something much more valuable: personality, individuality and a passion for the written word rather than the bottom line. (Portzline 2004, p. 10)

The considerable differences between independent book stores can be attributed to the personalities and priorities of their owners. Book lovers may enter with a particular purchase in mind, or just as often may wish to be stimulated by what is on display or what the bookseller personally recommends. In the case of books, often people don't know what they want to purchase, and while online sites invest enormous sums in software that suggests products customers may like, this cannot match the experience of immersion in a bookstore. The survival of independent stores relies on the need for third places, as discussed in Chap. 3:

> A[n independent] bookshop is like the old village well, where people can gather and have shared experiences … We like to see ourselves as more of a lifestyle business. You can come in and have a coffee, buy a book, sit on the couch and read, and in the evenings hear and meet your favourite writers. Independent bookstores have staff that know and love books. For the best advice on what's available, you still go to a local bookshop. (Concannon, in Brown 2011, p. 13)

Bookshop proprietors emphasize the importance of developing strong community networks, recommending nimble and creative thinking, focusing on author book signings, events and launches, lunchtime book chat sessions for young children and in-store book clubs, as well as embracing new technologies including social media, webs, blogging and e-books (Perkin 2010, p. 7). Beginning in 2011, hundreds of bookshops around Australia have celebrated National Bookshop Day on 20 August (Page 2013), marking the contribution of bookshops to the local economy, each bookshop's uniqueness, the visual and tactile experience they provide and their considerable value to Australian literature, culture and society. Independent bookshops reflect the diversity and individuality of their book-loving clientele, acting as important proxies for the community (Gould, personal interview, 2017; Glaas 2011) and providing a valuable form of literary profiling.

Books occupy a central place in the history and development of the Book Town Movement, and this chapter has revealed why books are both unusual and unique items of cultural consumption. Commentators such as Miller (2006, pp. 148–9) question whether we live in an epoch in which

> the bookshop is an institution suspended between 'the dying old society' and the 'society struggling to be born' ... It has few defenders ... Perhaps the bookshop belongs to the good things of the bourgeois epoch, like the rule of law, representative institutions, public liberties and the right of the *habeas corpus*, things from which there is a general benefit but which have been so much taken for granted that their beneficiaries have grown careless about their well-being ...

While that may be true in some urban precincts, books in book towns remain a privileged form of communication—one in which the genius of the written word can be embodied in an object that is at once a medium of expression, a means of communication and a work of art.

Books and their centrality to the global Book Town Movement affirm the importance of books in our lives. Many admirers of the hard-copy book who I met in book towns and through personal interviews for this research commented on the uniquely lasting nature of the book, its accessibility to all and its ability to be sentimentalized and personalized. In the words of Buzbee (2006, p. 202), 'The flexible and durable technology of the printed book – its quiet sensuality in the rustle of the pages – is still evidently desirable ... How do you press a wildflower into the pages of an e-book?' Books are laden with powerful associations—a familiar title will spark recognition; an idea or conversation will be recalled. Each book collection is unique and informs its owner's experience in surprising ways. Our traditional notion of a book is of a physical object, precious even if no longer hand-copied on sheepskin by cloistered monks. The very real boundaries of a book's materiality stand in contrast to the unlimited existence of the internet, leading to an experience of sensuality and an idealization of the book's materiality (Kurschus 2015, p. 56). For all these reasons, and others illustrated in this chapter, it is clear that the brilliant simplicity of the book is still valued in book towns, and the book remains regarded as a highly efficient random access device.

When books as artefacts unlike any other are amassed together in small rural locales, they are the change agents that make possible the re-emergence of territorial identities and 'personalities'. It is the infinite numbers of books that draw collectors and contemporary travellers, who in turn relish the local history, terrain and symbolically laden sites that are converted into distinctive regional place profiles. Over the last 20 years, thriving book towns have drawn on a common formula of success factors initially blueprinted by Tony Seaton for the judging of Scotland's National Book Town. As the next chapter demonstrates, those unable to ensure that their ventures were profitable and sustainable over time failed in part or in whole to take into account the combination of elements that contemporary travellers desire in a biblio-tourism experience.

Notes

1. Refer to https://www.bookedupac.com
2. City of Archer City, http://www.archercity.org/about-archercity.html
3. The sixteenth-century French nobleman Jean Grolier de Servières of Lyons, a man dedicated to beautiful books and bindings, collected a distinctive style of binding designs sourced during many diplomatic missions to Italy. Grolier possessed one of the finest private libraries of his time (and possibly any other time), consisting of some 3000 volumes contained within bindings of superlative richness and beauty. Grolier is considered the first modern bibliophile (Basbanes 1995, p. 81).
4. Sociologist and collector Professor Adrian Franklin was a panel member on the Australian ABC television series *Collectors* (2005–2011), which reinvigorated interest in collecting in Australia, including the 2012 Queensland Museum interactive exhibition *What Do You Collect?* See http://www.whatdoyoucollect.com.au
5. The close connection between books and memory and the book collector's 'DNA' is analysed by Hill (2009, p. 202), Marshall (2004, p. 281), Fadiman (1998, pp. ix–xi, 122), Zaid (2004, p. 11), Basbanes (1995, p. 9), Hazlitt (1928, p. 221), Steffens (2009, p. viii), Spufford (2002, p. 9) and a host of others.
6. Jacques de Decker, one time secretaire perpetual de l'Academie royale de langue et literature francaise de Belgique, wrote the preface to Nöel Anselot's (2004) book town memoir, *Redu*.
7. Australian bookshop proprietors are forced to buy from the Australian representatives of overseas publishing houses who dictate the price. According to Berkelouw, Australian book prices are much too high—a situation that needs to change (personal interview, 2012).

8. However, as previously explained, this is not necessarily the case in nations such as the United Kingdom and the United States.
9. For example, the total value of book sales in Australia grew by an annual average of 5.2% from 2005 to 2010—far higher than the growth rates in comparable international markets such as Canada, the United States and the United Kingdom, and other comparable Australian sectors such as creative industries (PriceWaterhouseCoopers Report 2011, quoted in White 2011, p. 3).
10. Refer to 'The State and Future of Independent Bookselling in the UK'. Ribbonfish, 17 June 2016, https://www.ribbonfish.co.uk/blog/the-state-and-future-of-independent-bookselling-in-the-uk

References

Adams, P. (2012, February 4). Shelf life. *The Weekend Australian Magazine*, p. 38.

Akerman, P. (2011, February 19–20). It's the human touch that matters for minnows: Bookshops have something the internet doesn't – Direct contact with people. *The Weekend Australian*, p. 3.

Anselot, N. (2004). *Redu: Un Village a Livres Ouverts: La Merveilleuse Histoire du Premier Village du Livre d'Europe Continentale*. Brussels: Editions Racine.

Barker, N. (2001). *A potencie for life: Books in society*. London: British Library Publishing.

Bartmanski, D., & Woodward, I. (2015). *Vinyl: The analogue record in the digital age*. London: Bloomsbury.

Basbanes, N. A. (1995). *A gentle madness: Bibliophiles, bibliomanes, and the eternal passion for books*. New York: Henry Holt.

Benjamin, W. (1999). *The Arcades Project*. Cambridge, MA: Belknap Press.

Benjamin, W. (2007 [1968]). Unpacking my library: A talk about book collecting. In *Illuminations: Essays and reflections* (pp. 59–67). New York: Schocken Books.

Benjamin, W. (2008). *The work of art in the age of its technological reproductivity and other writings on media*. Cambridge, MA: Belknap Press.

Brown, P. (2011, March 16–22). Brought to book: The printed page's days seem to be numbered. *Brisbane News*.

Buzbee, L. (2006). *The yellow-lighted bookshop: A memoir, a history*. Saint Paul: Graywolf Press.

Campbell, C. (1987). *The Romantic ethic and the spirit of modern consumerism*. Oxford: Basil Blackwell.

Clark, T. J. (2000). Reservation of the marvellous: *The Arcades Project* by Walter Benjamin. *London Review of Books, 22*(12), 3–9.

Clark, B. L. (2009, March 19). Cross border raid for books. *The Exile Bibliophile: Adventures in Book Collecting and Ephemera* [Weblog]. http://exilebibliophile.blogspot.com.au/2009/03/cross-border-raid-for-books.html. Accessed 17 Aug 2010.

Classen, C. (2012). *The deepest sense: A cultural history of touch*. Urbana: University of Illinois Press.

Collins, P. (2003). *Sixpence House: Lost in a town of books*. New York: Bloomsbury.

Disruption and innovation in the Australian book industry. (2016, February 9). Small Press Network. http://smallpressnetwork.com.au/australian-publishing-industry-is-fighting-back-against-digital-disruption. Accessed 8 Apr 2017.

Fadiman, A. (1998). *Ex Libris: Confessions of a common reader*. Harmondsworth: Penguin.

Franklin, A. (2008). *A collector's year*. Sydney: UNSW Press.

Gekowski, R. (2011, March 9). A fond farewell to secondhand bookshops. *The Guardian* [Books]. http://www.guardian.co.uk/books/booksblog/2011/mar/09/farewell-secondhand-bookshops. Accessed 12 Mar 2011.

Glaas, W. (2011, August 8). My name is Wendy and I'm a bookstore junkie. *Talking Writing: A Magazine for Writers*. http://talkingwriting.com/?p=22196. Accessed 18 Aug 2011.

Goldstone, L., & Goldstone, N. (1997). *Used and rare: Travels in the book world*. New York: St Martin's Press.

Hazlitt, W. (1928). On reading old books. In *The plain speaker: Opinions on books, men and things* (pp. 220–229). London: J.M. Dent and Sons.

Hill, S. (2009). *Howards End is on the landing: A year of reading from home*. London: Profile Books.

Horowitz, M. (1997, 12 July 12). Larry McMurtry's dream job. *New York Times* [Books]. http://www.nytimes.com/books/97/12/07/home/article2.html?_r=5. Accessed 7 Aug 2010.

Huckans, J. C. (2005, July/August). Book town revisited. *Book Source Magazine*. http://www.booksourcemagazine.com/showstory.php?sid=archive/e0507. Accessed 31 Oct 2009.

Jones, K. (1997, December). I've written enough fiction. *Texas Monthly*. http://www.texasmonthly.com/1997-12-01/feature6.php. Accessed 10 Aug 2010.

Jones, K. (1998, August). Larry McMurtry's next career. *Biblio* [USA], p. 50.

Kean, D. (2012). Ebooks: The unlikely saviour of the hardback. *Danuta Kean* [Weblog]. http://talkingwriting.com/my-name-is-wendy-and-im-a-bookstore-junkie. Accessed 1 Apr 2012.

Kells, S. (2011). *Rare: A life among antiquarian books*. Sydney: Folio.

Kurschus, S. (2015). *European book cultures: Diversity as a challenge*. Heidelberg: Springer.

Lindenberger, M. (2012, August 15). The great book sale of Texas: Larry McMurtry gives up his collection. *Time*, TIME.com. http://nation.time.com/2012/08/15/the-great-book-sale-of-texas-larry-mcmurtry-gives-up-his-collection. Accessed 4 July 2013.

Manguel, A. (1996). *The library at night*. New Haven: Yale University Press.

Manguel, A. (1997). *A history of reading*. London: Flamingo.

Marshall, A. (2004). *Fossicking for old books*. Melbourne: Bread Street Press.

McMurtry, L. (1999). *Walter Benjamin at the Dairy Queen: Reflections at sixty and beyond*. New York: Simon & Schuster.

McMurtry, L. (2008). *Books: A memoir*. New York: Simon & Schuster.

McMurtry, L. (2009a, January 20). Interview with Fritz Lanham. 'Author Larry McMurtry sees the end of book culture'. *Chron* [USA]. http://www.chron.com/disp/story.mpl/headline/features/6221607.html. Accessed 31 Aug 2010.

McMurtry, L. (2009b). *Literary life: A second memoir*. New York: Simon & Schuster.

McMurtry, L. (2011, September 22). How to run a bookstore: Neatness doesn't count. *Bloomberg Businessweek*. http://www.businessweek.com/printer/magazine/how-to-run-a-bookstore-09222011.html. Accessed 1 Oct 2011.

McShane, P. (2002). *To further Australia's understanding and involvement in the international booktown movement through a program of visits and interviews*. Winston Churchill Memorial Trust of Australia. http://www.booktown.com.au/ChurchillReport_Booktowns_2002.htm. Accessed 27 Feb 2010.

Merfeld-Langston, A. L. (2007). The *villages du livre*: Local identity, cultural politics and print culture in contemporary France. PhD thesis, Pennsylvania State University.

Merfeld-Langston, A. L. (2010). Celebrating literature to shape citizenship: France's 2007 *Lire en fête*. *Modern and Contemporary France, 18*(3), 343–356.

Miller, L. J. (2006). *Reluctant capitalists: Bookselling and the culture of consumption*. Chicago: University of Chicago Press.

Minet, P. (1989). *Late booking: My first twenty-five years in the secondhand book trade*. Old Knowle: Frantic Press.

Page, J. (2013, July 28). National bookshop day 2013 – In locations across Australia, bookshops will be celebrating. *Bite the book: Book reviews and industry views*. http://bitethebook.com/2013/07/28/national-bookshop-day-2013. Accessed 30 July 2013.

Perkin, C. (2010, July 24–25). Digital or not, a book is still a book. *The Weekend Australian* [Inquirer], p. 7.

Portzline, L. (2004). *Bookstore tourism: The book addict's guide to planning & promoting bookstore road trips for bibliophiles and other bookshop junkies*. Harrisburg: Bookshop Junkie Press.

Roberts, J. C. (2009, January). A Visit to Archer City: The site of *The Last Picture Show* doubles as a book-collecting mecca. *Caxtonian* [USA]. http://www.caxtonclub.org/reading/2009/jan09.pdf. Accessed 17 Aug 2010.

Rodger, N. (2008). Judging books by their covers: An examination of books as auratic objects in a digital era. BA (Hons) thesis, RMIT University.

Saikia, R. (2010). *Blue guide to Hay-on-Wye*. Taunton: Blue Guides.

Sartre, J.-P. (1964). *Words*. Harmondsworth: Penguin.

Shaw, M. (2011, January 19). A paler world: Book culture in a jiffy bag? *Killings: The Kill Your Darlings Blog* [weblog]. http://www.killyourdarlingsjournal.com/2011/01/1-paler-world-book-culture-in-a-jiffy-bag. Accessed 22 May 2011.

Sorensen, R. (2009, April 11–12). Reading the future. *The Weekend Australian Review*.

Spufford, F. (2002). *The child that books built*. London: Faber and Faber.

Steffens, J. (Ed.). (2009). *Unpacking my library: Architects and their books: Featuring an essay by Walter Benjamin*. New Haven: Yale University Press.

Striphas, T. (2009). *The late age of print: Everyday book culture from consumerism to control*. New York: Columbia University Press.

Strlic, M., Thomas, J., Trafela, T., Cséfalvayová, L., Kralj Cigić, I., Kolar, J., & Cassar, M. (2009). Material degradomics: On the smell of old books. *Analytical Chemistry, 81*(20), 8617–8622.

Sutherland, J. (2009, January 26). Interview with Ramona Koval, 'Magic Moments: Life Changing Encounters with Books, Music and Film'. *The Book Show,* ABC Radio National. http://www.abc.net.au/rn/bookshow/stories/2009/2770765.htm. Accessed 14 Apr 2011.

Ulin, D. (2010). *The lost art of reading: Why books matter in a distracted time*. Seattle: Sasquatch Books.

Urry, J. (2002). *The tourist gaze*. London: Sage.

Walker, B. (2010). *Reading by moonlight: How books saved a life*. Melbourne: Hamish Hamilton.

White, L. (2011, November 12–13). Franchise expansion good for readers. *The Weekend Australian* [Weekend Professional], p. 3.
Zaid, G. (2004). *So many books*. London: Sort of Books.

Interviews

Berkelouw, Leo. Eumundi, Queensland, 14 August 2012.
Gould, Lincoln. Wellington, New Zealand, 8 February 2017.
Muller, Laurie. Brisbane, Queensland, 17 August 2010 and 7 September 2010.
Nelson, Carole. Sedbergh, Yorkshire, United Kingdom, 9 September 2011; phone interview, 29 March 2017.
Sheahan-Bright, Robyn. Gladstone, Queensland, 24 August 2010.
Schiotz, Peter. Maleny, Queensland, 4 April 2012.

6

Occasional Errata: Book Towns That Fail or Falter

Only a small number of book town projects have failed, and in this chapter I demonstrate by close analysis of these examples that book towns cannot remain sustainable in circumstances where there is a congruence of geographical, social, cultural, financial, managerial and logistical challenges. In favourable circumstances, book towns offer exemplary models of sustainable peripheral tourism. The previous chapter demonstrated that the concept's success lies not only in the 'power of the secondhand economy' (Seaton 1999, p. 397), but also specifically in the particular essence, aura and material qualities possessed by books, as an unusually powerful sub-set of the secondhand economy. Books—which of course are at the heart of book town enterprises—are the inspiration for the clustering of bookshops, but also the ensuing chain of associated fairs, festivals, launches, author talks, workshops and other events, in a manner that would not draw a same degree of national and international attention if the focus were instead, for example, on vintage clothing or antiques. This is because books and book culture are culturally and socially significant in these peripheral hubs, and more is at stake than economic revival and the establishment of businesses. This is why it is important to address the issue of book town failure in a comprehensive account of the Book Town Movement.

J. Frank, *Regenerating Regional Culture*, Sociology of the Arts,
https://doi.org/10.1007/978-3-319-65036-4_6

At first glance, there would seem to be merit in any attempt to revive rural economies through book town developments, and Landry (2008, p. 10) has advocated 'creating something out of nothing' using a particular site-specific specialization to generate distinctiveness, which burgeoning book towns have certainly done. In the establishment of a book town, innovative and imaginative responses to varied demands involve risk and the possibility of failure, a condition shared with many other cultural projects. Officially, failure seldom occurs and is not frequently discussed. Yet Landry (2008, pp. 115, 152) argues that reflecting on the failure of cultural projects can be beneficial because a focus centred only on success can lead to complacency. In my interviews with book town founders and leaders (including McShane, personal interview 2010; Nelson, personal interview 2011; Turpin, personal interview 2011), there was acute awareness of the shortcomings of the three failed UK book towns—Blaenafon in Wales, Atherstone in England and Dalmellington in Scotland. An understanding of the specifics of those failures had become a learning device for their own projects. Landry distinguishes between competent and incompetent failure, linking incompetent failure to a lack of understanding of local circumstances and the causes of ineffectiveness, as well as a broad level of thoughtlessness. Incompetence of this type, he states, repeats acknowledged failures (2008, p. 152), and I would argue that this occurred when James Hanna—the entrepreneur who instigated the Blaenafon and Atherstone initiatives—failed to learn from the difficulties in Blaenafon, meaning that the Atherstone project, which commenced later, had no real chance of success.

However, it is important to clarify that sometimes failures are partially attributable to governments and other stakeholders. Governments have an obligation to monitor and evaluate book town projects to ensure that outside investors are delivering on their promises, and that the sustainability of the projects is being assessed from a holistic perspective. This duty of care and civic responsibility protects against the sense of loss and the drop in self-esteem when a community's hopes of reinvention are dashed by project failure. There are detrimental social effects brought about by poor planning, a lack of research and feasibility work and disproportionately raising the expectations of locals wishing to improve their social and economic environment. In the case of both Blaenafon and Atherstone, Chambers (personal interview 2011) and Playden (personal interview 2011) recounted the crushed expectations, frustration and degeneration of community pride and self-worth that occurred in both townships, resulting from the unviability of the project in which they had invested and Hanna's broken promises. It is also important to make the point that a disappointing book town experience from a tourist and visitor perspective reflects badly on other book towns because of the wider association between them as a specific type of leisure experience.

Seaton's studies of the fortunes of early book towns in Europe, as well as Hay-on-Wye, conclude that there are a number of critical success factors particular to book towns, which I will use in this chapter to identify the factors that were problematic in Blaenafon in Wales and Atherstone in England, that continue to hinder the ongoing sustainability of Graiguenamanagh in the Republic of Ireland. The following factors are adapted from Seaton (1999, pp. 394–5):

- Organizational strength and managerial capabilities
- Transformation scope—a large enough critical mass of book dealers to create a town of books, not just a town with a few bookshops in it
- Economic importance of the book town to the region
- Speed of implementation
- Method of attracting new dealers
- Strategic value to the region, state or nation in the location
- Existing book trade expertise—a nucleus for further expansion
- Scenic appeal of the town
- Ability to secure supplies of books
- Historic and cultural features of the town
- Suitable accommodation and tourism infrastructure (current and future potential)
- A cultural events programme to augment book town development
- Property availability and low-level rents, enabling affordability for book retailing

It is unlikely that a prospective book town will 'score highly' in every category (Seaton 1999, p. 395). In fact, none of the towns that expressed interest in being awarded the role of Scotland's national book town fitted all Seaton's criteria to qualify as the 'ideal town'. Rather, the 'assessment was a matter of balancing the respective strengths and weaknesses of the towns against each other' (p. 395). As well as a succession plan designed to transition book towns through the ageing of strong and passionate book town founders, there are three additional criteria for success that my research underscores. One of these is the need for financial support from the public sector, an entrepreneur or an alternate funding source over the duration of a book town's development, until the project becomes financially sustainable. Another is a high degree of need or hunger in the community to transform the town's circumstances. Towns that are already vibrant and affluent, I argue, are less likely to have communities that will coalesce, with outside assistance, behind a book town initiative. The locations most effectively transformed by a reinvigorated book town identity are towns and villages that have inherent charm, physical beauty or historical interest, but that may simultaneously be experiencing rural decline, physical dilapidation, closing of retail businesses, minimal tourism success and social problems such as unemployment and an inability to retain community members. Another important criterion for success is a book town's potential to engage with a younger demographic, as this is important to the ongoing viability and future sustainability of book towns over time.

Book Towns That Might Have Been: Blaenafon and Atherstone

Blaenafon in Wales and Atherstone in England were one-time book towns masterminded by an American from Mississippi, James Hanna, who for a short time was a business partner of Richard Booth's. Blaenafon is an industrial World Heritage Site located near Pontypool in Southern Wales. One of the world's largest producers of iron and coal in the nineteenth century, it is renowned for having made a significant contribution to the Industrial Revolution. Blaenafon's industrial past is still visible in the coal and iron ore mines, the shafts of which still honeycomb the surrounding hills. Quarries, a primitive railway system, furnaces and homes of the mining workers are still preserved in the area (Smith 2003, p. 108). The town's Big Pit site, the most intact ironworks in Western Europe, has been made into a museum, and a monument to industrial archaeology that Macaskill (2007) considers as compelling as the Acropolis, the Colosseum or any other iconic monument in world history. St Peter's Neo-Gothic church built by ironmasters in 1804 and the magnificent Blaenafon Workmen's Hall, housing a library, reading rooms and a concert hall, are also notable heritage sites in the town. However, like many other industrial sites that once boasted wealthy pasts, Blaenafon has suffered major economic decline in recent decades. In the late twentieth century, when the tide of prosperity ebbed and thousands of jobs were lost along with homes and businesses, there were more boarded-up shops than open ones in the main street, which had been nicknamed 'Plywood City' (*BBC News* 2003).

When the town was awarded Heritage Site status by UNESCO in 2000, ranked alongside the Egyptian pyramids in importance, it instilled local pride in past traditions and strengthened conservation and tourism development plans for the town (*BBC News* 2003). James Hanna's book town community revival project appeared on Blaenafon's radar three years later. Hanna claimed that bookshops would save Blaenafon and shake off the town's depressed image, building on the deep link between heritage and regeneration, and following in the footsteps of the town's miners—many of whom were keen readers and book hoarders (*BBC News* 2003). Kennedy (2003) described Hanna as 'an evangelist of the power of massed bookshops to transform local economies, in the style of Hay-on-Wye', and called his project 'a bold experiment to see if tourists can be lured into an obscure South Wales town to buy books'. Eight bookshops opened in June 2003 on World Conservation Day, promoting specialties such as film and theatre, cookery, photography and children's books. Torfaen Borough Council backed the scheme by making properties available, including the old NatWest bank premises for conversion into the Blaenafon Book Bank. For a period of time, there were more bookshops in Broad Street, Blaenafon, than in the book districts of some cities, but two years later Hanna had departed for Atherstone in North Warwickshire, and only two quality bookshops remained, one of which—Broadleaf Books—belonged to Joanna Chambers. When it was clear that the book town project had collapsed, Chambers relocated her bookshop to the nearby market town of Abergavenny.

Chambers, who had extensive knowledge of books prior to opening her business, was attracted to the generous start-up package Hanna offered. Prior to the book town opportunity, Chambers ran a market stall selling children's books in Abergavenny, but earlier had worked extensively in other bookshops. She heard of the project through 'word of mouth' and 'jumped at the opportunity because it was the only way I would ever have been able to afford a shop of my own' (personal interview 2011). Chambers described what was offered as a 'Three Point Plan consisting of a shop of 5000 books fully kitted with shelving, and back up support including technical assistance with IT'. She said the package was valued at £15,000 and that the books were supplied to Hanna from Richard Booth, so it was 'unlikely he had any choice about the type of books he received'. Optimistic despite the varying fortunes of the book town project, Chambers recalls that other bookshop owners 'had no kind of knowledge about books, only a dream. Anybody who works in, or has an interest in books knows that being reasonably well read helps'. Chambers was therefore the only stakeholder with book trade expertise involved in the project. Further, she believes the books allocated to new bookshops by Hanna were 'not the kind of books that would sell' and that inexperience made booksellers ignorant of these pitfalls. An absence of book trade understanding also meant that securing an ongoing supply of quality secondhand books to maintain sufficient levels of stock was another stumbling point, as Hanna provided no further assistance to business owners in this regard.

Chambers considered the book town's location problematic: the town's bleakness and working-class reputation made it unappealing to more prosperous Welsh residents and book lovers in nearby Abergavenny and other neighbouring towns:

> You could never get people to drive over the hill. It's only a hill, but people found the class differences a real barrier … it never bothered me and I always felt completely safe there, but the Blaenafon community was not a book-loving community. People used to say to me, 'We want shoes. We want clothes. We do not want books.' It is understandable. If you look at pictures of the main street in earlier times, it was a street full of busy shops full of produce and meat … of course, it all dried away with the industry

> and nothing was left. The locals were never going to be huge supporters of the [book town] initiative. (personal interview 2011)

While Blaenafon had significant historical points of interest from a mining perspective, it did not have the scenic appeal and charm that other successful book towns have to attract a range of visitors. Chambers commented that 'cultural heritage should have been an important component of the book town but it was not.' While a business named Browning Books hosted a number of book signings for authors, Chambers was unaware of other cultural events organized to enhance the book town's development. Chambers' business survived in Blaenafon for five years due to the online sales that came from having book town status, and that aspect of the trade was responsible for half her income. The Blaenafon book town project had not reached the level of sustainability that, according to Chambers, 'brings the boutiques, coffee shops, and other types of businesses that help a book town such as Hay-on-Wye create tourist appeal' (personal interview 2011).

Hanna also promoted the North Warwickshire town of Atherstone, without an identity since the loss of its historic millinery and coal mining industries after 2005. In a media release, Hanna claimed that Atherstone's Mayor Richard Meredith wanted to duplicate the early success of Blaenafon, which had for a short time kick-started the regeneration of that Welsh Valleys town. Although Atherstone is 'a lovely Georgian town right in the centre of England … rich in history and heritage with links to George Eliot, Michael Drayton, Boadicea and the Battle of Bosworth … with eleven or twelve universities within twenty miles', the huge potential market for book dealers failed to materialize (Meredith, in Hanna 2005). Like Blaenafon, Atherstone's book town project struggled for five or six years and then disappeared from sight.

Peter Playden, the proprietor of Throckmorton's Bookshop—one of the larger Atherstone bookshops and now an online business—told me that Atherstone was a graveyard of empty hat factories. The town was

> sitting on a pile of pith helmets made for the Boer War which unfortunately ended too soon for them to be sold … the town made every kind of hat you can think of, but ever since George V stopped wearing hats, this

> place has been in decline … the villages around here were about mining which again ended by the 1990s, so this is a sort of classic, depressed ex-market town. If you walk around town now, there's not a lot going on. The only work that's available locally is casual labour in the newer logistics industries, because of our location and the very good road links. Big companies use Atherstone as their European hub. We have ALDI and TNT. (Playden, personal interview 2011)

Playden was alerted to the book town opportunity through an article in the *Independent* newspaper while he was still living in Coventry. He and his wife had 'half-heartedly been looking for a business opportunity … a bookshop was one of the things that we'd discussed'. While Playden had no background in bookselling or book collecting, he claims to have been a 'voracious reader' and had found a cheap source of books in charity shops. While Playden found Hanna personable and a talented publicist, his dealings with Hanna and his company, Booktowns International, were never satisfactory. The Atherstone book town venture lacked ongoing funding and clear leadership:

> The project lacked guidance, somebody with experience to lead and advise booksellers, a plan to attract people to the location and a long-term budget … there were a number of missing factors. I think what was needed was for the local authority at a regional level or town level to take strategic control of the project and to manage, as well as possible, the aggregate of all the individual businesses … some training perhaps as well. I realised that if someone tells you they have a good business idea for you, they are actually selling you something they should be doing for themselves. (personal interview 2011)

Hanna was interested in a business opportunity but not engaged in the project to the same passionate extent as Booth, McMurtry, Nelson and Anselot, who all dealt in books themselves, led projects from within the book town communities in which they lived and had personally invested in the futures of the towns. Hanna deserted the project unexpectedly in mid-2006, only informing other stakeholders by email when he had returned to the United States.[1] Moreover, while securing financial support is not specified in Seaton's (1999, p. 398) list of success criteria, public sector backing was crucial to spearheading and funding the Wigtown book town project, and many book town projects in Europe have been enhanced through EU recognition—particularly the Telematics in Rural Areas initiative seeking to link book towns through effective IT networks.

The Atherstone Booktown project applied to the Market Towns Joint Action Group for a sum of £24,500 in November 2004. This sum was approved with matched funding of £5000 from both the Borough and County Councils. These grant monies covered the initial equipping of an office and the salaries of staff involved in administering the project. In-kind support was also provided by the Borough Council for the use of a warehouse on an industrial estate for the storage of books for a period of three years. A further sum of £500 was later provided for promotion and future events (Community and Environment Board Report 2006, pp. 2–6). This funding was insufficient for a project of such anticipated scale. Comparatively, Wigtown received subsidies—both financial and managerial advice—from the local government authority, Dumfries and Galloway Council, as well as Scottish Enterprise and the European Union. This support totalled £1.9 million. A book town office was established in Wigtown with a project officer and part-time staff for a ten-year period. In this establishment phase, these officers were responsible for marketing Wigtown as well as organizing the Wigtown Book Festival, a remit that has since been overtaken by the Wigtown Festival Company (Watson, personal interview 2011). Formal management and planning during book town establishment and development have established a secure base for growth that the failed book towns lacked. In correspondence with the North Warwickshire Borough Council, a bookseller from Wigtown named Moi McCarty stated:

> James [Hanna] flung himself into these projects [Blaenafon and Atherstone] not too long after he moved to Britain when his experience was only of Hay and he had no real knowledge of the workings of small businesses and local authorities … in Britain. He believes very strongly in the private funding of business. Nothing wrong with that but the truth is that all book towns in Europe except Hay were started with public funding. This money doesn't usually go to booksellers. It is generally used to market the town, in the first instance to booksellers to get them to start businesses and then to customers … the book shops are the draw but it's the food and

> accommodation providers, builders, consultants, garages, etc. who reap the largest benefit … Designation as a book town means being able to tap into funding for re-generation and cultural projects that benefits everybody. The media interest that is generated raises the recognition of the town …. (in Community and Environment Board Report 2006, pp. 7–8)

While Booth generated plenty of publicity for Hay-on-Wye, that book town's constant financial struggles can be attributed to the largely non-subsidized nature of the venture over many decades.

Property availability is an important criterion for success, and Playden highlighted how problematic it was for the book town project that one property developer had a monopoly in the Atherstone area, making acquiring suitable premises difficult for aspiring book dealers wishing to move there. This had also occurred in Wigtown, where many properties were owned by an absentee landlord, but prospective bookshop owners persisted in searching for alternative bookshop accommodation (Watson, personal interview 2011). Importantly, Playden noted that there had been failed attempts to promote the book town as a sustainable cultural tourism attraction. In his view, the link between tourism and book collecting is over-estimated:

> There's too much diversity for there to be a set pattern [of visitation to book towns] … the idea that you will make money out of middle class people who want to go somewhere nice for a day or weekend and who like boutique shops with old or specialized merchandise still relies on them finding the right items when they turn up. It's still pot luck … my most reliable customers are the old guys who buy railway books and have been [doing so] for 40 years. (personal interview 2011)

His opinion was that:

> People just collect whatever it is they're interested in and there are a myriad of people collecting specialized genres and sub-genres. People like yourself studying book towns need to get a picture of the diversity of experience. Both for people planning book towns and individuals who fancy it as a business, a lot more information should be provided than is currently available.

While, as discussed in other chapters, this understanding of specialized book interests is important to the book town concept, emphasis of the heritage aspects in book towns is also vital to creating ambience and an attractive and fulfilling visitor experience. Online selling may be an important 'bread and butter' sales component for some booksellers, but the charm and intrinsic appeal of a town should be central to the success of the initiative. Shops need an appealing 'face' that stimulates interest and creates street appeal. While Atherstone is not an unattractive town, my impression of it was neutral. There was nothing about Atherstone that distinguished it as particularly desirable or as a place I would seek to visit for leisure or recreation. After speaking with both Chambers and Playden, I concluded that the Blaenafon and Atherstone experiences were similar. Very few 'book' people were appointed or involved, there was no passionate leadership and there was minimal financial support from public-sector sources. Neither experiment matured to a point where the book town identity emerged strongly enough to make the town a sustainable tourist attraction. Hanna showed little persistence and kept moving to the next project and chance to benefit financially from people with idealism whose imagination had been captured by the book town vision he promoted. While prosperous book town developments might have been of value to these communities economically, and of strategic value to Wales and England based on their locations, many of the success factors intrinsic to other book towns' success were absent in both Blaenafon and Atherstone.

Graiguenamanagh: Almost Ireland's Book Town

While Graiguenamanagh, County Kilkenny, in the Republic of Ireland is without question a bookish destination, project founder Brian Roberts has struggled to transform the picturesque village of 800 residents settled by Cistercian monks in 1204 into a sustainable full-time town of books. While there is not yet a critical mass of bookshops to provide the immersive experience that satisfies bibliophiles, the town's inherent charm, quaintness, history and the natural attractiveness of the surrounding area make it a culturally rich site—unlike Blaenafon and Atherstone. Graiguenamanagh, meaning 'village of the monks', is a location of great tranquillity and scenic beauty at the foot of the imposing Brandon Hill. Life there centres on Edmund Spenser's 'goodly River Barrow', the 'whole village like an old grey mouse crouching on the little rivulet of the Duiske as it enters the Barrow' (Swayne 1995). The town is recognized for regular concert series in Duiske Abbey, featuring classical and traditional musicians from Ireland and beyond.

Despite the town's failure to create a year-long tourist attraction from bookshops, it is known for a successful annual book festival that, like Clunes, it hopes will enhance its reputation as a book centre. The Graiguenamanagh Town of Books (GTOB) Festival is now in its fourteenth year. It began following restaurateur Roberts' visit to Hay-on-Wye, from which he returned with a 'missionary zeal' (personal interview 2011) to replicate that town's formula in the village of Graiguenamanagh. Roberts could see many similarities between the two places, including eight empty shops—the same number with which Booth began in Hay-on-Wye (Roberts, personal interview 2011). However, while Booth could afford to buy vacant shops himself and fill them with books, Roberts was not in a position to do so. The project's future success therefore relies on attracting investment from governments or other individuals, as well as appropriate booksellers leasing or renting property. Developing methods of attracting new dealers has been a problem for Graiguenamanagh.

The commencement of the project coincided with a major economic downturn and banking crisis in Ireland in the mid-2000s. Project consultant Susan FitzGerald (2012) states in her *Feasibility Study for Graiguenamanagh Permanent Town of Books*:

> Many booksellers are nervous of opening a shop in this economic climate, especially in a rural village with just a small amount of current tourist trade and low resident population. They find the idea of renting much less appealing than owning, and are very wary of high rates … Many potential sellers wish to do so part-time as part of a lifestyle choice/retirement, and do not want to be fretting over their shop, or manning it full-time. In fact, they may often have to be absent to source fresh stock at estate sales … Unfortunately, in order to survive, many soon find working part-time is

> not possible … Their very real concerns must be addressed and solutions/support provided to encourage them to open in GTOB. Sharing shop space can be one way to address time and cost challenges.

Roberts describes the difficulties he encountered:

> The way I feel is that I'm trying to convince the [funding bodies] … that you have to look at a town of books project in Ireland and not as eight shops or 10 shops. You must look at it the way people look at Kilkenny Castle or at the Rock of Cashel – that it's one attraction, and that the entire town is a tourist attraction … They want to give us a small amount of money and walk away, but they'll be funding Kilkenny Castle forever. This thing needs support and will take quite a bit of time but then you will see a dividend in the B&Bs opening up, cafés and other shops opening up, and they must be drawn into a loop of money themselves. (personal interview 2011)

Increased specialization of booksellers and bookshops selling old and interesting books to attract international interest and real collectors would increase the bookishness of the town. I observed a disproportionate emphasis on remaindered titles and mixed merchandise in the permanent bookshops. However, when we met, Roberts (personal interview 2011) was already pursuing a strategy to both save on start-up costs and increase diversification of stock:

> One of the ideas I have is to involve lots of shops here like the veterinary shop, the coffee shop, and others. Can we match them with a bookseller so we could have a book department at the butcher? Books on meat! Let each restaurant have a wall of books. That way, those shops are established already and covering the cost of their rent and rates and not looking at the costs of starting up a new bookshop. They could do a deal with the bookseller on commission.

Another disadvantage likely to deter visitors to the town is limited tourism infrastructure, including insufficient accommodation and eating establishments. Dealers with whom I spoke at the book festival were also concerned about restricted public transport and the distance from major motorways. However, many other book towns have developed successful tourist profiles despite being located in peripheral locations, and Graiguenamanagh is no further from Dublin than Wigtown is from Edinburgh and Glasgow. A remote location is not necessarily a disqualification for success.

The GTOB Festival is a wide-ranging event held over three days that runs on a shoestring budget. Roberts' Waterside Restaurant and Guesthouse, the centre of many festival events, is a transformed nineteenth-century grain store, located right alongside the river, which exudes character and warmth (Fig. 6.1). In the same way as Clunes, the GTOB Festival attracts booksellers from Dublin, Kilkenny, London and Liverpool, as well as local shopkeepers selling their wares. In addition to the 30 temporary bookshops set up in shops and marquees at the festival, there was an engaging programme of special events aimed at serving the interests of a broad demographic. Sessions involved gardening experts, celebrity chefs and children's authors, with the highlight a presentation

Fig. 6.1 Graiguenamanagh, Republic of Ireland—almost Ireland's book town (2011) (Source: Photograph by author)

and poetry reading from then presidential candidate, Michael D. Higgins. Higgins spoke of the richness of Graiguenamanagh's 800-year-old Duiske Abbey as a central feature of what he believed would become Ireland's Town of Books and reflected on the synergy of the history of the location as a long-time centre of learning and literacy.

FitzGerald (2012) makes a valid argument in her report about the need for Graiguenamanagh to promote its unique characteristics as a tourist location:

> In these recessionary times, and as in-store physical book sales are falling, a GTOB must not 'trade' on simply being a book town. It must also trade heavily on its current assets in order to give it a critical mass as a destination – its mediaeval abbey and history, traditional woollen mill, outdoor activities and natural beauty, and Graiguenamanagh's timeless, nostalgic charm and friendly community spirit.

Thus she recommends that retailers, landlords and the community, as well as end consumers, need to embrace the project. To attract and retain booksellers, she recommends better publicity—'enticing information packs'—and better networks. She suggests that the GTOB Committee should build strong networks with non-book businesses, other book towns, other local destinations, tourism bodies, small businesses and book trade organizations, as well as the local community. While there is merit in building networks and exciting interest in the community for the project, the town is unlikely to progress its book town vision without an injection of funds in the way that Wigtown, Sedbergh and Clunes have done—an investment in its future. If the town were to be formally recognized as Ireland's book town, its status would attract new interest from book dealers elsewhere in Ireland and abroad, bookshops would open with incentives to encourage business investment, book collectors and curious tourists would support the initiative, and its ideal location, intrinsic history and charm would soon become apparent, and would blend with the new identity based around books.

It would also be advantageous for Graiguenamanagh to establish a relationship with the IOB and other book towns worldwide, a step that would possibly lead to increased national and international marketing. In her feasibility study, FitzGerald (2012) emphasizes the importance of Graiguenamanagh developing a strong Irish brand to absorb interest from the considerable American tourist market that identifies with Ireland. Establishing relationships with other key sectors, including education, libraries, health and wellness/sport and leisure, tourism, arts and culture and religion (related to the Abbey), might also lead to conference-based and other additional income for the town, an interest in events for writers and writers' retreats, and an annual writer-in-residence for the school. These links would assist accommodation and other businesses in the town in the winter months and provide a counterweight to the seasonal nature of Irish tourism. More focus on linking with Ireland's rich literary history and traditions would also help the town to maximize its potential. Just as Clunes has linked with Melbourne as a UNESCO City of Literature, Graiguenamanagh should similarly piggyback on Dublin's status as the fourth UNESCO City of Literature. Dublin has a unique literary heritage, already famous worldwide, and this should be used to draw people to associated book-related projects elsewhere in the country. It is full of monuments, statues, plaques, pubs and restaurants that celebrate literary figures, including Deane, Swift, Sheridan, Boucicault, Synge, Wilde, Joyce, Yeats, Shaw, O'Casey, Beckett, Kavanagh, Behan and O'Brien, as well as living writers such as Roddy Doyle, Anne Enright, Colm Tóibín, Eavan Boland and Joseph O'Connor. Ireland's great literary legacy, as Kerby (2010) attests, should be celebrated in a national book town. Roberts' reluctance to envisage the book town belonging in a literary tradition, as discussed in Chap. 4, is a drawback that needs to be reconsidered if the town is to attract the cultural tourist cohort.

Literary, bookstore and bibliophile tourism is a significant, growing and relatively uncharted global trend (Beale 2011; Portzline 2004, pp. 92–3), to which Ireland's book town can look as it has implications for book town expansion. Book towns blend well with other literary tourism attractions, appealing to the 'caprice and passion of the literati' (Robinson and Anderson 2004, p. 26). Increasingly for bibliophiles, visits to book towns and other locations with literary associations will impact on their collecting. Collecting books while travelling is about gathering objects that symbolize a place or person. Production, circulation and public consumption of books and other printed materials are vital to the health of the literary tourism industry. The books themselves 'provide a fixity to their imagined contexts, and their generally long shelf-life, assumed through increasingly well defined "secondhand" markets, maintains a powerful intergenerational dimension that feeds the concept of literary heritage' (Robinson 2004, p. 66). This type of tourism is also attributable to tourists creating a personal geography, where they immerse themselves in a dialogue with literary history. Purchasing books while travelling can be likened to others taking photographs or buying post-cards: 'books in the future will be souvenirs ... of your experience so you will buy a book because you want a tactile association' (McShane, personal interview 2010). It is possible to trace the history of this idea to Johannes Gutenberg in the 1450s—arguably the first prototype of today's book town entrepreneur and innovator, who traded books as souvenirs to pilgrims (McShane 2009). Ireland's book town is well positioned to become a place for literary tourists to purchase Irish literary materials, and the project should be promoted with this focus. It is advantageous for a book town like Graiguenamanagh to attract, where possible, literary pilgrims seeking to connect with nostalgic cultural landscapes, offering multiple entry points through experiences such as book shopping with an Irish literary focus, festivals featuring Irish writers, creative writing opportunities and other events.

Fading Book Town Leaders

Brian Roberts in Graiguenamanagh was a passionate project leader for a decade, unwilling to give up on transforming his Irish village into a permanent town of books. However, he spoke of the strain of managing the book town project as well as the impact on his hotel business, which provides the family's livelihood. Since our first interview in 2011, Roberts has relinquished the leadership role in Graiguenamanagh in favour of fellow town resident Martin O'Brien (Roberts personal interview 2017).[2] Like Roberts, many book town founders struggle to delegate, transfer or abdicate their leadership role. This is definitely the case in Gold Cities, Archer City and particularly Hay-on-Wye, where there was no one in the 'line of succession' easily able to replicate the unique blend of abilities of the book town founders. Until Elizabeth Haycox invested in Hay-on-Wye, the town's prospects had begun to seem somewhat diminished, given that Booth—an octogenarian whose speech has been slowed since a stroke 15 years ago—is now past directing the town's future. Even after Haycox's investments, one prominent bookseller stated:

> Sadly, under the weight of the new plutocracy, Hay's forgotten about its own ideal and its capacity to beguile the global press without a big PR budget. It was taught by a master of free publicity, and the lesson is now being ignored. (Harris 2012, p. 2)

While this situation was not entirely surprising, Sedbergh Book Town encountered unexpected difficulties (as mentioned in Chap. 4) related to leadership when four committee members fell ill within a short space of time, coinciding with funding reductions, so that some energy for the project waned as a result.

Following Noël Anselot's retirement in Redu, Belgium, that book town lacked the same energy with regard to marketing and publicity (McShane 2002, p. 21). Inspired leadership in existing book towns is fundamental to sustaining them and inspiring other towns to join the movement. Along with Booth, Anselot has been pivotal in assisting the planning and development of a number of French book towns, including Bécherel, Montolieu and Fontenay-la Joûte, as well as the Swiss book town of Saint-Pierre-de-Clages. Through his influential role, the IOB has undisputedly demonstrated leadership in encouraging the growth of the Book Town Movement worldwide. Anselot, an entrepreneur, businessman, ex-Cabinet minister and founder of Redu *village du livre* in Belgium, became 'a *de facto* foreign affairs minister to the international Book Town Movement' and offered more refined diplomatic skills which, according to McShane (2002, p. 21), provided a sharp 'contrast to the movement's maverick monarch, Richard Booth'. For example, Anselot advised the Malaysian government about the establishment of Kempung-Baku on Langkawi in the mid-1990s. With Booth and Henk Ruessink—the founder of Bredevoort book village in the Netherlands—Anselot was also a member of the panel that selected Wigtown in Scotland. Merfeld-Langston describes Anselot as 'Richard Booth's first disciple' and, like

Booth, an 'individual impresario' (2007, pp. 45–6). However, based on my discussions with Booth (personal interview 2011), he and Anselot started as close colleagues and business partners but soon came to be wary of each other as a result of their differing views about what makes a book town successful.

Following a trip to Wales in the early 1980s, during which he reclaimed an entire collection of thousands of books and manuscripts that Booth had acquired from a Belgian family estate, Anselot established the Redu *village du livre*. Booth had approached Anselot about a partnership, inspiring him to consider a book town in Belgium. Using his connections and book trade expertise to steer the project, Anselot and others developed the book town through a series of book fairs and other events, including Fete du Livre (Easter book festival), Nuit du Livre (night book festival) and Journees du Regionalisme (a book fair with a focus on local and regional history). These events raised funds to establish the project. The local council and various landlords have since prioritized bookseller involvement (McShane 2002, pp. 20–1). While the first bookshop opened in 1980 on the site of a converted snail farm, it was 1984 before the more expansive book town, with shops established in unused stables, barns and schoolrooms, came into being in this tiny rural location in the Ardennes Forest in the Francophone part of Belgium.[3]

The opening of the book village coincided with a twinning ceremony for the towns of Redu and Hay-on-Wye. While the twinning was obviously a product of the characters involved, and a physical manifestation of the sense of partnership felt by Booth and Anselot at that time, it was also appropriate in terms of the similar characteristics and conditions that underpinned each town's transformation into a book town. Like Hay, Redu had largely been dependent on farming, was experiencing economic decline, had an ageing population and could take advantage of different kinds of vacant buildings (Merfeld-Langston 2007, p. 47). According to Booth, the falling out between the two entrepreneurs was due to different opinions about the Montolieu book town project, for which they acted as joint advisers. While Booth claims to have preferred the notion of young *bouquinistes* trying a range of approaches, including mixed business and cooperative ventures as in the Galerie des Bouquinistes in Montolieu, Anselot preferred the development of small, privately owned shops (Booth 1999, pp. 252–3). Thus the issue of property became problematic for the relationship, as it did in the relationship between Booth and the American James Hanna. While the Montolieu book town survived these teething problems and now prospers, other book towns have not been so fortunate.

For example, one of the contenders in the Scottish National Book Town Competition was the town of Dalmellington, located north-west of Wigtown on the road to Ayrshire. The assessment panel, including Seaton, Anselot, Henk Reussink, Booth and others, recommended that thought be given to including some of the unsuccessful towns in a Scottish book trail, creating a triangle with Dalmellington in the north, Moffat in the east and Wigtown in the west (McShane 2002, p. 18). While this did not materialize, Dalmellington was started as a book town in 1997 after Booth fell out with the supporters of the Wigtown project (Goodenough 2006). However, Dalmellington struggled as a book town from the start. Booth kick-started the project as an act of defiance (McShane 2002)—not an ideal motivation for a project that required the whole community to be behind it and the wholehearted support of funding bodies. Originally the sole bookseller, Booth was later joined and bought out by a business named A Wheen o'Blethers, which later moved to nearby Newton Stewart. Following that development, two other booksellers joined the project, all trading from an old school building in the town prior to the collapse of the venture in January 2005 (Goodenough 2006). It would be true to say that the personalities of book town founders can be responsible for uncertainty about the viability of book town projects, but it is also true that the booksellers themselves can contribute to this.

Paul McShane, who met with Gary Stollery, founder of Gold Cities Book Town, in 2002, writes (2002, p. 12) of Stollery's 'stress and exhaustion … managing the seemingly inevitable and frequent tensions that occur among independently-minded booksellers', and identified in this book town a generic problem: the sometimes problematic relationship between the booksellers in the towns who need assistance to promote the venture, and the individual or group providing that service. The status of a founding figure, and their role over time, proved to be difficult issues with booksellers who seemed to be quick to criticize but slow to support them. While booksellers should not necessarily rely on an over-arching manager or leader in the development process, taking some ownership of the project themselves, a competent, motivated book town manager like Carole Nelson in Sedbergh, who attends to funding applications and marketing, is an asset. The existence of a broad, strategic plan for a book town development is the catalyst that is more likely to interest economic organizations with funding budgets, rather than the notion of shops full of old, musty books (Nelson, personal interview 2011).

Booksellers: The Last of the Bohemians

Collins (2003, pp. 104–5) states that 'once a town has forty booksellers, it becomes less likely that every one of them will get along, especially with a fellow who was one of the two living entries in a book titled *The World's Greatest Cranks and Crackpots*' (Nicholas 1982). Similarly, McShane (personal interview 2010) says that being 'self-centred and focused on his own plans, not really working in with a broader strategy'—as Booth was—is a common attribute of secondhand booksellers in many book towns he visited and that, by definition, booksellers are 'contrary and cantankerous people. They're secondhand booksellers basically because they can't fit in anywhere else … They're free spirits … always on the hunt for that deceased estate or that customer'. Seaton (1997, p. 15) also sums up these eccentric key stakeholders in book towns:

> Book dealers … are a unique breed. At worst, they are rapacious, pretentious, or snooty; at best, stoic in the face of poor sales, good humoured and almost always more broadly knowledgeable than academics, and often more knowledgeable in specialist ways. Moreover, in our over-bureaucratized world of management-speak and conformity, they might be considered the last of the Bohemians – often dressed like tramps, hopeless at business, and foolishly preferring to buy rather than to sell.

Their individualism is what makes book dealers more difficult to organize, and renders them hostile or apathetic to business procedures and management structures, as well as prone to personal rivalries and jealousies. The book trade provides 'a certain shelter for those whose humours might ill-suit them for work elsewhere' (Collins 2003, p. 140). A number of other interviewees made similar remarks: Playden (personal interview 2011) said it was 'very hard to get individual book businesses to work together' and that 'organizing booksellers is like herding cats … the kind of people that become booksellers are not the kind of people who want to work in a bureaucratically organized project'. Seaton (1996, pp. 12–13) argues that because booksellers are highly individualistic, they 'are happier to exist in the highly bohemian world of books rather than in the more institutionalized and bureaucratic organizations from which some of them have come'.

For example, in September 2009, the 'grumpy' booksellers of Hay-on-Wye, disgruntled with their so-called king, Richard Booth, staged a mock trial, conviction and beheading of an effigy of Booth. At the same time, Booth was apparently plotting to put up posters around town declaring the 'revolt of the peasants' (McShane, personal interview 2010; Sullivan 2010, p. 27). Schisms like these in book towns—where good leadership and management are crucial—provide a challenge according to McShane, especially given the notoriously prickly nature of secondhand booksellers. Merfeld-Langston (2007, p. 107) sees this individualism as a 'paradoxical contrast to the desire for social cohesion' wanted by project initiators. For this reason, Edmondson (personal interview 2011) says book towns are organic in their development, and it is not possible to 'make them too prescribed'. Collins also remarks that booksellers rely on many other community members to keep the main attractions—bookshops—open to draw tourist to the town. 'Hay seems like a town run by solitary eccentrics with their little bookstores, and yet there must be a secondary economy built around their needs, and mostly peopled by artisans, middlemen, and labourers; all, I'm sure, of vastly greater sense and practicality than the booksellers themselves' (Collins 2003, p. 30).

However, the concept of a secondhand bookshop as somehow timeless, a place that never alters, is now dated, as is the image of the antiquarian bookseller as a bearded, bespectacled, pipe-smoking gentleman in a worn tweed jacket that Brisebois (2008) comments was probably widely promoted via the cinema. In fact, the contemporary trade changes rapidly. Mandelbrote (2006) describes the role of antiquarian book dealers in the creation of taste and details their contribution to scholarship—something that has often been overlooked by experts in the history of the book. Many booksellers have chosen to move from somewhere else to 'start again'—a romantic notion, but the reality is a great deal more difficult. This line of work combines a high element of risk, 'with an attraction for round pegs wishing to vacate square holes, a combination that does not make for stability' (Minet 1989, p. 60). Book lovers mistakenly see selling books as a philosophy for life, not a business where ends need to be met. In Hay-on-Wye, Seaton (1996, p. 12) discovered that booksellers have highly unstable and volatile business lives, which are often unprofitable. The causes of this uncertainty are structural and inherent in the secondhand book market: variable supply, increased competition among a growing number of dealers and the relatively small support base of book buyers in the wider population—particularly at the expensive end of the market—which means profitable sales are infrequent. Book dealers invest significant sums in high-quality books and are then forced to retain the stock for long periods of time before suitable buyers are located. Booth's financial highs and lows are no secret; cash flow was an ongoing problem for his book empire, and at one time he needed to divest himself of a number of bookshops to remain solvent.

Despite these economic realities, there is much to attract the bookseller to a book town community—both the location and the business concept. There is a general awareness that the strength in cooperatives makes them more worthwhile than individual effort (Booth, personal interview 2011; Edmondson, personal interview 2011). Even when there is an aggregate of individual businesses rather than a fully fledged cooperative, book towns have marketing and networks that represent all the booksellers and therefore a stronger position in the marketplace. To avoid booksellers having to lead a 'hand-to-mouth existence', Seaton (1996, 13) recommends investment by way of development funds from public agencies to bolster the bookselling economy in Hay-on-Wye, and presumably other book towns. This support for bookshops as the generators of a range of other businesses would seem prudent, compared with what he refers to as investment in 'forlorn manufacturing' enterprises that are mostly immaterial to Hay's true economic requirements.

Acquiring book knowledge is a key component of working as a bookseller:

> The trade in rare or antiquarian books depends on knowledge; the more one knows about books, the better books one is likely to handle – and there is no fixed point, other than death, at which one has to stop increasing one's knowledge about books. This is one reason why the trade is so satisfying. (Playden, personal interview 2011)

Schiotz (personal interview 2012) agrees: 'What you buy makes an image of what you have in the shop. This is only possible through knowledge and experience; a lifetime of learning. Knowledge is power when it comes to secondhand books.' Both Schiotz (personal interview 2012) and Edmondson (personal interview 2011) speak of the skill involved in understanding what people are going to purchase, which is crucial to the success of the enterprise. Edmondson emphasizes that this is why it is important that he deal in books related to his own field—botany—because his in-depth knowledge of collectible botanical texts attracts interest from international collectors as well as British ones, and buyers actively seek his expertise. Nelson (personal interview 2011) agrees that, as a bookseller, you must buy what interests you because your enthusiasm translates into specialized knowledge over time. Nelson and Edmondson also stress the importance of the physical shop face—a real advantage for book town proprietors because books 'come to you', satisfying what they state is the number one rule of bookselling—finding good stock. People travel specifically to book towns to donate or sell books as well as purchase them, saving the bookseller trekking hundreds of kilometres a week to scour garage sales and flea markets, buying deceased estates, attending auctions, visiting other shops including charity shops and generally having to 'run books to earth', as booksellers not located in book towns (Schiotz and Marshall, for example) reported doing regularly. In contrast, Carole Nelson (personal interview 2011), the owner of The Sleepy Elephant in Sedbergh, claims that 'most of my books walk through the door', believing that book towns are 'front of mind when people are downsizing'. McShane (2002, p. 31) speaks of the challenges for secondhand booksellers of acquiring stock, also reporting that being based in a book town means a regular stream of books as customers transport them by car in the knowledge they will gain an optimum price. He mentions that in the *villages du livre*, the weekly cycle involves purchasing books from visitors throughout the week to sell at weekends.

Generational Change in Book Towns

The future of the Book Town Movement was a topic that generated heated discussion and a range of different viewpoints from interviewees. Turpin, Playden and Chambers believe the IOB model is somewhat out of step with the primary concerns of book towns, and that the model of book towns is evolving so that, for book towns to remain sustainable, they will need to continue to reinvent themselves. While key book town stakeholders, such as Nelson in Sedbergh and Booth, obviously see definite benefits in belonging to the IOB, Turpin, the Wigtown festival director (personal interview 2011), states that despite Wigtown being a member of the IOB, an international focus is not his book town's central tenet. The impetus in Wigtown is directed more towards local, regional and national interests. While Turpin certainly doesn't oppose the IOB and its work—Wigtown, after all, hosted an IOB international conference in May 2004—his view is part of a shift in emphasis that he describes as 'generational'. He regards the IOB as primarily related to Richard Booth and his various book town projects and concerns. Further, he queries whether the primary motivation should be having an International Organization of Book Towns that celebrates the fact that all these places sell books, because, 'We now have an internet that connects places all round the world' (Turpin, personal interview 2011). This line of argument is related to Turpin's over-arching view that book towns need to broaden their appeal and be 'of their time', serving multiple purposes rather than simply selling books. He advocates conferences, residencies and creative writing courses to build advantage out of geographical remoteness, as these activities foster sustainability. While Turpin fully accepts bookselling as a key part of the book town experience, and 'a perfectly reasonable kind of leisure activity', he believes that internet selling has impacted on Booth's original vision:

> I don't think you can have a book town without bookshops, but you need something else and you need a concept around that ... in a sense you have to take that idea of the book town, not taking the meaning of the book as a physical object to be sold. That's only part of it. You have to look at culture ... you create this sense of 'here's this little centre of culture that is interested in literature, it's interested in literacy, other cultural activity' ... I think if the book town idea is going to work long term, they almost have to brand themselves more like mini university towns without universities. (Turpin, personal interview 2011)

Turpin promotes the idea of encouraging book towns to be micro centres of intellectual activity, innovation and learning, 'but not on the grand scale of a university'. He foresees ongoing problems for book towns that are bound to a model where they have a set number of bookshop owners and nothing else to distinguish them in their role as a town of books. He believes many book towns are trapped in a model that may not be the right or best one moving forward:

> It is impossible not to come to the conclusion that the economic model on which book towns were set up has completely changed. In 1997 [in Wigtown], the idea was that by having a collection of book shops this would be a magnet. However, the days when secondhand bookshops were the only place to find a book you could not get in a high street store are long gone. Any model that relied on that is obsolete ... I think we need to really start re-thinking what these towns are about and, to some extent, that is being done already. I think the way forward for us is to think of a book town as not just about books as physical objects but as a place where ideas are traded – and not just literary ideas. (Turpin, in Rinaldi 2012)

Turpin envisages a more totalizing experience that includes not only books themselves, but the process of writing and other cultural forms that intersect with books being part of a wider cultural spectrum. Many book towns have taken their first steps to broaden out the concept, 'whether consciously or unconsciously', by adopting festivals and events. However, this is challenging economically because festivals only boost a book town's economy for a short time period—a point of agreement with Turpin, Booth and Edmondson.

I discussed the issue of potential cross-cultural learning with Turpin, seeking to understand how this could be an advantage to book towns. While Turpin regards the IOB as a useful connection point for individual booksellers, he considers the different languages of IOB member book town members to be problematic with regard to the extent of learning and sharing that can potentially occur. Turpin considers the IOB to be related primarily to Booth and his various book town projects and concerns. However, even Booth commented that having a common language is a significant advantage for book towns to learn from one another, citing his difficulties communicating business concepts and providing advice in the French town of Montolieu, compared with the relative ease of relating to Gary Stollery in the United States. Booth admits that this is an ongoing challenge for the IOB despite the good work it does to promote international links. However, Watson (personal interview 2011), proprietor of The Old Bank bookshop in Wigtown, was approached by the book town of Bécherel to participate in a joint venture and set up a transnational project, which she enjoyed as a French speaker. The project involved a creative cultural exchange with reciprocal delegational visits. Likewise, Clunes completed a cultural exchange with Korean book town colleagues from Paju BookSori in 2015 and was awarded a grant from the Australia Korean Foundation to fund joint creative exchanges and reaffirm this cross-cultural relationship.[4]

On the question of the IOB's role in the future of book towns, Merfeld-Langston (2007, p. 16) and Edmondson (personal interview 2011) believe the purely international role of the IOB to be a potential pitfall, both seeing the need for some national forms of control. Edmondson (personal interview 2011) argues for a national analogue of the IOB groupings, including Scotland, Wales, England and the Republic of Ireland, based on language. He feels that such a practical application would 'fill a gap that the IOB's current structure is unable to plug'. Such a body would assist, for example, in circumstances such as Hay-on-Wye's location being chosen for the Hay Festival. He says this would overcome the town having been:

> picked off as an isolated entity rather than part of a network … you need some sort of over-arching network or national entity that legitimizes and controls the activities. If the Book Town Movement was stronger, as a network, it [Hay-on-Wye] would be more able to fight this injustice off.

Merfeld-Langston is concerned that there is no precise definition established for a *village du livre* in France—a contradiction, considering that France is a nation that favours precisely defined labels and classifications:

> No national organization oversees the development of these endeavours [book towns], perhaps owing to the newness of the phenomenon. Consequently, there are no specific guidelines to follow and each town seems resolute about asserting its uniqueness and independence.

The example is used of Montmorillon's local government's efforts to homogenize business practices among bookstores. These restrictions met with resistance from shop proprietors who argued that a lack of defined boundaries needed to be understood in the context of France's continuing struggle for decentralization since the 1980s (Merfeld-Langston 2007, p. 16).

The issue of regulation is a point of broader disagreement for the future of book towns. Due to the wide diversity of cultures and book town models, any regulation of book towns would need to be responsive to the strategic models that are working for the particular mix of businesses and local conditions in any given initiative. IOB members tend to be concerned about definitional issues such as whether it is important to purely sell books in book towns. Obviously, a functioning rural township needs to sell a range of items so that people can live their daily lives, so this is a matter of striking a balance between books and by-products. However, book towns such as Hay-on-Wye, for example, have also developed other specializations such as antiques and visual art, which blend well with books but also slightly dilute the immersive nature of the desired book town theme. This issue has been at the heart of a debate within the organization for years because some members advocate an unqualified focus on books, while others take a more pragmatic approach. It is also a problem that there is a contrast between what local governments are proposing, in some instances, and how booksellers prefer to operate, and such mismatches reduce the effectiveness of the book town model. If used positively, regulation could be used as a means to encourage regional innovation based on regional needs and resources. The argument for regulation in book towns would be its potential to reduce administrative burdens, widen the scope for joint marketing and increase the potential for the creation of a global book town brand that could have a positive impact on productivity and overall recognition of the concept. The risk of regulation would, however, be that it would represent a diversion towards compliance and away from creativity and innovation (BERR Report 2008, p. vii). Further, control by a central authority, as has been stated, is not to the taste of many freedom-loving, locally focused booksellers, so this scenario is unlikely to materialize. The organic nature of the international Book Town Movement will be an intrinsic challenge in terms of governance, communication and achieving sustainability of book towns over time.

A potential for active engagement with youth is a criterion for success that I consider should be added to the list of factors that enhance book town viability. The importance of engaging with a younger demographic and their families was a topic that recurred in my conversations with book town founders and other stakeholders. While McShane believed book towns would only be supported in the future by older generations because younger generations use other ways of engaging with culture (personal interview 2010), most interviewees considered that the intergenerational nature of the book added to its sustainability. Booksellers revealed that a surprising number of young people are keen readers and book buyers, despite the wide interest in online culture that exists. Schiotz (personal interview 2012) believes carrying the right book under your arm is still part of the younger generation communicating a certain image to their peer group. Tapping into contemporary interests in books is evidenced in European book towns, where genres are promoted that interest young people, including collectible graphic novels and comic books.

Graiguenamanagh, for example, excels in engaging with a younger demographic. FitzGerald (2012, p. 10) prioritizes promotion via social media channels and web marketing, and is vigilant in her efforts to endorse the area as a natural 'off-the-beaten-track' paradise, adventure activity centre and honey pot of cultural heritage, not just a place with a bookish focus. The GTOB Festival included a book treasure trail for families, a secondary schools debate titled 'The Paper Book is Dead, Kindle is King', an exhibition of local children's writing, children's river craft workshops and a disco, rowing races on the river, nature walks, circus street performances and a children's circus skills workshop. The image of the river is central to the marketing of the event and is used as a background for book town experiences that promote books alongside physical adventure. This is a positive feature, and one that has also been used to advantage in both Wigtown and Clunes in particular.

In south-west Scotland, where Wigtown in located, literature for youth is also a key component of the developing identity of the Dumfries and Galloway region. A region-wide schools programme provides links between education and literature, including virtual reality literature development delivered via a Scottish programme called GLOW, the world's first national intranet. It was developed exclusively for Scotland's schools community, enabling a breaking down of geographic and social barriers. A role based in the Wigtown Book Town Festival office provides support to build a regional programme of writing for youth, but also to programme the Wigtown Children's Book Festival (Yates, personal interview 2011). Since 2013, the Wigtown Book Festival has run its own parallel youth events, separate from the children's festival, for youth aged 15–25, coordinated and chosen by a committee of young people aged from 15 to 16 years, who liaise with members of the main festival board but are not dependent on them. They have their own venue, The Booth, and their own programme, enigmatically named WTF (Wigtown the Festival). The Festival, in recognition that schools in Dumfries and Galloway are often geographically disparate, runs an outreach programme delivering well-known authors to schools themselves during the festival period. The region is working to distinguish itself not only as the site of Scotland's book town, but as a hub for children's literature and home to a cultural centre for storytelling and myths, focused on Gaelic and Scots language in particular, that is supported by a national policy for creative industry partnerships. A charitable organization, the Peter Pan Moatbrae Trust, aims to restore one of the most beautiful and significant historic buildings in Dumfries as a centre for children's literature, reinventing the garden for play and active learning. J.M. Barrie attended Dumfries Academy, and in 1924 described the garden of his friend Stuart Gordon, Moatbrae House, as an 'enchanted land to me … the genesis of that nefarious work'—referring to the play *Peter Pan*. The Trust therefore aims to return the house to its original condition as a landmark and attraction for the region, providing the opportunity for a new generation of children to explore a magical landscape in the footsteps of Peter Pan. Discussion about the resonance of books—and book towns—in the lives of younger residents and visitors (Yates, personal interview 2011; Swales, personal interview 2011) suggested a positive future for this particular—and perhaps unexpected—materialization of print culture in the twenty-first century. This optimism seemed well founded because the Trust appointed its first Education Officer in 2015 and in March 2017, in cooperation with the Wigtown Book Festival, organized its first children's book festival, Big DoG, running a series of book events for children and young adults in Dumfries.

In 2014, for the first time, Clunes Book Town presented a children's book festival, Clunes Booktown for Kids 2014, with a day dedicated to school activities and another to families. With the theme of transporting children 'back to the world before Vegemite'—to the early 1900s—this festival offered 5–12-year-olds an opportunity to experience, through books, readings, writing workshops and opportunities to meet authors and illustrators, a particular period of Australian history up close. In particular, the event featured a Children's Village of Lost Trades, where traditional artisans such as coopers, fletchers, bodgers and blacksmiths demonstrated their work in a village atmosphere. The book town established a Clunes Book Town for Kids Advisory Panel to oversee this festival, which includes children's authors, illustrators, local community members and the principal of the town's primary school.

Book Towns Grow Out of Need

It is unlikely that a book town project will work in a town that already has a strong tourist profile and a multiplicity of riches. Book town success is more probable when there is a high level of need for the project to reinvigorate a town that has lost its major industries and is experiencing economic and social downturn. Hay-on-Wye, Sedbergh, Wigtown and Clunes are all towns that were transformed by their book town-themed identities and now re-experiencing economic buoyancy. Nor is it necessarily sufficient that a town has many bookshops and a community with a deep regard for books and literary culture. McShane (personal interview 2010), Muller (personal interview 2010), Booth (personal interview 2011) and others regard South-East Queensland as an ideal location for pursuing the future development of a book town, and Muller in particular considers that Maleny and the surrounding villages in the Blackall Ranges would ideally suit the book town model evidenced around the world. Maleny has long been recognized as a rural centre for books, readers and writers, although it doesn't officially call itself a book town. It is the home of two writers' festivals—Outspoken and Celebration of Books Maleny. It is also home to five new and secondhand bookstores in its main street. There is a thriving library culture in the town, as many as 50 book clubs, a number of poetry groups, Jill Morris's book farm and a range of festivals and other literary events and celebrations. Over 500 artists of all kinds live in the hinterland, many of them writers. This book culture is attractive to many for its stimulation, but a landscape and temperate climate that provide a home for rich flora and fauna are also a huge drawcard, providing an attractive intersection of landscape and literature.

Four years ago, environmentalist and author Steven Lang and antiquarian book dealer Chris Francis established Outspoken—an extended literary festival taking the form of occasional conversations with writers. More than forty of these events have now occurred, and Lang has been successful in securing big names like Geraldine Brooks, Richard Ford, Alexander McCall Smith, A.C. Grayling, Thomas Keneally, Richard Flanagan, Kate Grenville, Karen Joy Fowler, Ruth Ozeki and Cate Kennedy. While local people are keen participants, there are also regular attendees from Brisbane and the nearby Sunshine Coast.

At a public meeting held as part of a series of artists' talks by the Maleny Arts Council in 2012 to discuss the future of Maleny as a book town, inspired by my research, local booksellers made it clear that the idea of theming the town was unattractive to them as there was much to lose. While they acknowledged the town as 'an unofficial book town', from a business and marketing perspective they preferred the multiple identities the town currently reflects to visitors: an organic food town, a wedding destination, a place with a vibrant arts community, a place known for national parks and wilderness, a place for short breaks 'that offers something to everyone'. Real estate in Maleny is becoming increasingly expensive, and the example of escalating property values in Hay-on-Wye that have accompanied the book town's success was raised. A Maleny bookseller stated:

> There is some risk Hay might find in the future that it becomes a victim of its own success … Maleny lacks cheap real estate. It lacks cheap rent and it's not a dying rural town. Maleny, or Australia for that matter, is not densely populated like in Europe and the UK where they had great success with book towns. We're not motivated to become a book town to save the economy of the town. (Maleny Public Meeting 2012)

Instead of pursuing the idea of a book town development, a group of like-minded book lovers later collaborated to create an annual event celebrating Maleny's love of books, reading and writing. Celebration of Books Maleny features workshop events, book launches, films, interviews with writers, a writers' marketplace, a book club gathering and a book swap tree in Cooke Park in Maleny's main street, where you actually hang a book you've enjoyed on a tree and select another one. What became clear to me from the community meeting and from research and observation is that it is unlikely book towns will propagate and thrive in places like Maleny, which derive their sustainability as places that provide the 'conspicuous consumption' to which Ragusa (2013, p. 110) refers—simply comfort and urban replication, in many respects, for day trippers and weekenders. An up-market weekend escape and a book town experience might overlap, but they are fundamentally different things. A book town will not survive if it is merely an example of transplanted urban living in another place. A smaller, needier community like Clunes or Featherston, with leaders and community members driven to create a new vitality for a town, is a far stronger motivation for the success of a book town project.

In summary, ambitious plans to recreate communities as book towns are insufficient to drive success, as the cases of Atherstone, Blaenafon, Dalmellington and Graiguenamanagh demonstrate. Book towns require founders with personal and financial investment in projects or management teams able to access public funding while also possessing resourcefulness and energy grounded in community cooperation. There are very few examples of failed book towns because idealistic projects of this nature are usually initiated by someone influential who is prepared to think differently, persuade others of the need for change and sell the notion of an 'imagined community'. While Seaton's criteria are practical and useful for any community embarking on such a venture, it is also vital that a book town embraces a local as well as a wider vision, which adapts the basic steps to emphasize the unique values of the town. Rather than merely adapting an off-the-shelf formula, successful book towns devote attention to the motivational factors that generate interest from visitors to visit a peripheral community: they take a lead in the conversation about books, ideas and how the future will be shaped.

Notes

1. It has since been reported that Hanna was arrested on his return to America, facing numerous counts of rape and sexual indecency, and has now been imprisoned (Sanders and Gaskell 2013, p. 1).
2. While Roberts explained there is still no progression to a permanent town of books, he believes the 2016 event was the strongest yet. Positively, the current Book Town Committee has undertaken to share more of the burden of responsibility for administrating the annual festival between its members. Roberts was more optimistic about reports of reduced reliance on Kindles and other electronic reading devices, and buoyed by evidence of a resurgence in paper book sales (personal interview 2017).

3. Anselot gives an account of his book town journey in a bibliomemoir about Redu, published in 2004 to mark the community's twentieth anniversary as a book village. The organizers combined the twinning celebration with Europe's first 'space film' festival, in homage to the European Space Agency satellite station, also located in Redu ('Belgium's Book Town' 2004).
4. The initial cultural exchange was centred on a project featuring the work of Clunes-born photographer George Rose (1861–1942), who took a series of 'historically potent streetscapes of Korea' in 1904. The photographs have since been exhibited in both book towns. Korean artists and authors also attended Clunes Booktown Festival in both 2014 and 2015: http://clunesbooktown.com.au/international-program

References

Atherstone Booktown update and progress. (2006, October 30). Report of the Assistant Director (Planning and development), Atherstone [UK] Community and Environment Board, pp. 1–7.

Beale, N. (2011). *Literary tourist*. http://literarytourist.com. Accessed 26 Oct 2011.

Belgium's Book Town. (2004). Expatica Belgium. http://www.expatica.com/be/leisure/travel_tourism/belgiumsbook-town-12329.html?ppager=0. Accessed 6 Aug 2010.

BERR (Department for Business Enterprise and Regulatory Reform). (2008). *Impact of regulation on productivity: BERR occasional paper no. 3*.http://www.cses.co.uk/UPI/File/Impact-of-regulation-on-productivity.pdf. Accessed 16 Apr 2015.

Bookish Blaenavon opens new chapter. (2003, June 27). *BBC News*. http://news.bbc.co.uk/2/hi/uk_news/wales/3023862.stm. Accessed 25 May 2011.

Booth, R. (1999). *My kingdom of books*. Ceredigion: Y Lolfa Cyf.

Brisebois, M., & Mandelbrote, G. (Ed.). (2008). *Out of print and into profit: A history of the rare and secondhand book trade in Britain in the twentieth century* [Book Review]. Papers of the Bibliographical Society of Canada, 22 March. http://www.thefreelibrary.com/Giles+Mandelbrote,+ed.+Out+of+Print+%26+Into+Profit%3A+A+History+of+the...-a0183983011. Accessed 22 July 2012.

Collins, P. (2003). *Sixpence House: Lost in a town of books*. New York: Bloomsbury.

FitzGerald, S. (2012). *Feasibility study for a Graiguenamanagh permanent town of books*. Submitted as an application for Leader Funding from the Irish National Rural Network, Moate, Co. Westmeath, Republic of Ireland.

Goodenough, M. (2006, April 11). Dalmellington book town: On the road to nowhere. *The Book Guide* [UK]. http://www.inprint.co.uk/thebookguide/shops/dalmellington_book_town.shtml. Accessed 7 Aug 2010.

Hanna, J. (2005, June 10). *Atherstone bids for new identity as England's National Book Town* [Media Release]. http://www.inprint.co.uk/thebookguide/shops/atherstone_press_release_2.1.htm. Accessed 22 May 2011.

Harris, P. (2012). UK: Is the book town of Hay-on-Wye dying? *Sheppard's Confidential: News and Events in Antiquarian and Second-Hand Books, Ephemera, Prints and Maps*, 19 April.

Kennedy, M. (2003, March 10). Books could help town to turn over new leaf. *The Guardian*. http://www.guardian.co.uk/uk/2003/mar/10/books.artsnews-temporary. Accessed 30 June 2010.

Kerby, J. (2010, August 4). Moneytimes with Jill Kerby. *The Anglo-Celt*. http://www.anglocelt.ie/opinion/columnists/articles/2010/08/04/3999038-moneytimes-with-jill-kerby. Accessed 25 Nov 2011.

Landry, C. (2008 [2000]). *The creative city: A toolkit for urban innovators*. London: Earthscan.

Macaskill, H. (2007, March 24). The complete guide to book towns. *The Independent* [UK]. http://www.independent.co.uk/travel/uk/the-complete-guide-to-book-towns-441542.html. Accessed 22 Feb 2010.

Maleny Arts Council (2012, March 13). Maleny – A book town? *Public Meeting, Maleny RSL Hall*.

Mandelbrote, G. (Ed.). (2006). *Out of print and into profit: A history of the rare and secondhand book trade in the twentieth century*. London: British Library and Oak Knoll Press.

McShane, P. (2002). *To further Australia's understanding and involvement in the international booktown movement through a program of visits and interviews*. Winston Churchill Memorial Trust of Australia. http://www.booktown.com.au/ChurchillReport_Booktowns_2002.htm. Accessed 27 Feb 2010.

McShane, P. (2009, December 10). *BookTown Australia: The international book town experience – An Australian perspective*. Monash University Seminar: Book Towns and Writer's Festivals. http://arts.monash.edu.au/blogs/events/2009/12/10/seminar-book-towns-and-writers-festivals. Accessed 14 Mar 2011.

Merfeld-Langston, A. L. (2007). The *villages du livre*: Local identity, cultural politics and print culture in contemporary France. PhD thesis, Pennsylvania State University.

Minet, P. (1989). *Late booking: My first twenty-five years in the secondhand book trade*. Old Knowle: Frantic Press.

Nicholas, M. (1982). *The world's greatest cranks and crackpots*. London: Octopus Books.

Portzline, L. (2004). *Bookstore tourism: The book addict's guide to planning & promoting bookstore road trips for bibliophiles and other bookshop junkies*. Harrisburg: Bookshop Junkie Press.

Ragusa, A. T. (2013). Downshifting or conspicuous consumption? A sociological examination of treechange as a manifestation of slow culture. In N. Osbaldiston (Ed.), *Culture of the slow: Social deceleration in an accelerated world*. London: Palgrave Macmillan.

Rinaldi, G. (2012, October 6). How do book towns survive in the age of the e-reader? *BBC News South Scotland*. http://www.bbc.co.uk/news/uk-scotland-south-scotland-19814700. Accessed 5 Dec 2012.

Robinson, M. (2004). Between and beyond the pages: Literature–tourism relationships. In M. Robinson & H. Andersen (Eds.), *Literature and tourism: Essays in the reading and writing of tourism* (pp. 39–79). Andover: Thomson Learning.

Robinson, M., & Andersen, H. (2004). Reading between the lines: Literature and the creation of touristic spaces. In M. Robinson & H. Andersen (Eds.), *Literature and tourism: Essays in the reading and writing of tourism* (pp. 1–38). Andover: Thomson Learning.

Sanders, A., & Gaskell, S. (2013, January 13). Welsh town left stunned by US paedophile James Hanna's conviction. *Wales Online*. http://www.walesonline.co.uk/news/wales-news/welsh-town-left-stunned-paedophile-2497133. Accessed 24 Mar 2015.

Seaton, A. V. (1996). *Book towns and rural tourism development: Hay on Wye 1961–1996*. Glasgow: University of Strathclyde.

Seaton, A. V. (1997, April). Scandinavia, the Fatherland, and Bonnie Scotland: International book towns, Part Three. *Biblio*, pp. 12–15.

Seaton, A. V. (1999). Book towns as tourism developments in peripheral areas. *The International Journal of Tourism Research, 1*(5), 389–399.

Smith, M. (2003). *Issues in cultural tourism studies*. New York: Routledge.

Sullivan, J. (2010, January 16). Villagers hawk their literary lure. *The Age*, p. 27.

Swayne, S. (1995). *'The old grey mouse': Graiguenamanagh remembered*. Graiguenamanagh: The Abbey Centre.

Interviews

Booth, Richard MBE. Hay-on-Wye, Wales, 20 September 2011.

Chambers, Joanna. Abergavenny, Wales, 20 September 2011.

Edmondson, John. Graiguenamanagh, Republic of Ireland, 17 September 2011.

McShane, Paul. Bowral, New South Wales, Australia, 9 July 2010.

Muller, Laurie. Brisbane, Queensland, 17 August 2010 and 7 September 2010.

Nelson, Carole. Sedbergh, Yorkshire, United Kingdom, 9 September 2011; phone interview, 29 March 2017.

Playden, Peter. Atherstone, Warwickshire, United Kingdom, 13 September 2011.

Roberts, Brian. Graiguenamanagh, Republic of Ireland, 17 September 2011; phone interview, 28 March 2017.

Schiotz, Peter. Maleny, Queensland, 4 April 2012.

Swales, Gill. Sedbergh, Yorkshire, 8 September 2011.

Turpin, Adrian OBE. Wigtown, Scotland, 4 September 2011; via email, 15 March 2017.

Watson, Joyce and Cochrane, Ian. Wigtown, Scotland, 4 September 2011.

Yates, Carolyn. Wigtown, Scotland, 4 September 2011.

7

Book Towns: An Unfolding Story

Book towns are growing sites of cultural diversity. The Book Town Movement has experienced significant international expansion since Seaton's first crucial input, motivated as it was by specific economic development and tourism agendas, such as those he utilized to engineer the establishment of Scotland's National Book Town (Seaton 1996a, b, c, 1997, 1999). While urban centres still play an important role in contemporary print culture and more broadly in cultural life, the ways in which people engage with arts and cultural debates are in a process of transformation. Less conventional spaces on the rural periphery—book towns—are emerging as vital hubs of artistic creation, festival culture and consumption. Wigtown and Clunes—unlike cosmopolitan urban centres like Edinburgh and Melbourne, which are particularly rich in artistic production and consumption—have not traditionally been associated with iconic authors or landmark events. However, the fertile artistic activity now occurring as a matter of course in these small bookish communities is recontextualizing the whole notion of artistic places, signifying a changing balance between modes of engagement and urban and rural life. The very remoteness of book towns in fact protects them from domination by metropolitan centres.

J. Frank, *Regenerating Regional Culture*, Sociology of the Arts,
https://doi.org/10.1007/978-3-319-65036-4_7

This book's aim, in particular, has been to recognize the cultural life of the book in book towns and highlight the multiple points of connection between book towns and changing cultural expression and celebration, subsequent impacts on community life and the role played by book towns in sharpening the regional identity of peripheral locations in many parts of world. Fundamental to this shift is the fact that books in book towns are both linking mechanisms and symbolic entities. The book is a device that synthesizes aspects of our culture and history: the places where we live, our understandings of ourselves, our cultural industries that bring vitality. The book is therefore a vehicle of interconnectedness, and book towns are increasingly materializing as a means of locating and expressing that interconnectedness.

Terms used to describe the qualities of books such as aura, *objet d'art* and patina—a surface appearance of something grown beautiful with age or use—actually describe the interactive relationship inherent in the book as an object and the physical infrastructures, cultural practices, regional applicabilities and constructed meanings that surround it. Books are the products of our human, physical and cultural evolution. Even now, as we build relationships with technology, it is the human element that perpetuates a longing for material forms. We yearn for sensual, bodily experiences and, through these yearnings, search out tangible engagements with objects such as books. In turn, these interactions with books contribute to a book's provenance, shaping its individual path through history.

Book towns are thriving in the digital age because the tangible boundaries of the book's materiality are in stark contrast to the infinite possibilities of the internet. At the heart of the success of book town projects are books themselves: satisfying physical objects, not only capable of transmitting ideas and information but the culmination of traditional artistry and expertise that tie them to history, culture and place. Books in book towns symbolically integrate print culture and distinct local heritage. Ensuring books' survival is a primary motivation of many book town entrepreneurs. Book towns not only assure the continued existence of millions of antiquarian and secondhand books, but also the survival of the craft skills that produced them. Yet, as well as preserving past technologies, book towns actively participate in contemporary global communications. They are therefore both products of current technological change and places that react to change by protecting the past.

Rather than simply offering books in shops as products for sale, book towns increasingly offer interactive experiences. Literary topics are ingeniously mixed with popular cultural offerings that reflect a sense of particularity and local place to create a breadth of experiences. Fluidity therefore exists for book lovers to move between more traditional and unconventional places and topics for books on their own terms, curating their own book-based experiences and cultural identities. Through its exploration of reader-tourist motivations and behaviours, this book has also located book towns as important locales together with, or alongside, identifiable literary landscapes and sites with strong links to literature and popular culture. They embrace both 'high' and 'low' cultural forms, often thriving on the contrast between the two. Where there are literary affiliations, they foster cultural attachment in book towns, and book and literary festivals foster temporary communities that build lasting connections. Collecting books is a hobby open to all, regardless of age, race, position or formal education. The collector understands, cherishes and preserves the concept and the ideal of the book, understanding its historical and sentimental value.

Chapter 5 emphasized that each person has a unique literary DNA, or connection to a unique trajectory of different books that is established throughout a lifetime. The only common features observable in people who collect books are that they have a certain intellectual curiosity and distinctive interests. These egalitarian values need to be preserved:

> One of my impressions of [Hay-on-Wye] was that it's genuinely egalitarian and non-elitist and if you're not careful with festivals and even bookshops, you can gravitate up the elite end and alienate the ordinary folk from it, but it seemed it just fitted in with the place and all the ordinary folk just went on as normal … Never under-estimate ordinary folk and their interest in writers and their strong views on them, and their generosity of spirit. Never talk down to them. That's one of the keys in publishing in my view as well. And certainly, that's the strong impression I had of Hay-on-Wye. It was a town that wasn't 'up itself', but thoroughly enjoyed doing what it was doing. Everyone was welcome. You could check your ego in at the border. (Muller, personal interview 2010)

This study has updated the somewhat restricted view of Seaton and others that book towns are sites of gentrification, supported primarily by upper income and highly educated individuals, instead arguing that book town culture is egalitarian. The democratization of book culture that has occurred more broadly through engagement with book festivals, book clubs and online publisher and author blogs is reflected in the way book towns are supported and by whom. This argument takes its departure from Richard Booth's earliest observations that book towns, because they were established as 'economies of poverty', spring from adversity and offer every individual a unique opportunity to affordably pursue special interests and purchase books, as discussed in Chap. 2.

Book town audiences are a blend of cultural tourists, post-tourists and local communities. However, tourist profiles are never entirely static (Smith 2006), so someone may choose to be a cultural tourist at one time and a leisure tourist at another. The growing focus on book towns as centres of cultural activity symbolizes a juncture at the heart of a serious interrogation of the concept of tourism itself. As Rojek and Urry (1997, p. 1) ask, 'Where does tourism end and leisure or culture or hobbying or strolling begin?' The blurring of tourism with a wide range of other pursuits is part of the cosmopolitan attraction of book towns. Their cultural versatility provides a means of reconsidering the motivations of tourists and the ways in which these destinations can be made appealing. The situation favourable to book towns has also developed as a response to the greater sophistication and travel experience of a broader number of people and the declining popularity of other traditional tourist attractions and forms of tourism, as well as new approaches to international cultural development.

As I have identified, eccentricity has emerged as an important thread that runs through the success of the Book Town Movement. Right from the outset, book towns were the brainchildren of unconventional, entrepreneurial and committed founders whose ingenuity increasingly has been adopted by governments and development organizations. These organizations have both social and economic objectives. They want to harness social capital to foster sustainable communities by capitalizing on the multiplier effect that accrues from tourism in book towns. Future policy regarding book towns will need to take account of both creativity and diversity. While book towns have proliferated, it is evident from the case studies in this book that a book town must have an intrinsic reason for its creation and ongoing existence—whether that be the economic survival of a small, failing peripheral village, a means of expressing unique regional distinctiveness and skill, or the utopian ideal of building a better alternative society based around books in a country area.

The freedom for book towns to pursue these visions is expanding, and recent changes to regional and cultural funding acknowledge the cultural and multiple contexts in which tourism and art are being positioned. Funding agendas directed at the geographical periphery are heightening opportunities for book towns to become places of cultural production and participation, in line with democratization of culture more holistically, thus contributing to their sustainability. It helps that arts and cultural activities centred on print culture are a flexible, cost-effective and responsive mechanism for engagement. Existing premises in these villages are able to be converted into book establishments, requiring refurbishment rather than costly new construction like other tourist initiatives. Due to the infinite array of secondhand books in circulation, bookshops and book events are constantly self-renewing attractions, providing a refreshing experience for repeat visitors. It is the cultural resources of previously depressed communities that are cleverly harnessed in book towns: skills, traditions, ideas, communal stories, self-reliance of populations, charming buildings and cultural heritage.

Through creative and cultural activity, social bonds in book towns are strengthened and the identity of the town and region is enhanced. This is achieved not only by writers and artists, but by ordinary community members through a sense of obligation and pride in their community. Book towns deliver positive outcomes at a community level that are inherent in the arts experiences available to members of that community. These include both the benefits that occur at the time of the experience, such as the communal meaning arising from mass participation at a rural locale, and those that accrue over time, such as preserving cultural heritage and fostering cultural diversity. Book towns' multiplier effects generate the reinvigoration of other industries—not only those directly related to books and print culture, but also hotels, restaurants and other retail businesses. The diversification of economic activity appeases non-book appreciating sectors of the community, contributing to increased social cohesion, lively civic engagement and a sense of shared achievement. Regeneration is not an end in itself; it is about people and the quality of the lives they will be able to lead. Unless book town projects involve, and win, the support of local people, they cannot be sustained over time.

One particular challenge for book towns is to maintain their distinctiveness, while at the same time developing commercially viable enterprises. This combining of culture and tourism is a complex and strategic activity for book town leaders, requiring a high level of sensitivity to the social eco-system of the community. Book town communities are complex entities, comprising many different groups and stakeholders. These groups have different values, attitudes and perspectives. The community in a book town should therefore not be treated as a single entity with a homogenous attitude towards book town tourism development. In today's rapidly changing environment, project initiators require an understanding of how community development and empowerment can be achieved. Book town communities do not simply exist in a physical geographic dimension, such as a number of streets heavily populated with bookshops, but through the shared aspirations of book town founders, booksellers, other business owners and community members. Book town leaders such as Nelson, McShane, Turpin and Gould have succeeded in establishing networks and connections, particularly with authors and the publishing sector, thereby harnessing this targeted publicity to germinate book events and build for them a sustainable profile of attraction.

Book towns host events in spaces with warmth and resonance of community—distinctive places that allow a merging of individual and common interests. Chapter 3 asserted that bookshops and intimate book gatherings in book towns generate a conviviality vital to the strengthening of community. Those people who visit book towns escape their frenetic city lives and enjoy meaningful experiences that deliver a sense of belonging in a rural locale and with other like-minded participants. The bookshops themselves act as third places where outsiders can make connections and feel like insiders. By making these links, book towns open dialogues with both visitors and locals, drawing them together to consider a broad range of issues with the book as the constant backdrop. Book villages are small, approachable and non-intimidating in comparison with some urban events and festivals, which have stronger connections to nineteenth-century high-art ideologies.

From my own observations of book town visitors, participants are engaging in what qualifies as a lifestyle experience at one level, and a more deeply cultural experience at another. Tourists can simply shop, or they can immerse themselves in book culture at a meaningful level: book towns provide opportunities that are simultaneously ordinary and extraordinary. They successfully manufacture some experiences to cater to the cosmopolitan expectations of urban visitors. Therefore, a book town needs to demonstrate that it can meet certain lifestyle expectations without losing the essence of its distinctive rural experience. As Turpin (personal interview 2011) explained, there is an important balance to establish between the slightly quirky and quaint local events and the more straightforward large event in the main tent that resemble what would be offered at an event like the Edinburgh Book Festival. However, book town events in a village like Wigtown are a drawcard for their pop-up aesthetic. Urban visitors enjoy events in unusual rural locations like nearby Cardoness Castle, the ruined RAF station or the Galloway Forest Park under dark skies, as the case study in Chap. 4 revealed. Festival directors like Turpin are succeeding because they are aware of the importance of authenticity as a motivator. They understand that not all aspects of cosmopolitanism are necessarily progressive. I have argued that successful book towns avoid the threat of inequality between cosmopolitans and 'the rest', keenly aware that sections of town populations feel uneasy about the presence of books and the intellectual connotations that accompany the bookish nature of book towns. Dealing with negativity is an ongoing challenge, but, as Turpin (personal interview 2011) and Nelson (personal interview 2011) confirmed, the wider social and economic benefits of Wigtown and Sedbergh have, over time, reinforced book town projects as positive solutions to peripheral sustainability (Fig. 7.1).

Book towns fit particularly well with the 'slow' paradigm that embraces slow books, slow reading, slow food and slow travel, allowing a leisurely immersion in distinctive regional cultures and *terroir*. Book towns answer the need for purposeful activities and personalized consumption experiences related to sensory needs. As I explained in Chap. 3, book towns allow an opportunity for participants to be part of a life-affirming dialogue that requires an investment of time. The book town image is syn-

Fig. 7.1 Wigtown, Scotland's National Book Town, during Wigtown Book Festival week (2016) (Source: Photographer Colin Tennant (used with permission of Wigtown Festival Company))

onymous with a 'core piece of goodness': not only are books discussed, ideas are also traded. Their philosophy embraces a growing interest in ethical, 'green', meaningful and special-interest travel. Book town pilgrimages meet a need for self-development. The move away from material values in the late twentieth century to a more 'post-materialistic' way of thinking is reflected in the way book towns acknowledge that economic goals need to accommodate other aspirations to do with the quality of people's lives. There is a shift from being 'well off' to a concentration on wellbeing. An environmental consciousness also motivates tourists to increasingly search out and compare different places in terms of their perceived character, but the growth of the Romantic gaze that celebrates nature is also responsible for helping to spread the notion of book town tourism worldwide. This is why book towns appeal as sites of retreat from city-based relentlessness to more idealistic, rural, community-focused lifestyles, promising people more perfect lives. The book town ethos therefore attracts creative individuals with previous book experience originating from urban centres, whose expertise, tolerance of diversity and fresh approaches contribute the oxygen that drives such projects forward and excites local people to action.

This is why, in book towns, we witness the cultural mobility of both books and people, manifested in locations that celebrate independent and artistic values. This unique engagement with print culture in book villages delivers status and cultural authority to previously marginalized places, and offers literary immersion for 'true book believers'—serious collectors, and book and literary devotees. These explorations, discoveries and personal experiences in real social spaces cannot, at this time, be replicated by ever more sophisticated online markets. The book town phenomenon reinforces the book as a resilient medium, and an iconic and potent object. For many people to whom I talked as part of this research, book towns are self-contained and self-enriching universes where there is veneration for the written word. What is yet unknown is whether the surprising success of the Book Town Movement, continuing as it is into the early twenty-first century, reflects the amalgamation of number of unique circumstances that bracket the close of the industrial age and the start of the digital age. While it is uncertain whether books in the future will have the same power to drive community regeneration, if and when they no longer constitute as significant a part of our individual memory and daily lived experience, the evidence presented here indicates that book towns will continue to fulfil a number of important social, cultural and economic needs in society.

References

Rojek, C., & Urry, J. (1997). *Touring cultures: Transformations of travel and theory*. London: Routledge.

Seaton, A. V. (1996a). *Book towns and rural tourism development: Hay on Wye 1961–1996*. Glasgow: University of Strathclyde.

Seaton, A. V. (1996b). *Book towns and rural tourism development: The new European book towns 1984–1996*. Glasgow: University of Strathclyde.

Seaton, A. V. (1996c). Hay-on-Wye, the mouse that roared: Book towns and rural tourism. *Tourism Management, 17*(5), 379–385.

Seaton, A. V. (1997, July). The book town concept: Retail specialization and rural tourism. *Insights* [British Tourist Authority/English Tourist Board].
Seaton, A. V. (1999). Book towns as tourism developments in peripheral areas. *The International Journal of Tourism Research, 1*(5), 389–399.
Smith, M. (2006). Entertainment and new leisure tourism. In D. Buhalis & C. Costa (Eds.), *Tourism business frontiers: Consumers, products and industry* (pp. 220–227). Burlington: Elsevier Butterworth Heinemann.

Interviews

Muller, Laurie. Brisbane, Queensland, 17 August 2010 and 7 September 2010.
Nelson, C. Sedbergh, Yorkshire, United Kingdom, 9 September 2011; phone interview, 29 March 2017.
Turpin, A. OBE. Wigtown, Scotland, 4 September 2011; via email, 15 March 2017.

References

A Global Community of Educators. (2011). *Wandering educators*. http://www.wanderingeducators.com/learn-more.html. Accessed 29 Oct 2011.

About Hay Castle Trust and the plans for Hay Castle. (2017). *Hay Castle Trust*. http://haycastletrust.org/ourvision.php#ad-image-0. Accessed 17 Mar.

About Slow TV. (2010). *The Monthly: Australian Politics, Society and Culture*. http://www.themonthly.com.au/about-slowtv. Accessed 10 Aug 2010.

Adams, P. (2012, February 4). Shelf life. *The Weekend Australian Magazine*, p. 38.

Aitchison, C., MacLeod, N., & Shaw, S. (2002). *Leisure and tourism landscapes: Social and cultural geographies*. London: Routledge.

Akerman, P. (2011, February 19–20). It's the human touch that matters for minnows: Bookshops have something the internet doesn't – Direct contact with people. *The Weekend Australian*, p. 3.

Anselot, N. (2004). *Redu: Un Village a Livres Ouverts: La Merveilleuse Histoire du Premier Village du Livre d'Europe Continentale*. Brussels: Editions Racine.

Ashworth, G. J., & Graham, B. (Eds.). (2005). *Senses of place; senses of time*. Aldershot: Ashgate.

Atherstone bids for new identity as England's National Booktown. (2005, June 10). *Booktowns International Press Release*. http://www.inprint.co.uk/thebookguide/shops/atherstone_press_release_2.1.htm. Accessed 14 Mar 2011.

J. Frank, *Regenerating Regional Culture*, Sociology of the Arts,
https://doi.org/10.1007/978-3-319-65036-4

Atherstone Booktown update and progress. (2006, October 30). Report of the Assistant Director (Planning and Development), Atherstone [UK] Community and Environment Board, pp. 1–7.

Austin, J., et al. (2006). Social and commercial entrepreneurship: Same, different or both? *Entrepreneurship Theory and Practice, 30*(1), 1–22.

Australian Bureau of Statistics. (2004). *Australian social trends 2004: Seachange – New coastal residents.* Cat no. 4102.0. Canberra: ABS.

Australian Bureau of Statistics. (2007, October 25). *2006 census Quickstats: Clunes.* http://www.censusdata.abs.gov.au/census_services/getproduct/census/2006/quickstat/UCL210000. Accessed 3 May 2010.

Back to Booktown. (2010). Website. http://www.booktown.clunes.org. Accessed 6 Feb 2010.

Bagshaw, M., & Mills, C. (2010). *Alastair Sawday's slow North Yorkshire: Moors, dales and coast, including York.* Chalfont St Peter: Bardt.

Barker, N. (2001). *A potencie for life: Books in society.* London: British Library Publishing.

Barthes, R. (1972 [1957]). *Mythologies.* London: Paladin.

Bartmanski, D., & Woodward, I. (2015). *Vinyl: The analogue record in the digital age.* London: Bloomsbury.

Basbanes, N. A. (1995). *A gentle madness: Bibliophiles, bibliomanes, and the eternal passion for books.* New York: Henry Holt.

Beale, N. (2011). *Literary tourist.* http://literarytourist.com. Accessed 26 Oct 2011.

Bedford, Y. N. (2012). The '"Peace Gardens", Featherston, South Wairarapa and the chor-farmer'. *Australian and New Zealand Environmental History Network, 5*(2). https://environmentalhistory-au-nz.org/2012/12/the-peace-gardens-featherston-south-wairarapa-and-the-chor-farmer. Accessed 20 Mar 2017.

Beeton, S. (2005). *Film-induced tourism.* Clevedon: Channel View.

Beeton, S. (2006). *Community development through tourism.* Melbourne: Landlinks Press.

Belgium's Book Town. (2004). *Expatica Belgium.* http://www.expatica.com/be/leisure/travel_tourism/belgiums-book-town-12329.html?ppager=0. Accessed 6 Aug 2010.

Benjamin, W. (1999). *The Arcades Project.* Cambridge, MA: Belknap Press.

Benjamin, W. (2007 [1968]). Unpacking my library: A talk about book collecting. In *Illuminations: Essays and reflections* (pp. 59–67). New York: Schocken Books.

Benjamin, W. (2008). *The work of art in the age of its technological reproductivity and other writings on media.* Cambridge, MA: Belknap Press.

Bennett, A., & Woodward, I. (2014). Festival spaces, identity, experience and belonging. In A. Bennett, J. Taylor, & I. Woodward (Eds.), *The festivalization of culture* (pp. 11–25). Farnham: Ashgate.

Bennett, A., Taylor, J., & Woodward, I. (Eds.). (2014). *The festivalization of culture*. Farnham: Ashgate.

Benson, M., & O'Reilly, K. (2009). *Lifestyle migration: Expectations, aspirations and experiences*. Aldershot: Ashgate.

BERR (Department for Business Enterprise and Regulatory Reform). (2008). *Impact of regulation on productivity: BERR occasional paper no. 3*. http://www.cses.co.uk/UPI/File/Impact-of-regulation-on-productivity.pdf. Accessed 16 Apr 2015.

Birkerts, S. (1995). *The Gutenberg Elegies: The fate of reading in an electronic age*. Winchester: Faber and Faber.

Blainey, G. (1983). *The tyranny of distance: How distance shaped Australia's history*. Melbourne: Sun Books.

Book town on Timbuktu shortlist. (2006, November 13). *BBC News*. http://news.bbc.co.uk/2/hi/uk_news/wales/mid_/6144034.stm. Accessed 13 Apr 2010.

Booked Up. (2010). Website. http://www.bookedupac.com/id12.html. Accessed 17 Aug 2010.

Bookish Blaenavon opens new chapter. (2003, June 27). *BBC News*. http://news.bbc.co.uk/2/hi/uk_news/wales/3023862.stm. Accessed 25 May 2011.

Booktown South Africa. (2008). *KZN literary tourism*. http://www.literarytourism.co.za/content/view/174/1. Accessed 13 Oct 2008.

BookTownNet. (2014). *Redu, Village du Livre*. http://members.tripod.com/redu/english/booktown.htm. Accessed 20 Apr 2014.

BOOKtrail. (2010). *Southern Highlands NSW.* http://www.southern-highlands.com.au/booktrail. Accessed 17 Oct 2010.

BOOKtrail Southern Highlands NSW. (2014). *The wonderful book world of the Southern Highlands*. http://www.booktown.com.au/shbookworld.htm. Accessed 20 Apr 2014.

Booth, R. (Ed.) (1976). *The country life book of book collecting*. London: Hamlyn.

Booth, R. (1977). *Independence for Hay*. Cusop: Richard Booth Publications.

Booth, R. (1983a). *An address by the King of Hay in the Black Mountains of Wales to Russell means, spiritual leader of the Lakota people in the Black Hills of the Dakotas*. Cusop: Richard Booth Publications.

Booth, R. (1983b). *Bureaucracy in Brecon and Radnor: With reference to a horse ride through Cusop Dingle*. Cusop: Richard Booth Publications.

Booth, R. (1983c). *Why Woolworth will destroy Brecon*. Cusop: Richard Booth Publications.

Booth, R. (1999). *My kingdom of books*. Ceredigion: Y Lolfa Cyf.

Borsch, O. J., et al. (2008). Resource configuration and creative practices of community entrepreneurs. *Journal of Enterprising Communities: People and Places in the Global Economy, 2*(2), 100–123.

Bourdieu, P. (1984). *Distinction: A social critique of the judgement of taste*. Cambridge, MA: Harvard University Press.

Bourdieu, P. (1986). *The forms of capital*. http://www.marxists.org/reference/subject/philosophy/works/fr/bourdieu-forms-capital.htm. Accessed 25 Nov 2010.

Bowie-Sell, D. (2012, October 1). Wigtown Book Festival 2012: Marek Kukula, Martin Dorey and James Attlee. *The Telegraph*. http://www.telegraph.co.uk/culture/books/wigtown-book-festival/9578887/Wigtown-Book-Festival-2012-Marek-Kukula-Martin-Dorey-and-James-Attlee.html. Accessed 21 Nov 2012.

Bradshaw, T., & Nichols, B. (2004). *Reading at risk: A survey of literary reading in America*. Washington, DC: National Endowment for the Arts.

Brady, T. (2011, March). *Clunes Back to Booktown and the writer*. Victorian Writers Centre. http://www.snodger.com.au/tessbrady/images/pdfs/Writer-in-community-VWC.pdf. Accessed 20 June 2012.

Brady, T. (2012, September). Clunes address. *Paju Booksori: World Booktown Symposium*. https://clunesbooktown.com.au/ Accessed 10 July 2013.

Brewster, D. (1996). *Wigtown: The story of a royal and ancient burgh*. Wigtown: The Galloway Gazette.

Briedenhann, J., & Wickens, E. (2004). Rural tourism: Meeting the challenges of the new South Africa. *The International Journal of Tourism Research, 6*(3), 189–203.

Brisebois, M., & Mandelbrote, G. (Ed.). (2008). *Out of print and into profit: A history of the rare and secondhand book trade in Britain in the twentieth century* [Book Review]. Papers of the Bibliographical Society of Canada, 22 March. http://www.thefreelibrary.com/Giles+Mandelbrote,+ed.+Out+of+Print+%26+Into+Profit%3A+A+History+of+the...-a0183983011. Accessed 22 July 2012.

Brown, P. (2011, March 16–22). Brought to book: The printed page's days seem to be numbered. *Brisbane News*.

Bryman, A. (1995). *Disney and his worlds*. London: Routledge.

Burnett, K. A. (1998). Local heroics: Reflecting on incomers and local rural development discourses in Scotland. *Sociologica Ruralis, 38*(2), 204–224.

Burnley, I., & Murphy, P. (2004). *Sea change: Movement from metropolitan to Arcadian Australia*. Sydney: UNSW Press.

Burns, P. (2001). Brief encounters: Culture, tourism and the local/global nexus. In S. Wahab & C. Cooper (Eds.), *Tourism in the age of globalization* (pp. 290–305). London: Routledge.

Burns, P., & Novelli, M. (2008). *Tourism and mobilities: Local/global connections*. Cambridge, MA: CAN International.

Burwood, N. (2010). International booktowns. *News and Trivia Archive*. http://www.anyamountofbooks.com/narchive.html. Accessed 23 Aug 2010.

Butler, B. D. (2010, 17 June). What's your favourite book town? *Travel Between the Pages: The Intersection of Travel, Books & Art*. http://travelbetweenthepages.com/2010/06/17/whats-your-favorite-book-town. Accessed 18 Aug 2010.

Butler, R. W., & Hall, C. M. (1998). Image and re-imaging of rural areas. In R. Butler, C. M. Hall, & J. Jenkins (Eds.), *Tourism and recreation in rural areas* (pp. 115–122). Chichester: John Wiley and Sons.

Buzbee, L. (2006). *The yellow-lighted bookshop: A memoir, a history*. Saint Paul: Graywolf Press.

Calhoun, C. (2002). The class consciousness of frequent travelers: Toward a critique of actually existing cosmopolitanism. *The South Atlantic Quarterly, 101*(4), 869–897.

Campbell, C. (1987). *The Romantic ethic and the spirit of modern consumerism*. Oxford: Basil Blackwell.

Campbell, J. (2014). *The bookshop book*. London: Constable and Robinson.

Carrière, J.-C., & Eco, U. (2011). *This is not the end of the book: Two great men discuss our digital future*. London: Harvill Secker.

Carter, D., & Galligan, A. (Eds.). (2007). *Making books: Contemporary Australian Publishing*. Brisbane: University of Queensland Press.

Castells, M. (1997). *The power of identity: The information age: Economy, society and culture* (Vol. 1). Oxford: Blackwell.

Celebration of Books Maleny. (2015). Website. http://www.celebrationofbooksmaleny.com. Accessed 4 May 2015.

Chappel, S., & Brown, L. (2006). Literary tourism beyond the city. In P. Whitelaw & B. O'Mahony (Eds.), *CAUTHE: To the city and beyond* (pp. 1764–1773). Melbourne: Victoria University School of Hospitality and Tourism.

Chenoweth, E. (2005, June 27). Making Hay-on-Wye. *Publishers Weekly* [New York], pp. 24–6.

City of Archer City. (2010). Website. http://www.archercity.org. Accessed 17 Aug 2010.

Claridge, C. L. (2010). *The Slow Movement: Making a connection.* http://www.slowmovement.com. Accessed 4 Oct 2010.

Clark, T. J. (2000). Reservation of the marvellous: *The Arcades Project* by Walter Benjamin. *London Review of Books, 22*(12), 3–9.

Clark, B. L. (2009, March 19). Cross border raid for books. *The Exile Bibliophile: Adventures in Book Collecting and Ephemera* [Weblog]. http://exilebibliophile.blogspot.com.au/2009/03/cross-border-raid-for-books.html. Accessed 17 Aug 2010.

Clarke, K. (2000). *The book of Hay.* Little Logaston Woonton Almeley: Logaston Press.

Classen, C. (2012). *The deepest sense: A cultural history of touch.* Urbana: University of Illinois Press.

Clement, B. (1999, May 4). Voting for a new Britain: King of Hay stands as a Scargillite. Unlikely ally sings Scargill's praises. *The Independent.* http://www.independent.co.uk/news/voting-for-a-new-britain-king-of-hay-stands-as-a-scargillite-unlikely-ally-sings-scargills-praises-1091383.html. Accessed 30 Oct 2009.

Clunes. (2015). *Victorian places 2015.* http://victorianplaces.com.au/clunes. Accessed 30 Mar 2017.

Clunes Booktown: For the love of books. (2015). Website. http://clunesbooktown.com.au. Accessed 6 July 2015.

Cogent Strategies International Limited. (2009). *The economic impact of StenaLine Wigtown book festival 2008: A report for the Wigtown Festival Company.* Glasgow: Cogent Strategies International Limited.

Cole, S. (2006). Cultural tourism, community participation and empowerment. In *Cultural tourism in a changing world: Politics, participation and (re)presentation* (pp. 89–103). Clevedon: Channel View.

Collins, P. (2003). *Sixpence House: Lost in a town of books.* New York: Bloomsbury.

Collits, P. (2000). *Small town decline and survival: Trends, success factors and policy issues.* Paper presented to Future of Australia's Country Towns. LaTrobe University, Bendigo. http://www.regional.org.au/au/countrytowns/global/collits.htm. Accessed 31 Aug 2010.

Constantoura, P. (2001). *Australians and the arts.* Sydney: Federation Press.

Cooke, P., & Lazzeretti, L. (Eds.). (2008). *Creative cities, cultural clusters and local economic development.* Cheltenham: Edward Elgar Publishing Ltd.

Coser, L. (1992). Introduction: Maurice Halbwachs 1877–1945. In L. Coser (Ed.), *On collective memory* (pp. 1–34). Chicago: University of Chicago Press.

Craddock, K. (1993, July–November). An introduction to book collecting. *Antiques and Art in Victoria*, n.p.

Craik, J. (2001). Cultural tourism. In N. Douglas, N. Douglas, & R. Derrett (Eds.), *Special interest tourism: Context and cases* (pp. 113–139). Brisbane: John Wiley & Sons.

Cresswell, T. (2004). *Place: A short introduction*. Oxford: Blackwell.

Cuers, S., & Hewston, J. (Eds.). (2006). *Strong communities handbook: In what ways can urban and regional planning contribute towards high levels of social capital and community strengths in new and re-developing communities?* Brisbane: Queensland University of Technology.

Cumbria Economic Plan. (2007). *Copeland Borough Council*. http://copeland.gov.uk/attachments/cumbria-economic-plan-2007. Accessed 9 Oct 2011.

Darnton, R. (1999, March 18). The new age of the book. *The New York Review of Books*. http://www.nybooks.com/articles/546. Accessed 30 Oct 2009.

Darnton, R. (2009). *The case for books: Past present and future*. New York: Public Affairs.

De Certeau, M. (1984). *Notes from the practice of everyday life*. Berkeley: University of California Press.

Derrett, R. (2001). Special interest tourism: Starting with the individual. In N. Douglas, N. Douglas, & R. Derrett (Eds.), *Special interest tourism: Context and cases* (pp. 1–28). Brisbane: John Wiley & Sons.

Dewailly, J.-M. (1998). Images of heritage in rural regions. In R. Butler, C. M. Hall, & J. Jenkins (Eds.), *Tourism and recreation in rural areas* (pp. 123–137). Chichester: John Wiley and Sons.

Dickenson, J., & Lumsden, L. (2010). *Slow travel and tourism*. London: Earthscan.

Dickenson, J. E., Robbins, D., & Lumsden, L. (2010). Holiday travel discourses and climate change. *Journal of Transport Geography, 18*, 482–489.

Disruption and innovation in the Australian book industry. (2016, February 9). Small Press Network. http://smallpressnetwork.com.au/australian-publishing-industry-is-fighting-back-against-digital-disruption. Accessed 8 Apr 2017.

Douglas, N., Douglas, N., & Derrett, R. (Eds.). (2001). *Special interest tourism: Context and cases*. Brisbane: John Wiley & Sons.

Dowling, C. (2004). *Seachange: Australians in pursuit of the good life*. Sydney: Exisle.

Earl, B. (2008). Literary tourism: Constructions of value, celebrity and distinction. *International Journal of Cultural Studies, 11*, 401.

Eltham, K. (2009, January 7). Where the bloody hell are you? *Electric alphabet: Writing and publishing in the digital near-future* [Weblog]. http://electricalphabet.wordpress.com/2009/01/07/where-the-bloody-hell-are-you. Accessed 31 Aug 2010.

Engler, M. (1994). Theme towns: The pitfalls and alternative of image making. *Small Town, 25*(1), 4–7.

European Institute of Cultural Routes. (2006, January 18). *Cultural routes and landscapes: A common heritage of Europe*. http://www.culture-routes.lu. Accessed 10 Mar 2010.

Evans, G., & Shaw, P. (2004). *The contribution of culture to regeneration in the UK: A review of evidence*. A Report to the Department for Culture, Media and Sport. London: DCMS.

Fadiman, A. (1998). *Ex Libris: Confessions of a common reader*. Harmondsworth: Penguin.

Fentress, J., & Wickham, C. (1994). *Social memory*. Oxford: Blackwell.

Finkelstein, D., & McCleery, A. (Eds.). (2002). *The book history reader*. London: Routledge.

FitzGerald, S. (2012). *Feasibility study for a Graiguenamanagh permanent town of books*. Submitted as an application for Leader Funding from the Irish National Rural Network, Moate, Co. Westmeath, Republic of Ireland.

Flipo, F., & Schneider, F. (Eds.). (2008). *Proceedings of the first international conference on economic degrowth for ecological sustainability and social equity*. Paris, 18–19 April. Research & Degrowth, INT, 322p.

Florida, R. (1995). Toward the learning region. *Futures, 27*(5), 527–536.

Florida, R. (2002). *The rise of the creative class: And how it's transforming work, leisure, community and everyday life*. New York: Basic Books.

Florida, R. (2008). Who's your city? New York: Basic Books.

Foundation for Rural and Regional Renewal (FRRR). (2012). Website. http://www.frrr.org.au. Accessed 25 July 2012.

Francis, R. (2004, November 19). Making conversation: The rise of literary festivals. *Flakmagazine*. http://www.flakmag.com/books/litfest.html. Accessed 1 Feb 2011.

Frank, J. (1996). Does regionalism have an impact on the arts practice of a community? MBus (Arts Mgt), Queensland University of Technology.

Franklin, A. (2008). *A collector's year*. Sydney: UNSW Press.

Franklin, A., & Crang, M. (2001). The trouble with tourism and travel theory. *Tourist Studies, 1*(1), 5–22.

Frederickson, L., & Anderson, D. (1999). A qualitative exploration of the wilderness experience as a source of spiritual inspiration. *Journal of Environmental Psychology, 19*, 21–29.

Frenkel, S., & Walton, J. (2000). Bavarian Leavenworth and the symbolic economy of a theme town. *Geographical Review, 90*(4), 559–584.

Fullagar, S. (2010). *Creating slow travel cultures: Cycle touring as an alternative hedonism*. Paper presented to Creative Communities II Conference. Griffith University, Gold Coast, 23 September.

Gablik, S. (1993). Toward an ecological self. In R. Hertz (Ed.), *Theories of contemporary art* (2nd ed.). Englewood Cliffs: Prentice Hall.

Gardiner, N. (2009). A manifesto for slow travel. *Hidden Europe Magazine, 25*, 10–14.

Garnett, A. M., & Lewis, P. E. T. (2007). Population and employment changes in regional Australia. *Economic Papers, 26*(1), 29–43.

Gekowski, R. (2011, March 9). A fond farewell to secondhand bookshops. *The Guardian* [Books]. http://www.guardian.co.uk/books/booksblog/2011/mar/09/farewell-secondhand-bookshops. Accessed 12 Mar 2011.

Gelder, K., & Jacobs, J. M. (1998). *Uncanny Australia: Sacredness and identity in a postcolonial nation*. Melbourne: Melbourne University Press.

Gelling, C. (2003). *Berrima, New South Wales*. Berrima: Berrima Courthouse Museum.

Gibson, C. (Ed.). (2012). *Creativity in peripheral places: Defining the creative industries*. London/New York: Routledge.

Gibson, C., & Connell, J. (Eds.). (2011). *Festival places: Revitalising rural Australia*. Bristol: Channel View.

Gibson, C., & Connell, J. (Eds.). (2012). *Music festivals and regional development in Australia*. Farnham: Ashgate.

Glaas, W. (2011, August 8). My name is Wendy and I'm a bookstore junkie. *Talking Writing: A Magazine for Writers*. http://talkingwriting.com/?p=22196. Accessed 18 Aug 2011.

Goffman, E. (1959). *The presentation of self in everyday life*. Garden City: Doubleday.

Goldschmidt, P. (2012). *The falling sky*. Glasgow: Freight Books.

Goldstone, L., & Goldstone, N. (1997). *Used and rare: Travels in the book world*. New York: St Martin's Press.

Goodenough, M. (2006, April 11). Dalmellington book town: On the road to nowhere. *The Book Guide* [UK]. http://www.inprint.co.uk/thebookguide/shops/dalmellington_book_town.shtml. Accessed 7 Aug 2010.

Goodey, B. (1975). Urban trails: Origins and opportunities. *The Planner, 61*, 29–30.

Gopnik, A. (2015, June 12). When a bookstore closes, an argument ends. *The New Yorker*. http://www.newyorker.com/news/daily-comment/when-a-bookstore-closes-an-argument-ends. Accessed 18 June 2015.

Grado, S. C., Strauss, C. H., & Lord, B. E. (1997). Antiquing as a tourism recreational activity in south western Pennsylvania. *Journal of Travel Research, 35*(3), 52–56.

Graiguenamanagh – Town of Books. (2009). *Graiguenamanagh – Town of books, book festival*. http://www.booktownireland.com. Accessed 26 Oct 2009.

Grant-Marshall, S. (2012, November 23). From sad "nothing" town to book town. *BDLive.com*. http://www.bdlive.co.za/life/travel/2012/11/23/from-sad-nothing-town-to-book-town. Accessed 25 Jan 2013.

Grauman, B. (2008, October 29). Words, mountains, architecture form unique city of books. *Bloomberg*. http://www.bloomberg.com/apps/news?pid=newsarchive&sid=aNrGkzc99VXU&refer=home. Accessed 18 Nov 2010.

Green, C. (1992). Unofficial world: Postcolonialism and the metropolis. *Art and Text, 43*(38–41), 96–97.

Green, R. (2000). Notions of town character: A coastal community responds to change. *Australian Planner, 37*(2), 76–86.

Green, S. (2010). "The rainbow bridge": Writing and teaching in a regional context. *Text, 14*(1). http://www.textjournal.com.au. Accessed 7 Apr 2011.

Gretzel, U., Fesenmaier, D. R., & O'Leary, J. T. (2006). The transformation of consumer behaviour. In D. Buhalis & C. Costa (Eds.), *Tourism business frontiers: Consumers, products and industry* (pp. 9–18). Burlington: Elsevier Butterworth-Heinemann.

Griswold, W. (2008). *Regionalism and the reading class*. Chicago: University of Chicago Press.

Hall, C. M. (2009). Degrowing tourism: Décroissance, sustainable consumption and steady-state tourism. *Anatolia: An International Journal of Tourism and Hospitality Research, 20*(1), 46–61.

Hall, D., Roberts, L., & Mitchell, M. (2003). *New directions in rural tourism: Local impacts, global trends*. Farnham: Ashgate.

Halseth, G., Market, S., & Bruce, D. (2010). *The next rural economies*. Wallingford: CABI.

Hanna, J. (2005, June 10). *Atherstone bids for new identity as England's National Book Town* [Media Release]. http://www.inprint.co.uk/thebookguide/shops/atherstone_press_release_2.1.htm. Accessed 22 May 2011.

Hanna, J. (2009). *Booktowns*. http://www.booktown.org.uk/booktowns.html. Accessed 31 Oct 2009.

Harris, C. (2015, October 15). Featherston becomes New Zealand's first booktown with new festival this weekend. *Stuff*. http://www.stuff.co.nz/dominion-post/news/73050630/featherston-becomes-new-zealands-first-booktown-with-new-festival-this-weekend. Accessed 26 June 2016.

Harris, P. (2012). UK: Is the book town of Hay-on-Wye dying? *Sheppard's Confidential: News and Events in Antiquarian and Second-Hand Books, Ephemera, Prints and Maps*, 19 April.

Harvey, D. (1996). *Justice, nature and the geography of difference*. Oxford: Blackwell.
Harvey, D. (2000). *Spaces of hope*. Edinburgh: Edinburgh University Press.
Hay Festival. (2011). Website. hayfestival.org. http://www.hayfestival.com. Accessed 22 Oct 2011.
Hayes, D., & MacLeod, N. (2007). Packaging places: Designing heritage trails using an experience economy perspective to manage visitor engagement. *Journal of Vacation Marketing, 13*(1), 45–58.
Hazlitt, W. (1928). On reading old books. In *The plain speaker: Opinions on books, men and things* (pp. 220–229). London: J.M. Dent and Sons.
Hill, S. (2009). *Howards End is on the landing: A year of reading from home*. London: Profile Books.
Hodgkinson, T. (2011). *The Idler*. http://idler.co.uk. Accessed 22 Oct 2011.
Holman, T. (2006, June 30). Out and about in book town: Sedburgh in Cumbria has been designated England's first official book town. *The Bookseller*, p. 30.
Honoré, C. (2004). *In praise of slowness: How a worldwide movement is challenging the cult of speed*. New York: HarperCollins.
Hopkins, J. (1998). Commodifying the countryside: Marketing myths of rurality. In R. Butler, C. M. Hall, & J. Jenkins (Eds.), *Tourism and recreation in rural areas* (pp. 139–156). Chichester: John Wiley and Sons.
Horne, D. (2002). *Keynote address: The arts, the regions and the economy*. Paper presented to Groundswell: Regional Arts Surging Forward. Regional Arts Australia National Conference, Albury Wodonga.
Horowitz, M. (1997, 12 July 12). Larry McMurtry's dream job. *New York Times* [Books]. http://www.nytimes.com/books/97/12/07/home/article2.html?_r=5. Accessed 7 Aug 2010.
Howie, F. (2003). *Managing the tourist destination*. London: Continuum.
Huang, Y.-H., & Stewart, W. P. (1996). Rural tourism development: Shifting basis of community solidarity. *Journal of Travel Research, 34*(4), 26–32.
Huckans, J. C. (2005, July/August). Book town revisited. *Book Source Magazine*. http://www.booksourcemagazine.com/showstory.php?sid=archive/e0507. Accessed 31 Oct 2009.
Huff, S. (2008). Identity and landscape: The reification of place in Strasbourg, France. In D. C. Knudsen et al. (Eds.), *Landscape, tourism and meaning*. Bloomington: Ashgate.
Hugo, G. (1996). Counterurbanisation. In P. Newton & M. Bell (Eds.), *Population shift: Mobility and change in Australia* (pp. 126–146). Canberra: Australian Government Publishing Service.

Huigen, P. P. P., & Meijering, L. (2005). Making places: A story of De Venen. In G. J. Ashworth & B. Graham (Eds.), *Senses of place; senses of time*. Aldershot: Ashgate.

Inglis, F. (2000). *The delicious history of the holiday*. London: Routledge.

International booktowns. (2015). *The international booktowns movement*. http://booktown.com/International BKtowns.htm. Accessed 20 Aug 2015.

International League of Antiquarian Booksellers (ILAB). (2012). http://www.ilab.org. Accessed 10 Jan 2012.

IOB – International Organization of Book Towns. (2009). *Booktown.Net: World of books*. http://www.booktown.net. Accessed 5 Mar 2009.

Irshad, H. (2009). *Clusters: A key to rural prosperity*. Alberta: Government of Alberta.

Isserman, A. M., Fesser, E., & Warren, D. E. (2009). Why some rural places prosper and others do not. *International Regional Science Review, 32*, 300–342.

Jansen, A., & Skogseid, I. (2003). Book towns and the network society: New perspectives on developing rural enterprise. In S. Krishna & S. Madon (Eds.), *The digital challenge: Information technology in the development context*. Farnham: Ashgate.

Jones, K. (1997, December). I've written enough fiction. *Texas Monthly*. http://www.texasmonthly.com/1997-12-01/feature6.php. Accessed 10 Aug 2010.

Jones, K. (1998, August). Larry McMurtry's next career. *Biblio* [USA], p. 50.

Kahn, B. M. (1987). *Cosmopolitan culture: The gilt-edged dream of a tolerant city*. New York: Atheneum.

Kampung Buku Book Village Malaysia. http://www.bookvillagemalaysia.com Book *Village Foundation Malaysia*. Accessed 3 Nov 2009.

Karel, E. (2009, June 30). Brittany's booktown. *France Today*. http://www.francetoday.com/articles/2009/06/30/brittany-s-booktown.html. Accessed 30 June 2010.

Kean, D. (2012). Ebooks: The unlikely saviour of the hardback. *Danuta Kean* [Weblog]. http://talkingwriting.com/my-name-is-wendy-and-im-a-bookstore-junkie. Accessed 1 Apr 2012.

Kells, S. (2011). *Rare: A life among antiquarian books*. Sydney: Folio.

Kendall, G., Skrbis, Z., & Woodward, I. (2009). *The sociology of cosmopolitanism*. London: Palgrave Macmillan.

Kennedy, M. (2003, March 10). Books could help town to turn over new leaf. *The Guardian*. http://www.guardian.co.uk/uk/2003/mar/10/books.artsnews-temporary. Accessed 30 June 2010.

Kennedy, M. (2010). *Research audit: Clunes back to booktown 2010*. Bendigo: La Trobe University Planning and Development Program. http://www.booktown.clunes.org/documents/latrobe.pdf. Accessed 20 June 2012.

Kennedy, M. (2011). Binding a sustainable future: Book towns, themed place-branding and rural renewal. A case study of Clunes' "*Back to Booktown*". In J. Martin & T. Budge (Eds.), *The sustainability of Australia's country towns: Renewal, renaissance, resilience* (pp. 207–226). Ballarat: VURRN Press.

Kenner, H. (1998). *The elsewhere community: A grand tour of the world, and the mind*. Sydney: Allen & Unwin.

Kerby, J. (2010, August 4). Moneytimes with Jill Kerby. *The Anglo-Celt*. http://www.anglocelt.ie/opinion/columnists/articles/2010/08/04/3999038-moneytimes-with-jill-kerby. Accessed 25 Nov 2011.

Kijas, J. (2002). A place at the coast: Internal migration and the shift to the coastal-countryside. *Transformations, 2*, 1–12.

Killion, L. (2001). Rural tourism. In N. Douglas, N. Douglas, & R. Derrett (Eds.), *Special interest tourism: Context and cases* (pp. 165–187). Brisbane: John Wiley & Sons.

Kleinart, S. (1991). Towards regionalism. *Eyeline: East Coast Contemporary Visual Arts, 14*, 17.

Kneafsey, M. (2000). Tourism, place identities and social relations in the European rural periphery. *European Urban and Regional Studies, 7*(1), 35–50.

Knudsen, D. C., et al. (Eds.). (2008). *Landscape, tourism and meaning*. Bloomington: Ashgate.

Kong, L., & O'Connor, J. (Eds.). (2010). *Creative economies, creative cities: Asian European perspectives*. New York: Springer.

Kurschus, S. (2015). *European book cultures: Diversity as a challenge*. Heidelberg: Springer.

Lade, C., & Jackson, J. (2004). Key success factors in regional festivals: Some Australian experiences. *Event Management, 9*, 1–11.

Landry, C. (2008 [2000]). *The creative city: A toolkit for urban innovators*. London: Earthscan.

Landry, C., et al. (1996). *The art of regeneration: Urban renewal through cultural activity*. London: Comedia.

Lang, S. (2015). *Outspoken*. http://www.outspokenmaleny.com. Accessed 4 May 2015.

Lanham, F. (2009, January 20). Author Larry McMurtry sees the end of book culture. *Houston Chronicle*. http://www.chron.com/entertainment/article/

Author-Larry-McMurtry-sees-the-end-of-book-culture-1741461.php. Accessed 31 Aug 2010.

Lavoie, D. (1991). The discovery and interpretation of profit opportunities, culture and the Kirznerian entrepreneur. In B. Berger (Ed.), *The culture of entrepreneurship*. San Francisco: ICS Press.

Lindenberger, M. (2012, August 15). The great book sale of Texas: Larry McMurtry gives up his collection. *Time*, TIME.com. http://nation.time.com/2012/08/15/the-great-book-sale-of-texas-larry-mcmurtry-gives-up-his-collection. Accessed 4 July 2013.

Lindores, S. (2010, May 31). Hay festival founder is sure books' future secure. *Reuters Business and Financial News*. http://www.reuters.com/article/2010/05/31/us-britain-hayfestival-idUSTRE64U1NJ20100531?pageNumber=1. Accessed 16 Feb 2011.

Löfgren, O. (1999). *On holiday: A history of vacationing*. Berkeley: University of California Press.

Löfgren, O. (2003). The new economy: A cultural history. *Global Networks, 3*(3), 239–254.

Lopez de Haro, A. (2011, April 26). Despite rapid rise of e-books, rare books aren't endangered. *Columbia News Service*. http://www.bendbulletin.com/slideshows/1411712-151/despite-rapid-rise-of-e-books-rare-books-arent. Accessed 21 Aug 2015.

Lowenthal, D. (1985). *The past is a foreign country*. Cambridge: Cambridge University Press.

Macaskill, H. (2007, March 24). The complete guide to book towns. *The Independent* [UK]. http://www.independent.co.uk/travel/uk/the-complete-guide-to-book-towns-441542.html. Accessed 22 Feb 2010.

MacCannell, D. (1999 [1976]). *The tourist: A new theory of the leisure class*. Berkeley: University of California Press.

MacCannell, D. (2011). *The ethics of sightseeing*. Berkeley: University of California Press.

MacLeod, D. V. L. (2003). Culture and the construction of a niche market destination. In D. V. L. Macleod (Ed.), *Niche tourism in question: Interdisciplinary perspectives on problems and possibilities*. Glasgow: University of Glasgow Press.

MacLeod, D. V. L. (2009). Scottish theme towns: Have new identities enhanced development? *Journal of Tourism and Cultural Change, 7*(2), 133–145.

MacLeod, D. V. L. (2010). Power, culture and the production of heritage. In D. V. L. MacLeod & J. G. Carrier (Eds.), *Tourism, power and culture: Anthropological insights* (pp. 64–89). Bristol: Channel View.

MacLeod, D. V. L., & Carrier, G. (2010). Tourism, power and culture. In D. V. L. MacLeod & J. G. Carrier (Eds.), *Tourism, power and culture: Anthropological insights* (pp. 64–89). Bristol: Channel View.

Maleny Arts Council (2012, March 13). Maleny – A book town? *Public Meeting, Maleny RSL Hall.*

Mandelbrote, G. (Ed.). (2006). *Out of print and into profit: A history of the rare and secondhand book trade in the twentieth century*. London: British Library and Oak Knoll Press.

Manguel, A. (1996). *The library at night*. New Haven: Yale University Press.

Manguel, A. (1997). *A history of reading*. London: Flamingo.

Markusen, A. (2014). Creative cities: A 10-year research agenda. *Journal of Urban Affairs, 36*(S2), 567–589.

Marshall, A. (1998). *Trafficking in old books*. Melbourne: Lost Domain.

Marshall, A. (2004). *Fossicking for old books*. Melbourne: Bread Street Press.

Martin, J. (2009, October 20). *Montereggio – A booktown in Italy*. Wandering Italy Blog [Weblog]. http://wanderingitaly.com/blog/article/548/montereggio-a-booktown-in-italy. Accessed 1 Sept 2010.

Martin, J., & Budge, T. (Eds.). (2011). *The sustainability of Australia's country towns: Renewal, renaissance, resilience*. Ballarat: Victorian Universities Regional Research Network Press.

McCarthy, K. F., Ondaatje, E. H., Zakaras, L., & Brooks, A. (2005). *Gifts of the muse: Reframing the debate about the benefits of the arts*. Santa Monica: RAND Corporation.

McClarence, S. (2009, May 17). The little town taking a leaf out of Hay's book. *The Observer* [UK]. http://www.guardian.co.uk/travel/2009/may/17/sedbergh-book-town-cumbria. Accessed 3 Apr 2011.

McCrum, R. (2006, January 15). E-read all about it. *The Observer* [UK]. http://www.guardian.co.uk/books/2006/jan/15/ebooks.technology/print. Accessed 3 Feb 2011.

McFadyen, W. (2005, June 25). Walking many a country aisle. *The Age* [Melbourne]. http://www.theage.com.au/news/victoria/walking-many-a-country-aisle/2005/06/23/1119321846994.html. Accessed 22 May 2011.

McGranahan, D., & Wojan, T. (2007). Recasting the creative class to examine growth processes in rural and urban counties. *Regional Studies, 41*(2), 197–216.

McGuire, F., et al. (1999). *Leisure and aging: Ulyssean living in later life*. Champaign: Sagamore.

McHenry, J. A. (2011). Art will save the city, but what about country towns? The role of the arts in rural towns of Western Australia's Mid West region. In

J. Martin & T. Budge (Eds.), *The sustainability of Australia's country towns: Renewal, renaissance, resilience* (pp. 327–349). Ballarat: Victorian Universities Regional Research Network Press.

McKercher, B. (2002). Towards a classification of cultural tourists. *The International Journal of Tourism Research, 4*(1), 29–38.

McMillan, H. (2013, October 2). The lore (of Galloway) and you. *Wigtown Book Festival.* http://wigtownbookfestival.com/blog/the-lore-of-galloway-and-you/7. Accessed 10 Dec 2013.

McMillan, H. (2014). *McMillan's Gallovidean encyclopaedia.* Wigtown: Wigtown Festival Company.

McMurtry, L. (1997, December). Interview with Kathryn Jones. *Texas Monthly.* http://www.texasmonthly.com/1997-12-01/feature6.php. Accessed 10 Aug 2010.

McMurtry, L. (1999). *Walter Benjamin at the Dairy Queen: Reflections at sixty and beyond.* New York: Simon & Schuster.

McMurtry, L. (2004, September). Interview with Evan Smith. 'Texas Monthly talks'. *Texas Monthly.* http://www.texasmonthly.com/2004-09-01/talks-2.php. Accessed 10 Aug 2010.

McMurtry, L. (2008). *Books: A memoir.* New York: Simon & Schuster.

McMurtry, L. (2009a, January 20). Interview with Fritz Lanham. 'Author Larry McMurtry sees the end of book culture'. *Chron* [USA]. http://www.chron.com/disp/story.mpl/headline/features/6221607.html. Accessed 31 Aug 2010.

McMurtry, L. (2009b). *Literary life: A second memoir.* New York: Simon & Schuster.

McMurtry, L. (2011, September 22). How to run a bookstore: Neatness doesn't count. *Bloomberg Businessweek.* http://www.businessweek.com/printer/magazine/how-to-run-a-bookstore-09222011.html. Accessed 1 Oct 2011.

McShane, P. (2002). *To further Australia's understanding and involvement in the international booktown movement through a program of visits and interviews.* Winston Churchill Memorial Trust of Australia. http://www.booktown.com.au/ChurchillReport_Booktowns_2002.htm. Accessed 27 Feb 2010.

McShane, P. (2009, December 10). *BookTown Australia: The international book town experience – An Australian perspective.* Monash University Seminar: Book Towns and Writer's Festivals. http://arts.monash.edu.au/blogs/events/2009/12/10/seminar-book-towns-and-writers-festivals. Accessed 14 Mar 2011.

Meetham, K. (2001). *Tourism in global society: Place, culture, consumption.* Basingstoke: Palgrave.

Merfeld-Langston, A. L. (2007). The *villages du livre*: Local identity, cultural politics and print culture in contemporary France. PhD thesis, Pennsylvania State University.

Merfeld-Langston, A. L. (2009). Montolieu, France, village of living books. In *A compendium of clusters in less populated places: Circumstances, interventions and outcomes* (pp. 41–42). Carborro: Regional Technology Strategies.

Merfeld-Langston, A. L. (2010). Celebrating literature to shape citizenship: France's 2007 *Lire en fête. Modern and Contemporary France, 18*(3), 343–356.

Merfeld-Langston, A. L. (2014). Judging a book town by its cover: Marketing French *villages du livre*. In P. Wallen & P. Young (Eds.), *Place and locality in modern France* (pp. 125–137). London: Bloomsbury.

Michael, E. (2002). Antiques and tourism in Australia. *Tourism Management, 23*, 117–125.

Michael, E. (2007). *Micro-clusters and networks: The growth of tourism*. Oxford: Elsevier.

Miedema, J. (2009). *Slow reading*. Duluth: Litwin Books.

Miller, L. J. (2006). *Reluctant capitalists: Bookselling and the culture of consumption*. Chicago: University of Chicago Press.

Minet, P. (1989). *Late booking: My first twenty-five years in the secondhand book trade*. Old Knowle: Frantic Press.

Ministry for Culture and Heritage, New Zealand. (2014). *Featherston Camp*. https://nzhistory.govt.nz/war/featherston-camp. 18 March 2017.

Monteiro, C. (2012, September). A literary celebration in Scotland's National Book Town 28 September–7 October 2012 [Press Release]. *Wigtown Book Festival* [News and Press]. http://www.wigtownbookfestival.com/news-and-press/press-release-september-2012. Accessed 21 Nov 2012.

Moscardo, G. (2006). Third-age tourism. In D. Buhalis & C. Costa (Eds.), *Tourism business frontiers: Consumers, products and industry* (pp. 30–39). Burlington: Elsevier Butterworth Heinemann.

Mulcock, J., & Toussaint, Y. (2002). Memories and idylls: Urban reflections on lost places and inner landscapes. *Transformations, 2*, 1–16.

Murphy, P. (2002). Sea change: Re-inventing rural and regional Australia. *Transformations, 2*, 1–12.

Murray, S. (2009, December 10). *The book beyond the page: Book fairs, screen festivals and writers' weeks*. Monash University Seminar: Book Towns and Writer's Festivals. http://arts.monash.edu.au/blogs/events/2009/12/10/seminar-book-towns-and-writers-festivals. Accessed 14 Mar 2011.

Murray, S. (2012). *The adaptation industry: The cultural economy of contemporary literary adaptation*. New York: Routledge.

Myers, R., Harris, M., & Mandelbrote, G. (2007). *Fairs, markets and the itinerant book trade*. Newcastle: Oak Knoll Press.

Nahapiet, J., & Ghoshal, S. (1998). Social capital, intellectual capital and the organizational advantage. *Academy of Management Review, 23*(2), 242–266.

National Tourism and Heritage Taskforce [Australia]. (2003). *Going places: Developing natural and cultural heritage tourism in Australia*. Canberra: EPHC.

Nicholas, M. (1982). *The world's greatest cranks and crackpots*. London: Octopus Books.

O'Neill, P., & McGuirk, P. (2007, June 15–17). Towards an antipodean theory of space. In B. Mitchell, et al. (Eds.), *Proceedings of the ARCRNSISS methodology, tools and techniques and spatial theory paradigm forums workshop* (pp. 207–216). University of Newcastle, Australia. Melbourne: RMIT Publishing.

OECD. (2016). *Tourism and the creative economy*. http://www.oecd.org/publications/tourism-and-the-creative-economy-9789264207875-en.htm. Accessed 17 Mar 2017.

Oldenburg, R. (1999). *The great, good place: Cafés, coffee shops, bars, salons and other hangouts at the heart of a community*. New York: Marlowe.

Ong, W. J. (1982). *Orality and literacy*. New York: Routledge.

Onyx, J., & Leonard, R. (2005). Australian grey nomads and American snowbirds: Similarities and differences. *The Journal of Tourism Studies, 16*(1), 61–68.

Onyx, J., & Leonard, R. (2007). The grey nomad phenomenon: Changing the script of aging. *International Journal of Aging and Human Development, 64*(4), 381–398.

Onyx, J., Leonard, R., & Maher, A. (2007). *New partnerships: Promoting development in outback towns through voluntary programs for Grey Nomads* [Report of Bingara Field Visit – April/May 2007]. Grey Nomad Volunteering Project. Volunteering Australia.

Osbaldiston, N. (2010). Elementary forms of place in seachange. *Journal of Sociology, 46*, 239–256.

Osbaldiston, N. (Ed.). (2012). *Seeking authenticity in place, culture, and the self: The great urban escape*. London: Palgrave Macmillan.

Osbaldiston, N. (Ed.). (2013). *Culture of the slow: Social deceleration in an accelerated world*. London: Palgrave Macmillan.

Paasi, A. (1991). Deconstructing regions: Notes on the scales of spatial life. *Environment and Planning A, 23*, 239–256.

Page, J. (2013, July 28). National bookshop day 2013 – In locations across Australia, bookshops will be celebrating. *Bite the book: Book reviews and industry views*. http://bitethebook.com/2013/07/28/national-bookshop-day-2013. Accessed 30 July 2013.

Perkin, C. (2010, July 24–25). Digital or not, a book is still a book. *The Weekend Australian* [Inquirer], p. 7.

Peterson, R. A., & Kern, R. M. (1996). Changing highbrow taste: From snob to omnivore. *American Sociological Review, 61*, 900–907.

Pine, B. J., & Gilmore, J. H. (1999). *The experience economy*. Cambridge, MA: Harvard Business School Press.

Pitman, J. (2007, May 26). A paradise for bookworms. *The Spectator*. http://findarticles.com/p/articles/mi_qa3724/is_20070526/ai_n19179483. Accessed 30 July 2013.

Ploughman, I. (2006). Innovation in rural Queensland: Why some towns thrive while others languish. http://www.plowman.com.au/Innovation_in_rural_Queensland.pdf. Accessed 22 Feb 2006.

Portinari, F. (1989). *The slow food manifesto*. http://wwwmichaelpollan.com/article.php?id=87. Accessed 15 Jan 2014.

Portzline, L. (2004). *Bookstore tourism: The book addict's guide to planning & promoting bookstore road trips for bibliophiles and other bookshop junkies*. Harrisburg: Bookshop Junkie Press.

Pow, T. (1999, October 11). Whisky and writers in Wigtown. *New Statesman*, p. 39.

Pratt, A. C. (2008). Creative cities: The cultural industries and the creative class. *Geografiska annaler: Series B – Human Geography, 90*(2), 107–117.

Press, S. (2001). Reading Wigtown: Place identities in a Scottish book town. MA thesis, University of Oregon.

Prosser, G. (2001). Rural tourism. In N. Douglas, N. Douglas, & R. Derrett (Eds.), *Special interest tourism: Context and cases* (pp. 165–185). Brisbane: John Wiley & Sons.

Pryor, C. (2008, May 2). Country viewpoint – Robert Campbell, Clunes, Victoria. *ABC Rural*. http://www.abc.nat.au/rural/telegraph/content/2006/s2233658.htm. Accessed 20 June 2011.

Putnam, R. (1995). Bowling alone: America's declining social capital. *Journal of Democracy, 6*(1), 65–78.

Putnam, R. (2000). *Bowling alone: The collapse and revival of American community*. New York: Simon & Schuster.

Queensland Museum. (2012). What do you collect? http://whatdoyoucollect.com.au. Accessed 15 Apr 2012.

Ragusa, A. T. (2013). Downshifting or conspicuous consumption? A sociological examination of treechange as a manifestation of slow culture. In N. Osbaldiston (Ed.), *Culture of the slow: Social deceleration in an accelerated world*. London: Palgrave Macmillan.

Rebanks, J. (2010, December 5). *Culture Cumbria: A review of the current position and future potential*. Rebanks Consulting Limited. http://rebanksconsulting.com/resources/Culture%20Cumbria.pdf. Accessed 8 Oct 2011.

Rinaldi, G. (2012, October 6). How do book towns survive in the age of the e-reader? *BBC News South Scotland*. http://www.bbc.co.uk/news/uk-scotland-south-scotland-19814700. Accessed 5 Dec 2012.

Roberts, J. C. (2009, January). A Visit to Archer City: The site of *The Last Picture Show* doubles as a book-collecting mecca. *Caxtonian* [USA]. http://www.caxtonclub.org/reading/2009/jan09.pdf. Accessed 17 Aug 2010.

Robinson, M. (2004). Between and beyond the pages: Literature–tourism relationships. In M. Robinson & H. Andersen (Eds.), *Literature and tourism: Essays in the reading and writing of tourism* (pp. 39–79). Andover: Thomson Learning.

Robinson, M., & Andersen, H. (2004). Reading between the lines: Literature and the creation of touristic spaces. In M. Robinson & H. Andersen (Eds.), *Literature and tourism: Essays in the reading and writing of tourism* (pp. 1–38). Andover: Thomson Learning.

Rodger, N. (2008). Judging books by their covers: An examination of books as auratic objects in a digital era. BA (Hons) thesis, RMIT University.

Rojek, C. (1993). *Ways of escape: Modern transformations in leisure and travel*. Basingstoke: Macmillan.

Rojek, C. (2000). *Leisure and culture*. Basingstoke: Macmillan.

Rojek, C. (2001). *Celebrity*. London: Reaktion Books.

Rojek, C., & Urry, J. (1997). *Touring cultures: Transformations of travel and theory*. London: Routledge.

Rollman, H. (n.d.). Richard, King of Hay. *Newfoundland and Labrador Independent*. http://www.richardkingofhay.com/articles-in-international-newspapers-and-journals.html. Accessed 19 Aug 2015.

Rosa, J., & Malter, A. J. (2002). E-(embodied) cognition and e-commerce: How physiological factors affect on-line sales of experiential products. *Journal of Consumer Psychology, 13*, 63–75.

Rose, N. (1999). *Powers of freedom: Reframing political thought*. Cambridge: Cambridge University Press.

Rural and Regional Committee, Parliament of Victoria. (2009). *Inquiry into regional centres of the future: Final report*. Melbourne: Minuteman Press.

Sack, R. D. (1992). *Place, modernity and the consumer's world*. Baltimore: Johns Hopkins University Press.

Saffer, C. (2016, May 6). OECD wants to take a leaf out of Booktown. *Mojo*. http://mojonews.com.au/oecd-wants-to-take-a-leaf-out-of-booktown. Accessed 22 Mar 2017.

Saikia, R. (2010). *Blue guide to Hay-on-Wye*. Taunton: Blue Guides.

Sanders, A., & Gaskell, S. (2013, January 13). Welsh town left stunned by US paedophile James Hanna's conviction. *Wales Online*. http://www.walesonline.co.uk/news/wales-news/welsh-town-left-stunned-paedophile-2497133. Accessed 24 Mar 2015.

Sapsed, J., & Salter, A. (2004). Postcards from the edge: Local communities, global programs and boundary objects. *Organization Studies, 25*, 1515–1534.

Sartre, J.-P. (1964). *Words*. Harmondsworth: Penguin.

Sassatelli, R. (2013). Creativity takes time, critique needs space: Re-working the political investment of the consumer through pleasure. In N. Osbaldiston (Ed.), *Culture of the slow: Social deceleration in an accelerated world* (pp. 154–177). London: Palgrave Macmillan.

Scott, A. J. (2006). Creative cities: Conceptual issues and policy questions. *Journal of Urban Affairs, 28*(1), 1–17.

Seaton, A. V. (1996a). *Book towns and rural tourism development: Hay on Wye 1961–1996*. Glasgow: University of Strathclyde.

Seaton, A. V. (1996b). *Book towns and rural tourism development: The new European book towns 1984–1996*. Glasgow: University of Strathclyde.

Seaton, A. V. (1996c). Hay-on-Wye, the mouse that roared: Book towns and rural tourism. *Tourism Management, 17*(5), 379–385.

Seaton, A. V. (1997a, July). The book town concept: Retail specialization and rural tourism. *Insights* [British Tourist Authority/English Tourist Board].

Seaton, A. V. (1997b, April). Scandinavia, the Fatherland, and Bonnie Scotland: International book towns, Part Three. *Biblio*, pp. 12–15.

Seaton, A. V. (1998). The history of tourism in Scotland: Approaches, sources and issues. In R. McLellan & R. Smith (Eds.), *Tourism in Scotland*. London: Thomson International.

Seaton, A. V. (1999). Book towns as tourism developments in peripheral areas. *The International Journal of Tourism Research, 1*(5), 389–399.

Seaton, A. V. (2002). Tourism as a metempsychosis and metensomatosis: The personae of eternal recurrence. In G. M. S. Dann (Ed.), *The tourist as a metaphor for the social world*. Wallingford: CAB International.

Seaton, A. V. (2010, April 23–25). *Developing innovative products for Irish tourism – The McNally Tourism and Travel Archive*. Paper presented to Dromoland 2010: First Annual Tourism Policy Workshop. http://vimeo.com/11577877. Accessed 14 Mar 2011.

Seaton, A. V., & Alford, P. (2001a). The effects of globalization on tourism promotion. In S. Wahab & C. Cooper (Eds.), *Tourism in the age of globalization* (pp. 97–122). London: Routledge.

Seaton, A. V., & Alford, P. (2001b). Technology by the book: BookTownNet and SME cultural tourism networks. *Journal of Information Technology and Tourism, 4*(2), 107–123.

Sedbergh Book Town Limited and Sedbergh Book Town Literary Trust. (2008). *Growing and thriving joint business plan 2008–2011*. Sedbergh: Sedbergh Book Town Limited.

Seffrin, G. (2006). Emerging trends in contemporary festival practice: Exemplifying the modern festival through the praxis of boutique festival initiation and management at the Queensland Performing Arts Centre. PhD, QUT, Brisbane City.

Selwyn, T. (Ed.). (1996). *Myths and myth-making in tourism*. Chichester: John Wiley and Sons.

Shapiro, M. (2007a, May 10). Making Hay out of bookstores: Welsh town's self-titled king rules over realm of bibliophiles. *SFGate*. http://articles.sfgate.com/2007-05-10/entertainment/17243084_1_river-wye-hardback-books-hay-castle. Accessed 18 Aug 2010.

Shapiro, M. (2007b, May 3). The used-book King of Hay on Wye. *Los Angeles Times* [Travel section]. http://travel.latimes.com/articles/la-trw-wye6may06. Accessed 18 Aug 2010.

Sharpley, R., & Jepson, D. (2011). Rural tourism: A spiritual journey? *Annals of Tourism Research, 38*(1), 52–71.

Shaw, M. (2011, January 19). A paler world: Book culture in a jiffy bag? *Killings: The Kill Your Darlings Blog* [weblog]. http://www.killyourdarlingsjournal.com/2011/01/1-paler-world-book-culture-in-a-jiffy-bag. Accessed 22 May 2011.

Shaya, G. (2004). The flâneur, the badaud, and the making of a mass public in France, circa 1860–1910. *American Historical Review, 109*(1), 41–78.

Sheller, M., & Urry, J. (Eds.). (2004). *Tourism mobilities: Places to play, places in play*. London: Routledge.

Shields, R. (1991). *Places on the margin: Alternative geographies of modernity*. London: Routledge.

Shoemaker, S. (2000). Segmenting the mature market: 10 years later. *Journal of Travel Research, 39*, 11–26.

Short, J. R. (1991). *Imagined country: Environment, culture and society*. London: Routledge.

Silbergh, D., Fladmark, M., Henry, G., & Young, M. (1994). A strategy for theme trails. In J. M. Fladmark (Ed.), *Cultural tourism* (pp. 123–146). London: Donhead.

Skogseid, I., & Seaton, A. V. (1998). *BookTownNet – Book town status and user needs analysis* [BookTownNet Deliverable D3.1]. Stiftinga Vestlandsforsking VF-rapport 19/98.

Slow Movement. (2011). Website. http://www.slowmovement.com. Accessed 15 Oct 2011.

Smith, M. (2003). *Issues in cultural tourism studies*. New York: Routledge.

Smith, M. (2006). Entertainment and new leisure tourism. In D. Buhalis & C. Costa (Eds.), *Tourism business frontiers: Consumers, products and industry* (pp. 220–227). Burlington: Elsevier Butterworth Heinemann.

Soper, K. (2007). Rethinking the "good life": The citizenship dimension of consumer disaffection with consumerism. *Journal of Consumer Culture, 7*(2), 205–229.

Sorensen, R. (2009, April 11–12). Reading the future. *The Weekend Australian Review*.

Spufford, F. (2002). *The child that books built*. London: Faber and Faber.

Squire, S. J. (1994). The cultural values of literary tourism. *Annals of Tourism Research, 21*, 103–120.

Star, S., & Griesemer, J. (1989). Institutional ecology, "translations" and boundary objects. *Social Studies of Science, 19*(3), 387–420.

Starke, R. (2000). A festival of writers: Adelaide Writers' Week 1960–2000. PhD thesis, Flinders University of South Australia.

Steffens, J. (Ed.). (2009). *Unpacking my library: Architects and their books: Featuring an essay by Walter Benjamin*. New Haven: Yale University Press.

Stephenson, M., & Tate, A. S. (2015). *Arts and community change: Exploring cultural development policies, practices and dilemmas*. New York/London: Routledge.

Stewart, C. A. (2009). The culture of contemporary writers' festivals. MA (Lit Studies) thesis, QUT, Brisbane.

Striphas, T. (2009). *The late age of print: Everyday book culture from consumerism to control*. New York: Columbia University Press.

Strlic, M., Thomas, J., Trafela, T., Cséfalvayová, L., Kralj Cigić, I., Kolar, J., & Cassar, M. (2009). Material degradomics: On the smell of old books. *Analytical Chemistry, 81*(20), 8617–8622.

Stuart, M. B. (2016, July 19). The food of love: How festivals support local communities. *AAT Comment.* http://www.aatcomment.org.uk/the-food-of-love-how-festivals-support-local-communities. Accessed 25 Mar 2017.

Sullivan, J. (2010, January 16). Villagers hawk their literary lure. *The Age*, p. 27.

Sutherland, J. (2009, January 26). Interview with Ramona Koval, 'Magic Moments: Life Changing Encounters with Books, Music and Film'. *The Book Show,* ABC Radio National. http://www.abc.net.au/rn/bookshow/stories/2009/2770765.htm. Accessed 14 Apr 2011.

Swayne, S. (1995). *'The old grey mouse': Graiguenamanagh remembered.* Graiguenamanagh: The Abbey Centre.

Szerszyncki, B., & Urry, J. (2002). Cultures of cosmopolitanism. *Sociological Review, 50*(4), 461–481.

Szerszyncki, B., & Urry, J. (2006). Visuality, mobility and the cosmopolitan: Inhabiting the world from afar. *The British Journal of Sociology, 57*(1), 113–131.

The E.C. and tourism: Economically and culturally important sector is vital to Europe. (1988). *Europe, 276*, 24.

The Project: Creating our own enchanted land and restoring one of the most beautiful buildings in Dumfries. (2011). *Peter Pan Moat Brae Trust.* http://www.peterpanmoatbrae.org/theproject. Accessed 6 Oct 2011.

The state and future of independent bookselling in the UK. (2016, June 17). *Ribbonfish.* https://www.ribbonfish.co.uk/blog/the-state-and-future-of-independent-bookselling-in-the-uk. Accessed 8 Apr 2017.

Thomas, H. (2014, May 29). Hay-on-Wye: A town of books or festivals? *BBC News.* http://www.bbc.com/news/uk-wales-mid-wales-27624226. Accessed 17 Mar 2017.

Timmons, J. A. (1997). Opportunity recognition. In W. D. Bygrave (Ed.), *The portable MBA in entrepreneurship* (pp. 27–53). New York: John Wiley and Sons.

Trotter, R. (2001). Regions, regionalism and cultural development. In D. Carter & T. Bennett (Eds.), *Culture in Australia: Policies, publics and programs* (pp. 334–335). Melbourne: Cambridge University Press.

Tuan, Y. (1974). *Topophilia: A study of environmental perception, attitudes and values.* Englewood Cliffs: Prentice Hall.

Turpin, A. (2008, September 21). Putting the big in Wigtown. *Scotland on Sunday*. http://scotlandonsunday.scotsman.com/sos-review/Putting-the-big-in-Wigtown.4512771.jp. Accessed 18 Aug 2010.

Turpin, A. (2009, September 13). The missing magic. *Herald Scotland*. http://www.heraldscotland.com/comment/guest-commentary/the-missing-magic-1.919454. Accessed 11 Apr 2012.

Turpin, A. (2011, September 12). Twitter, poems and Michael D. Higgins combine at the Town of Books Festival. *Md Media*. http://www.mdmedia.ie/index.php/2011/09/12/twitter-poems-and-michael-d-higgins-combine-at-the-town-of-books-festival. Accessed 5 Oct 2011.

Ulin, D. (2010). *The lost art of reading: Why books matter in a distracted time*. Seattle: Sasquatch Books.

UNESCO. (2010). What is the creative cities network? *UNESCO Culture*. http://portal.unesco.org/culture/en/ev.php. Accessed 13 Apr 2010.

Urry, J. (1988). Cultural change and contemporary holiday-making. *Theory, Culture and Society, 5*(35), 35–55.

Urry, J. (1994). Cultural change and contemporary tourism. *Leisure Studies, 13*(4), 233–238.

Urry, J. (1995). *Consuming places*. London: Routledge.

Urry, J. (2000). *Sociology beyond societies: Mobilities for the twenty-first century*. London: Routledge.

Urry, J. (2002). *The tourist gaze*. London: Sage.

Urry, J. (2007). *Mobilities*. Cambridge: Polity Press.

Using GLOW and ICT. (2011). Education Scotland. http://www.education-scotland.gov.uk/usingglowandict/index.asp. Accessed 10 Nov 2011.

Vik, J., & Villa, M. (2010). Books, branding and boundary objects: On the use of image in rural development. *Sociologia Ruralis, 50*(2), 156–170.

Voights, J. (2008). Sedbergh's book town: Festival of books and drama. *Wandering Educators*. http://www.wanderingeducators.com/books-film/books/sedberghs-book-town-festival-books-and-drama.html. Accessed 10 June 2011.

Vukonić, B. (1996). *Tourism and religion*. Oxford: Pergamon Press.

Walker, B. (2010). *Reading by moonlight: How books saved a life*. Melbourne: Hamish Hamilton.

Wang, N. (2000). *Tourism and modernity: A sociological analysis*. Oxford: Pergamon Press.

Wanhill, S. (1997). Peripheral area tourism: A European perspective. *Progress in Tourism and Hospitality Research, 3*, 47–70.

Wearing, S., Stephenson, D., & Young, T. (2010). *Tourist cultures: Identity, place and the traveller*. London: Sage.

Weaver, D., & Lawton, L. (2006). *Tourism management* (3rd ed.). Brisbane: John Wiley and Sons.

Welcome to glorious Galloway and so much more. (2011). http://www.gloriousgalloway.com. Accessed 1 Oct 2011.

What is Slow Travel?. (2011). *Slow Movement*. www.slowmovement.com/slow_travel. Accessed 15 Oct 2011.

Wheatley, J. (2011, May 26). Elizabeth Haycox, the new Queen of Hay. *The Times*. http://www.thetimes.co.uk/article/elizabeth-haycox-the-new-queen-of-hay-nq9qtmfghc8. Accessed 17 Mar 2017.

Wheeler Centre for books, writing and ideas. *Arts Victoria*. http://www.arts.vic.gov.au/content/Public/About_Us/Major_Projects_and_Initiatives/City_of_Literature/The_Wheeler_Centre_for_Books_Writing_and_Ideas.aspx. Accessed 13 Apr 2010.

White, L. (2011, November 12–13). Franchise expansion good for readers. *The Weekend Australian* [Weekend Professional], p. 3.

Wickerman Festival. (2013). http://www.thewickermanfestival.co.uk. Accessed 8 Sept 2013.

Wigtown Book Company 2001. (2010). *Scottish Arts Council*. http://www.scottisharts.org.uk/1/professional/audiences/casestudies/literature/wigtown2001.aspx. Accessed 21 July 2010.

Wigtown Festival Company. (2010). *Wigtown Book Festival 2010 post event outcome report* [submitted to EventScotland]. Wigtown: Wigtown Festival Company.

Wigtown Booktown Initiative: An Evaluation [Final Report]. (2003, June). Glasgow: The Market Specialists.

Wigtown Festival Company. (2017, April 3). *Business plan 2017–2021*. Wigtown.

Williams, R. (1989a). Metropolitan perceptions and the emergence of modernism. In *The politics of modernism: Against the new conformists*. London: Verso.

Williams, R. (1989b). *Resources of hope: Culture, democracy, socialism*. London: Verso.

Winter, J. (2006). *Remembering war: The Great War between memory and history in the twentieth century*. New Haven: Yale University Press.

Wojan, T., & McGranahan, D. (2007). *Creative class codes*. Washington, DC: USDA. http://www.ers.usda.gov/data-products/creative-class-county-codes.aspx. Accessed 15 July 2012.

Wojan, T. R., Lambert, D. M., & McGranahan, D. A. (2007). The emergence of rural artistic havens: A first look. *Agricultural and Resource Economics Review, 36*(01), 53–70.

Wood, E., & Thomas, R. Festivals and tourism in rural economies. In J. Ali Knight, et al. (Eds.) *International Perspectives of Festivals and Events* (pp. 149–158). Oxford: Elsevier.

Words in Winter. (2012). http://wordsinwinter.com/event. Accessed 20 July 2012.

World Tourism Organization. (1995). *Global tourism forecasts to the year 2000 and beyond: Europe*. Madrid: World Tourism Organization.

Young, S. (2007). *The book is dead (long live the book)*. Sydney: UNSW Press.

Zaid, G. (2004). *So many books*. London: Sort of Books.

Interviews

(Personal interviews except where stated otherwise.)

Bakes, Pamela. Clunes, Victoria, Australia, 30 April 2010.

Berkelouw, Leo. Eumundi, Queensland, 14 August 2012.

Booth, Richard MBE. Hay-on-Wye, Wales, 20 September 2011.

Buckridge, Patrick. Brisbane, Queensland, 17 May 2011.

Chambers, Joanna. Abergavenny, Wales, 20 September 2011.

Derrett, Ros OAM. Brisbane, Queensland, 2 June 2011.

Edmondson, John. Graiguenamanagh, Republic of Ireland, 17 September 2011.

Gould, Lincoln. Wellington, New Zealand, 8 February 2017.

Gschwind, Daniel. Brisbane, Queensland, 15 July 2011.

Hauritz, Bill. Brisbane, Queensland, 29 November 2011.

McShane, Paul. Bowral, New South Wales, Australia, 9 July 2010.

McShane, Paul and Rosa, Steve. Mittagong, New South Wales, 8 July 2010.

Mead, Kate. Featherston, New Zealand, 8 February 2017.

Muller, Laurie. Brisbane, Queensland, 17 August 2010 and 7 September 2010.

Nelson, Carole. Sedbergh, Yorkshire, United Kingdom, 9 September 2011; phone interview, 29 March 2017.

Nioa, Anne. Maryborough, Queensland, 4 September 2010.

O'Hara, Jane. Telephone Interview, Brisbane, Queensland, 9 December 2011.

Playden, Peter. Atherstone, Warwickshire, United Kingdom, 13 September 2011.

Roberts, Brian. Graiguenamanagh, Republic of Ireland, 17 September 2011; phone interview, 28 March 2017.
Sharkey, Ted. Clunes, Victoria, 30 April 2010.
Sheahan-Bright, Robyn. Gladstone, Queensland, 24 August 2010.
Schiotz, Peter. Maleny, Queensland, 4 April 2012.
Swales, Gill. Sedbergh, Yorkshire, 8 September 2011.
Turpin, Adrian OBE. Wigtown, Scotland, 4 September 2011; via email, 15 March 2017.
Watson, Joyce and Cochrane, Ian. Wigtown, Scotland, 4 September 2011.
Williams, David. Brisbane, Queensland, 2 August 2011.
Yates, Carolyn. Wigtown, Scotland, 4 September 2011.

Ephemera

Secondhand and Antiquarian Booksellers, Printsellers and Bookbinders 2011 to 2012 [brochure], Hay-on-Wye, Wales: Addyman Books, 2011.
Secondhand and Antiquarian Booksellers, Printsellers and Bookbinders 2017 to 2018 [brochure], Hay-on-Wye, Wales: Addyman Books, 2017.

Index[1]

[1]Note: Page numbers followed by "n" refer to notes.

J. Frank, *Regenerating Regional Culture*, Sociology of the Arts,
https://doi.org/10.1007/978-3-319-65036-4

M

N

FSC
www.fsc.org
MIX
Papier | Fördert gute Waldnutzung
FSC® C083411

Kolibri 360 GmbH
Ferdinand-Jühlke-Straße 7
99095 Erfurt, Deutschland
produktsicherheit@kolibri360.de